In Our Own Hands

A mother California quail, the state bird, stands sentinal over her young. (Photo by Charles Kennard)

In Our Own Hands

A Strategy for Conserving California's Biological Diversity

Deborah B. Jensen

Margaret S. Torn

John Harte

UNIVERSITY OF CALIFORNIA PRESS

Berkeley / Los Angeles / London

University of California Press
Berkeley and Los Angeles, California

University of California Press
London, England

Library of Congress Cataloging-in-Publication Data

Jensen, Deborah B.
  In our own hands : a strategy for conserving California's biological
diversity / Deborah B. Jensen, Margaret S. Torn, John Harte.
    p.   cm.
  Includes bibliographical references and index.
  ISBN 0–520–08015–7 (alk. paper). — ISBN 0–520–08016–5 (alk.
paper)
  1. Biological diversity conservation—California.   2. Biological diversity conservation—Government policy—California.   3. Biological
diversity—California.   I. Torn, Margaret S.   II. Harte, John, 1939–.
III. Title.
QH76.5.C2J46   1993
333.95′16′09794—dc20   93–12135
                                                                 CIP

Printed in the United States of America

1 2 3 4 5 6 7 8 9

Contents

Preface

California is facing many challenges: rapid population growth, tax shortfalls, crime, faltering schools, homelessness, AIDS, plus natural disasters like the Loma Prieta earthquake and six years of drought. Some of the toughest policy battles are being waged over natural resources; these disputes range from the north coast to the south coast, from the Central Valley to the deserts. These issues are often presented as battles pitting one region's interests against another, or human welfare against natural resource conservation, even though we all depend on California's biological diversity. Unfortunately our growth and economic successes are contributing to the loss of precious natural resources. By attending to the problem and making intelligent choices, we can have both growth and a healthy environment.

Protecting biological diversity for ourselves and for future generations is a complicated business. In 1989, I decided that to make wise conservation policy we needed more information. As chair of the Senate Natural Resources and Wildlife Committee, I convened the first Senate hearing on Natural Diversity. At that hearing, we heard testimony from the authors of this book, *In Our Own Hands*. They presented data on the status of biological diversity in California and described both actions threatening biodiversity and the failures of our institutions to prevent losses. Their work broadened our understanding of the technical complexity of biodiversity conservation and convinced me of the need for a more comprehensive view of both the problems and the potential solutions. I invited the authors back, and they have spoken at every subsequent Senate Natural Resources and Wildlife Committee Natural Diversity Forum. In addition, their research was published as a report and distributed to the legislature by the California Policy Seminar in 1990. This book is based directly on that report.

By listening to their research findings, and reading their report, policy makers in Sacramento have learned that conservation of biodiversity is not merely a matter of protecting a few endangered species. First, endangered species cannot be protected unless we protect habitats and ensure clean air and clean water. Furthermore, unless we want to confront a new list of endangered species every year—and create a constantly shifting regulatory setting for the state's economy in response—we must begin now to plan for the protection of genetic and habitat diversity along with species. Our goal must be to protect healthy, functional ecosystems that support populations of California's wild species and maintain genetic diversity well into the twenty-first century.

Achieving broad and enduring goals requires a comprehensive strategy. Our conservation tools must include many types of policies in addition to the traditional reliance on acquisition of parks and open space. Unfortunately, parks cannot protect everything. Fortunately, we do have other tools. Parks and open space can, and must, be supplemented with wise stewardship of our wildlands, sensible balancing of conservation and development in our urban areas, and enhanced conservation in agriculture and other industries. Only with a multifaceted approach can we succeed.

In the years since this report first came out, there have been many exciting developments in conservation policies at the state level. New policies for sustainable timber harvest practices are being designed by a collaboration between the environmental community and the timber industry. The state and federal resource management agencies have signed an agreement to work together in a coordinated effort to protect biological diversity. Local and regional efforts to plan for biological conservation are springing up around the state. Habitat protection efforts and multispecies conservation projects are being attempted, and an Endangered Habitats Act is being considered in the California Legislature. The report resulting in this book led the way in calling attention to the major conservation opportunities. It is both rare and valuable in the policy world to do as these authors have done, to identify the problems and to envision practical yet far-reaching solutions, to inform our legislative efforts. Many of this book's recommendations are reflected in current policy proposals, albeit altered somewhat through the political process.

As chair of the California Senate Natural Resources and Wildlife Committee, I am striving to assure that the laws of the state ensure the long-term conservation of our biological diversity. Legislators and their staff work hard to keep up on changes in science that may be important to policy choices. Typically, we become informed about the importance of an issue through a series of disconnected information flows including news stories, seminars, technical reports, and meetings with specialists. Sometimes we get lucky, and a report or book comes along that clarifies the issues and identifies the key components of both the problem and the solution. Read this book and you will learn a great deal about California's natural resources. It will convince you we must change our path if we want to ensure that the beauty and natural resources of California persist for our children to enjoy and benefit from. This book has already influenced the thinking of the policy makers in Sacramento and of elected officials in local governments in several California communities.

We can envision a future California that conserves our precious natural resources and wildlands both for the commodities they produce and for the many ways they enrich our quality of life. We can also imagine a future California that has lost these treasures. The problems we face are not solely technical or scientific in their nature. They touch many aspects of our society: economic development, our vision of California's future, our knowledge of the natural world, and our concern for other forms of life. To make wise choices everyone needs to understand how their lives are enriched by, and yet are despoiling, California's natural resources. This takes education for all of us. Read on and discover the nature and importance of these choices.

Senator Dan McCorquodale

Authors' Note

This book grew from informal discussions we had late in 1986. Aware of dramatic changes affecting California's ecosystems, we became concerned that limited attention was being focused on understanding the forces causing loss of biodiversity, or on finding solutions. In spring 1987 we approached the California Policy Seminar (CPS) with a research proposal. Our goal was to investigate the status of biological diversity and obstacles to its protection and, on the basis of that research, to formulate a coherent strategy that might possibly be implemented at the state level in the political arena. To our delight, the CPS, a joint program of the University of California and state government that supports University research on policy issues in California, funded our proposal. Two and a half years later, in 1990, we had completed the research and prepared a report to the CPS that set forth our findings. That report was the basis for this book.

Our intended audience then was policy makers in the state government, as well as resource managers. We were gratified that the report was widely read and that it did exert an influence. So in late 1991, when we were approached by the University of California Press to consider republishing the report as a book, we agreed to undertake the necessary additional work. Our hope was that, as a book, the results of our research would be accessible to a wide range of Californians, not necessarily just those involved in government, resource management, or academia. Moreover, we felt that here was an opportunity to reach an audience in other states, where many of the issues we raised here are also pertinent.

Any policy document is a static snapshot of a dynamic, changing system. Our biggest challenge in producing a book from our 1990 report was to evaluate its currency in 1992. In the mere two years since we concluded our research, a new governor had been elected and many significant new developments had occurred in conservation policy in California. Some of these new conservation developments could, in part, be attributed to our 1990 report, whereas others originated independently. We found that much of the content of the work and its fundamental arguments were still sound, and so remain unchanged. The bleak economic picture of the state in 1992 is not reflected in the tone of our 1990 work, yet we have not attempted to write a "recession version." However, the book differs from the report in two major ways. First, we have updated and reorganized the factual background material on the status of and threats to biological diversity in California, rendering these sections more complete and, we hope, more readable. Second, we have written an epilogue that characterizes several significant new trends in the evolving policy dialogue about protecting California's biological diversity.

In chapter 1 we introduce the topic of biodiversity, defining the concept and portraying its importance in our lives. Setting the stage for subsequent chapters, we also explain why time is short for creating policies that will protect biodiversity. In chapter 2 we present four case studies of habitat and species loss in California during the past one hundred years. From these case studies we draw generalizations about both the causes of habitat and species loss and the barriers to protection of biodiversity in the state. In chapter 3 we summarize the current status of ecosystem, species, and genetic diversity, describing both how much is left and how fast it has been disappearing. We turn next to threats, both present and future, in chapter 4, where we provide an extensive analysis of the sources of these threats and the social, political, and scientific issues that will influence how potent they are likely to be in the future. Picking up from the discussion in chapter 2 of barriers to protecting biodiversity, we expand the list of such barriers in chapter 5 and provide a more detailed analysis of the importance and recalcitrance of these barriers. This then provides the framework for chapter 6, in which we set forth our "Strategy for Protecting Biodiversity in California." This strategy consists of a coherent set of policy recommendations designed to overcome the barriers delineated in chapter 5. Finally, in the epilogue, we review current policy trends critical to the design and implementation of a biodiversity strategy, providing insight into proposals and controversies that we think will color the conservation debate in the future.

Berkeley, California
June 1992

Acknowledgments

Although three names appear on the title page, this book is the product of many hands and minds. Many people contributed time, expertise, and data to this project, both in the research stage and by reviewing the draft. Their efforts and encouragement greatly improved the quality of this book. Five individuals deserve special thanks. Ted Bradshaw, research sociologist with the Institute of Urban and Rural Development, University of California, Berkeley, provided insights into how California state and local governments work; this enlivened us at every stage of the research. Karina Garbesi, while a graduate student at the Energy and Resources Group at University of California, Berkeley, collaborated with us in the proposal writing process and subsequently undertook the challenge of analyzing the threat to habitats and wildlife from selenium, ozone pollution, and pesticide poisoning. Her summaries appeared as appendices in the original report. Sharon Selvaggio reviewed the effectiveness of coastal protection afforded by the Coastal Commission to aid our thinking on alternative institutional structures. Joyce Gutstein assisted in gathering and organizing data for material used in chapter 3. Tony Fisher, professor of Agricultural and Resource Economics at University of California, Berkeley, provided us with many useful insights into the possibilities and limitations of economic incentives for protecting biodiversity.

In addition, we extend heartfelt thanks to William Ahern, Dan Airola, Susan Anderson, Steve Bailey, Reg Barrett, Ken Berg, Anne Bicklé, Roxanne Bittman, Frank Boren, Robert Callaham, Susan Cochrane, Andy Cohen, Chelsea Congdon, Dean Cromwell, Don Dahlsten, Gretchen Daily, Ray Dasmann, John Ellison, Robert Ewing, Phyllis Faber, Christopher Foe, Larry Ford, Alisya Galo, Karen Garrison, Vivian Gratton, Andy Gunther, Michael Hanemann, Lynn Hawkins, Alexis Harte, Mary Ellen Harte, Ed Hastey, Deborah Hillyard, John Hopkins, Mark Hoshovsky, Mari Jensen, Elizabeth Kersten, Barbara Leitner, Ralph Lightstone, Susan Mahler, Steve Malloch, Michael Mantell, Julia May, Darlene McGriff, Patrick McGuire, Connie Millar, Stephen Moore, Robert Motroni, Pam Muick, Dennis Murphy, Linda Nash, Steve Nicola, Richard Norgaard, William Pease, Susan Quishi, Judith Redmond, Larry Riggs, Gene Rochlin, Bitty Roy, Dale Sanders, Steve Sanders, Mary Schallenberger, Carrie Shaw, Joseph Skorupa, Michael Soulé, Richard Spotts, Jim Steele, Ron Stork, Kim Taylor, Irene Tomasi, Kathy Tonnessen, Ted Trzyna, Johanna Wald, Walt Westman, Jim Williams, John Willoughby, Sami Yassa, Cathy Zabinski, Laurie Zander, Dave Zeiner, and Seth Zuckerman. We extend thanks and an apology to those whose names we may have inadvertently omitted from this list.

Finally, we thank the California Policy Seminar, the Pew Charitable Trusts, and the Switzer Foundation for the financial support that made this book possible.

CHAPTER ONE

Biodiversity Basics

California is a state of superlatives. It possesses a spectacular thousand-mile coastline, the tallest peak and the lowest valley in the contiguous continental United States, massive giant sequoias, ancient bristlecone pines, twenty million acres of desert, ten million acres of cropland, and nearly twenty million acres of productive timberland. California has one of the ten largest economies in the world and produces half of the United States' agricultural produce. The state is a world leader in the manufacture of advanced electronic products and, as of the early 1990s, home to thirty million people. The combination of Mediterranean climate, rich geologic history, complex topography, and diverse soils has produced a region of extraordinary biological richness.

California's wealth of biological resources is sometimes splendidly apparent, as when the deserts flower in the spring or when, in the winter sunset, millions of migratory birds descend on the coastal lagoons and inland wetlands. More often, however, these riches go unperceived, for California's patchwork of habitats can best be grasped by a trained eye aloft, and the genetic wealth lodged in its wild species must be viewed with microscopic vision.

Whether visible or hidden, California's biological wealth is the wellspring of the state's economic wealth and its worldwide fame as a desirable place to live. The importance of the visible resources is apparent to all: logs to cut, food crops to harvest, fish to catch, and redwoods to stand in awe of. But these are only a few of the benefits Californians receive from their biological resources. Like people everywhere, Cali-

1

fornians owe the richness of their soils, the beauty and productivity of their forests, and the cleanliness and productivity of their waters—in short, the health of their environment and the wealth it produces—to a diversity of biological resources that often go unnoticed.

Unfortunately, all is not milk and honey in the Golden State. From the Sierra to the Pacific coast, from the deserts to the northern conifer forests, human activities are threatening the natural beauty and biological riches that characterize California. As more and more people seek to derive more and more wealth and other benefits from the state's biological bounty, many of the superlatives we came to California to find are being destroyed. Indeed, California is increasingly becoming known for a new set of superlatives, such as the listing of over sixty National Priority Superfund toxic waste sites, the most polluted air basin in the nation, and the largest number of endangered species of any state in the continental United States.

We have contaminated the air and water, dammed and diverted the rivers, filled in the wetlands, and plowed under the native vegetation. An alarming 90 percent of the interior wetlands and Central Valley riparian forests have been destroyed and nearly all the aquatic habitats in California have been altered or degraded. As a result of urban conversion, the Santa Barbara song sparrow, the showy Indian Clover, the Mendocino bush mallow, and many other native plants and animals have already been lost forever, and with them their unique, distinguishing genetic characteristics. Even more sobering, nearly one in three vertebrate species and one in ten of California's native plants are in serious danger of extinction.

Alterations of the landscape are accelerating. Almost three-quarters of a million people now join California's population every year (figure 1.1). As cities become more congested, residential developments mushroom in suburban and rural areas. Currently, an area the size of San Francisco is converted from natural vegetation or agricultural land to residential or commercial use every six months; every four years an area the size of Orange County is similarly developed. And even while habitat conversion and other traditional stresses on our biological resources increase as the population grows, new phenomena such as global warming pose additional threats to California's biological resources.

Although the State of California has many laws and agencies that regulate the use of natural resources, there are numerous barriers to the effective protection and wise management of our biological heritage. Agencies rarely work in concert to protect resources. Threats to our native ecosystems now arise not only from activities within California,

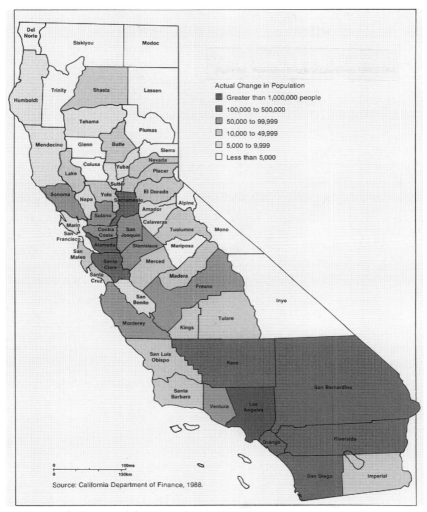

Actual Change in Population

■ Greater than 1,000,000 people
■ 100,000 to 500,000
▨ 50,000 to 99,999
☐ 10,000 to 49,999
☐ 5,000 to 9,999
☐ Less than 5,000

Source: California Department of Finance, 1988.

1.1. *Population growth by county from 1980 to 1987.*

but from worldwide activities that are beyond the direct reach of state law. Although some threats, such as large oil spills, result in dramatic impacts that cannot fail to attract attention, many insidiously sow destruction in small but accumulating steps. As a result, biological resources get nibbled away in small, barely noticeable, pieces before appropriate regulatory action can be taken. The California Endangered Species Act, designed to protect species pushed to the brink of extinction, contains various loopholes, allowing imperiled species to fall through the legal safety net. In other cases, such as protection of critically rare habitats, the needed legislation is lacking. Other laws are well-crafted, but they are not adequately enforced. Within the agencies, the day-to-day needs for quick responses to crises often overwhelm efforts to develop and put in place adequate long-term plans.

In some instances, the scientific knowledge needed to make wise resource decisions is lacking. Within the universities, research on applied topics such as conservation biology is often undervalued in comparison with currently more fashionable trends in science. Knowledge of the environment must not be merely acquired, it must also be conveyed. Educational barriers to effective protection of biological resources are part of a much bigger national problem—environmental ignorance. Environmental education is needed for all citizens, not just for science majors. Lack of ecological understanding fosters the myth that ecosystems are infinite and resilient, leading to short-term economic choices that are in conflict with longer term societal, economic, and ecological goals. A people who neither know how their food is produced nor how their water reaches their faucets cannot make the wise decisions required for their grandchildren to live as well as they do.

Because the threats are diverse and complex and the existing organizational structure is incapable of comprehensively addressing the problems, tactical remedies will treat, but not cure, the problem. Instead, a creative strategic vision for the future is called for if California is to sustain the biological diversity that remains. The time has clearly come to chart a course of action that will guarantee the long-term future of California's biological wealth. This book describes our efforts to accomplish exactly that. In subsequent chapters, we evaluate the status of the state's biological riches and determine what threatens them. Then we examine the barriers to protection and devise a strategy that will overcome those barriers. In the remainder of this chapter, we explain the ways in which the quality of all our lives and those of our descendants are linked to the success of this effort.

What Is Biological Diversity and Why Should We Care about It?

The aforementioned biological riches are part of a complex web that we call *biological diversity*. Simply stated, biological diversity is the variety of life. Because there are different levels and components to this variety, a more detailed definition is useful. *Biological diversity means the full range of variety and variability within and among living organisms, and the ecological complexes in which they occur; it encompasses ecosystem or community diversity, species diversity, and genetic diversity.*

Genetic diversity is the combination of different genes found among individuals within a population of a single species and the pattern of variation found in different populations of the same species. Adaptation to local conditions such as the summer fog along the coast or hot summer days in the Sierra results in genetic differences between the coastal and Sierran populations of Douglas fir. Species diversity is the variety and abundance of different types of organisms that inhabit a region. A ten-square-mile area of Modoc County contains different species than does a similar size area in San Bernardino County. Ecosystem diversity encompasses the variety of habitats that occur within a region, or the mosaic of patches found within a landscape. A familiar example is the variety of habitats constituting the San Francisco Bay–Delta ecosystem: grasslands, wetlands, rivers, riparian forests, and estuaries.

Protecting biological diversity (often called biodiversity) requires attention to all three different scales: ecosystems, species, and genes. If efforts are focused at only one scale, such as the conservation of an individual species, ecosystem patterns and processes are likely to be ignored or overlooked, leading to ecosystem degradation and loss of diversity at the landscape scale. Similarly, if species diversity is the focus, the genetic diversity found in different populations of the same species may be overlooked because it is only noticeable at a finer scale of resolution. Significant loss of biodiversity at one level can result in loss at the other levels because the components of biological diversity are dependent on each other. Clearly, if a species goes extinct the genes it contained will be lost. Less obvious, but equally important, loss of genetic diversity within a species increases the risk of extinction.

We benefit from biodiversity in myriad ways, one of the most obvious of which is recreation. Biological resources provide Californians with opportunities for nature observation, hiking, rafting, fishing, and hunting. Over three million California fishing licenses and stamps were sold in 1990, indicating the enormous popularity of just this one activity. Wildlife viewing activities are rapidly gaining in popularity. Just as few bird watchers or deer hunters would find a zoo or a managed game park a suitable substitute for wildlands, the visitors to California's undeveloped deserts, mountains, lakes, rivers, or coastline do not find TV nature documentaries and coffee-table books sufficient.

Because of this yearning to experience relatively undisturbed nature,

Table 1.1. *Levels of Biodiversity and Benefits*

Ecosystem	watershed maintenance
	climate moderation
	water quality
	air quality
	soil maintenance
	species habitat
	aesthetics
	recreation
Species	food
	lumber
	paper
	clothing
	medicine
	horticultural products
	recreation
	aesthetics
	medical knowledge
Genetic	pharmaceuticals
	agricultural improvements
	bioengineering raw materials
	adaptive choices for future environmental change

Californians enjoy an economic bonanza. Entire regional economies, such as those of Big Sur, the Mendocino coast, and Yosemite, are based on income from tourists seeking to discover the natural splendor of our ecosystems. In 1989, State Park and Recreation areas received nearly eighty million visitors; income from sales of outdoor recreational equipment and services provided to travelers (often from out-of-state) to our parks and wildlands has been on the order of hundreds of millions of dollars annually.

Many benefits that Californians receive from natural ecosystems are less widely recognized than are those from recreational uses of these ecosystems. Human society is sustained by a wealth of life-supporting goods and services provided by natural ecosystems and for which no practical substitutes exist.

"Ecosystem goods" refers to the biological produce—the food and fiber—with which natural ecosystems enrich our lives. Natural ecosystems contain a kind of library of diverse species and, within each species, of diverse genetic types. Californians draw upon these species and genetic varieties to meet many of their material needs. Chinook salmon and redwood trees are examples of wild species that benefit the lives of Californians, providing, respectively, a delicacy and an important building material. The list of wild species that we exploit for food and fiber is large, but in fact, even our domestic agricultural crops and animals originated from wild species. Plant breeders and genetic engineers hope to convert many wild species into tomorrow's crops, and some ranchers are even looking to wild animal species for better grazing stock for the future. About half of the medicines Californians use derive from wild plant species (Newman 1990). Although most of these were found in the tropics, future medicines may well be lying hidden in California's vegetation. The yew trees of the old growth forests of the Pacific northwest provide a spectacular example of how such riches lurk in unexpected places. The bark of this hitherto ignored, seemingly useless, species contains a substance, called taxol, that appears remarkably effective in treating some cancers. Industrial products may also have biological sources. A desert shrub found in our state, the jojoba, is a source of high-grade oil used in high temperature lubricants, replacing sperm whale oil.

Genetic diversity is important to our future well-being, for it provides the information that will enable species to cope with future change. For example, in the warmer climate predicted for the coming decades we will require trees and fish that can tolerate the new climatic conditions. Within wild populations, a wide variety of genetic combinations exist among individuals in populations and among different populations. Included in those combinations are undoubtedly genes that confer fitness for a warmer climate. Although the monocultures of today's commercial forests incorporate only a tiny subset of that genetic diversity—and probably lack the gene combinations we will require in the future—if we protect genetic diversity in native forests, we can turn to wildlands for seed stock containing more adaptive genetic combinations. Thus we can sustain future commercial biological resources, provided that the native biodiversity is left intact.

Although Californians are dependent upon ecosystem goods, in part because of the enormous role harvested natural resources now play in the state's economy, we benefit most from a different kind of natural resource harvest—one we reap not by sawing, fishing, or threshing, but rather by protecting natural ecosystems so that they continue to provide us with a host of free "ecosystem services" that we could not replace with technology at any conceivable price. These services are less tangible to most people than are ecosystem goods and easier to take for granted. But we ignore them at our peril.

One such service is climate moderation. Consider, for example, San Francisco Bay. Just as a person keeps cool by perspiring water, so does a geographic region. The Bay extends the cool, coastal climate far inland, keeping the region cool in summer. Forests play a similar role in other areas of the state, moderating temperatures and even augmenting rainfall in some cases. In many regions of the world, such as the slopes above the eastern Mediterranean and in western Michigan, people have learned by hard experience that when you destroy forests you impose a drier, less tolerable climate on future generations.

Inland and coastal wetlands play a role in sewage treatment, for the living creatures in these habitats detoxify many discharged wastes and carry out the equivalent of biological waste water treatment by assimilating inorganic nutrients. Marsh water can also help sustain drinking water supplies by recharging ground water in coastal regions, thereby reducing seawater intrusion into fresh groundwater supplies.

Natural ecosystems regulate the hydrologic cycle, the massive natural engine that irrigates our landscape. Vegetation and soil regulate the flows of water and maintain the levels of water in both natural and artificial reservoirs, including the aquifers that store groundwater. Floods are reduced because vegetation permits precipitation to soak slowly into the soil and then either into groundwater reserves or into delayed stream flow. This both reduces the rate at which storm runoff rushes downhill in flood stage and provides more water for human use in dry periods. Watershed vegetation also reduces soil erosion by slowing the flow of storm water through surface soils. Moreover, roots bind soil and foliage acts as a wind barrier, both of which reduce soil erosion and thus protect water quality.

Wild populations of birds and other predators kill vast quantities of insect pests, thus protecting our crops against insect damage and ourselves against bites and diseases. Other natural predators control rodent populations far more effectively than we can with our traps and poisons. Indeed, the phrase "the balance of nature" means not only the sustenance of creatures we like to look at but the prevention of outbreaks of those we dread.

Ecosystems maintain the composition of gases in the atmosphere, thereby sustaining the chemical conditions that we and other living creatures require. For example, soils and live vegetation store carbon that would otherwise reside as carbon dioxide in the atmosphere where

A freshwater wetlands in the Golden Gate National Recreation Area. (Photo by Charles Kennard)

it would heat the planet. Even the amount of ozone in the stratosphere (upper atmosphere), which protects us from harmful ultraviolet radiation, is regulated by nitrous oxide, a gas produced by microorganisms in soil and water in a natural biological process called denitrification.

Some ecological services, such as the regulation of the atmosphere, can be provided by either native or non-native species. Many others cannot. Native biological diversity provides biota adapted to the local conditions and therefore better able to resist disease, droughts, and fires. Native species provide habitat and food for other native species, resulting in a tendency for native species to develop resilient interactions that help sustain ecosystems. Native ecosystems have proven they can provide a diverse collection of services. No species can replicate or replace all of the unique characteristics of another, nor can any population contain exactly the same genetic combinations of another. Maintaining native ecosystems, species, and genes is the most certain means of assuring the continuation of the benefits of California's biological diversity.

The value to Californians of ecological goods and services is immense, for without the services provided by natural ecosystems, the state would lack the climate, water, and soil needed to sustain many of its productive economic activities. As measured solely by income from sale of resource commodities, our farms alone yield an annual gross income of over $15 billion.

But the true value of these goods and services exceeds that economic measure. How much is it worth to have natural air conditioning provided by a nearby water body or forest? Or to live with the security that flooding is unlikely in your valley because upslope vegetation regulates the hydrocycle? If we were to replace nature's free services with air conditioners, pesticides, additional reservoirs, sewage treatment plants, floodwalls, ultraviolet radiation shields, more medical treatment, and the like, the costs would be staggering. But the costs of these replacement activities would not simply reflect the cost to manufacture, put in place, and maintain the material replacements; they also would include the indirect costs stemming from the side effects of these technical fixes, such as the health effects of increased reliance on pesticides, and the unpleasantness of living in a plastic world. Here and there, estimates have been made of the direct dollar cost of replacing a natural service with a manufactured one. The main point, however, is not the enormous expense of replacing nature's services but the impossibility of doing so. Time and again, experience shows that people live degraded lives when natural services are degraded—they do not and cannot find satisfactory replacements.

These economic and welfare arguments are reason enough to preserve natural ecosystems, but biodiversity has other values that economic theories may never be able to satisfactorily address. Not only is it difficult to determine a dollar figure for the aesthetic and cultural value biodiversity provides, but two additional features render a solely economic valuation incomplete: the potential renewability of life and the irreversibility of its loss. Biological systems continue to grow and evolve, producing more goods, whereas extinction is forever. When we degrade natural ecosystems, and particularly when we cause the extinction of species or populations, we are bequeathing to future generations an irreversibly diminished world. We are depriving our descendants of the benefits that our ancestors left us.

One of the most difficult benefits to evaluate is the profound impact that wilderness and other living beings have on our psyche. The indigenous peoples of California derived, and continue to derive, spiritual sustenance from the natural world. Many people today find certain places in nature sacred, or life affirming. In a more general sense, the intricate patchwork of a wild landscape and the variety of living forms it sustains exert a deep appeal. To many people, wildlands provide intangible, even spiritual, returns—respite from the routine worries of life, a source of wonder about creation. For them, there simply are no substitutes; destroy wildlands and you destroy a piece of the gift of life.

Finally, biological systems have intrinsic value, beyond any measure of benefit to human society. A growing number of citizens find extinction ethically unacceptable. They are disquieted by the increasing loss of species, habitats, and genes. They question the morality of human actions that result in these losses. Simply having the power and ability to cause extinctions and in other ways interfere in evolutionary processes does not give humanity the right to use that power.

The Need for Action

Through careless exploitation, the thin fabric of soil, air, and water that sustains all life on earth is rapidly fraying. Growing human numbers, growing demands to satisfy luxurious as well as basic human needs, and deployment of a growing technological capacity to bend nature to human whim have forced the world to confront a dilemma of epic proportions: the most technologically sophisticated and most productive people ever to populate the planet are threatening the life-support system that has up to now sustained their economic growth and, more generally, their quality of life. California epitomizes this situation. We lead the world in the success with which we have been able to extract the bounty of nature to create agricultural and industrial wealth. But our successes have come at a cost to the resource base that sustained them.

The need to act is urgent. Historic demands on our biological resources have already led to dramatic transformations of our lands and waters; some habitats are on the verge of disappearing and with them will vanish many of the populations of species they sustain. These demands are sharply increasing because of California's increasing human population and the burgeoning demands that each Californian places on the state's natural resources. If we do not act now, it is likely that within decades, not centuries, the habitat destruction we are causing will lead to a massive wave of extinctions among the state's flora and fauna and a demonstrable decline in the quality of life of its citizens.

Adding to this urgency is a different and rarely discussed dimension of the problem. As children, many of today's adults enjoyed plentiful access to open spaces and recall thrilling encounters with wildlife. The landscape possessed a natural integrity, unmarred by tract homes stretching to the horizon; most rivers flowed undammed, most wetlands had not yet been filled. The natural beauty of the state has been part of its allure and a prime reason for its popularity. In our experience, the memories of that earlier ecological abundance are part of the motivation for the many people who today are joined in the effort to preserve biodiversity. What will motivate the adults of tomorrow if, as children, they lack such opportunity? We fear that loss of biodiversity will beget further loss; our children will not even know what they are missing.

Recent years have seen a change both in the public's awareness of the importance of the natural environment and in resource specialists' knowledge about the fragility of ecosystems and methods of sustainably managing them. Together these have led to a call for a new focus on biological diversity. Our proposed ten-part strategy for state action provides a framework for a future California where growth and development can occur in concert with the conservation and enhancement of biological resources. Biodiversity conservation must be an ongoing process and, as such, will require an ongoing commitment of time, energy, funding, and wisdom. We are at a critical juncture—the decisions made in the next ten years will decide the fate of many of the species and ecosystems in California. In doing so, we decide our own fate, and the fate of Californians forever. The choice is in our hands.

CHAPTER TWO

How Biodiversity Is Lost

Day by day, human activities are degrading the quality and shrinking the area of the natural habitats of California. The threats that these activities pose to plants and animals are varied, as are the many ways ecosystems can deteriorate in response to them. To provide a sense of the magnitude of the current level of deterioration as well as insight into the underlying causes and patterns of habitat degradation and species extinction, we present here case studies of four of California's threatened habitats, emphasizing the various ways in which each has responded to an onslaught of threats.

Lessons from California's Recent Past

RIPARIAN FORESTS

Flying over California on a clear day, one can see occasional sinuous strips of lush vegetation that provide a welcome break in the visual monotony of the arid or irrigated lands below. These strips of land are home to numerous plants and animals found in no other habitats. The lush vegetation results from the presence of a river and the strips are called riparian habitat (after *ripa,* meaning river in Latin).

Riparian forests used to be found along the banks of all the permanent waterways and many of the intermittent waterways of California.

A riparian forest in a Nature Conservancy preserve along the McCloud River. (Photo by Walt Anderson)

In the Central Valley these forests were composed of oaks, cottonwoods, sycamores, ashes, and willows extending as much as two to three miles from the river's edge. The understory was a tangle of shrubs, blackberries, wild grapes, and herbs. These riparian forests were critical to wildlife. They provided food and shelter, as well as relief from the hot summer sun. They stabilized the river banks and slowed the speed of flood waters. They provided habitat to a richer collection of terrestrial vertebrates than any other ecosystem in the state.

Great blue herons, ringtail cats, Swainson hawks, and tree frogs are only a few of the 225 different species of birds, mammals, reptiles, and amphibians that make use of California's remaining riparian forests (CDFG 1988a). In addition, the remaining vegetation along the shore is critical to the quality of the aquatic habitat and contributes significantly to maintaining healthy fisheries by providing shade, a source of food (insects that fall from the trees), and nutrients.

The Central Valley's riparian forests have been "modified with a rapidity and completeness matched in few parts of the United States" (Thompson 1961). Before the Gold Rush, there were over 921,000 acres of riparian forests in the Central Valley (Katibah 1984). These forests were cut for fencing, lumber, and firewood, including fuelwood to power the steamers that traveled up and down the Sacramento River. The rivers were dammed and the banks rip-rapped. In 1980, only 11 percent (102,000 acres) of this riparian forest remained (Katibah 1984). Of this, approximately 49,000 acres were in disturbed or degraded condition, and only 53,000 acres were considered to be mature forest. Even these last remnants of mature forest continue to be degraded or converted by human activities (CDF 1988). Much of the remaining acreage occurs as narrow stringers of vegetation along the rivers and streams. Few large tracts remain. Not surprisingly, the wildlife of the riparian habitat has been decimated. Some species, like the grizzly bear, were completely eliminated from the state. Others, like the yellow-billed cuckoo, are threatened with extinction.

A diverse array of activities have led to the demise of riparian habitat throughout California. Nearly all of the streams on the east side of the Sierra have been dammed and diverted. When this occurs the riparian forest above the diversion gets flooded and the downstream portion receives reduced flows. In the lower elevation reaches of streams on the east side of the Sierra, the riparian vegetation is being replaced by the arid-tolerant vegetation of the adjacent desert. Nearly every river flowing through Southern California has been dammed, diverted, or had its banks paved to form channelized waterways. Especially at low elevations, only small percentages of the original acreages of riparian vegetation remain (Faber et al. 1989). Flood control projects utilizing concrete or rip-rap have led to additional losses of riparian vegetation, despite growing evidence that there exist alternative and more effective flood control methods that retain vegetation.

In every region, grazing in riparian zones has caused the widening of stream banks, trampling of vegetation, and the muddying of streams, affecting the aquatic life. Problems are occurring on both private and federal lands. The U.S. General Accounting Office (USGAO) surveyed the status of riparian habitat on federal land in ten western states and found thousands of miles in degraded condition. In some areas, such as the Modoc National Forest, 78 percent of the streams are in poor to fair condition (USGAO 1988*b*). Private land does not fare better. In California, 21,498 miles of streams are suffering from stream-bank erosion problems (USDA 1984).

Even though the threats to riparian forests have been well documented, efforts to protect and restore riparian forests have not overcome local political and public resistance. Most low-elevation riparian forests are privately owned, and few local governments have ordinances protecting riparian habitat. Currently, California's laws and agencies provide few means of protecting the remaining habitat, particularly when federal authorities have responsibility for flood control projects or when new and better methods of managing resources have not yet been widely excepted within state agencies.

WETLANDS

California's inland wetlands provide the wintering grounds for millions of migratory waterfowl, its coastal wetlands are the nurseries for numerous forms of marine life, and both inland and coastal wetlands remove pollutants and excess nutrients from water, thereby providing society with a natural service that is of enormous (and undervalued) economic importance. Throughout California, however, and indeed throughout the United States, wetlands have been filled, dredged, and degraded. The plight of wetlands is now a familiar story and one that sheds light on the linkages between habitat loss and species endangerment.

California once boasted five million acres of permanent and seasonal interior wetlands that supported a rich array of waterfowl, shorebirds, tule elk, grizzly bears, and other wildlife species. The Central Valley

Saratoga Springs in Death Valley National Monument, sole habitat for the endangered Saratoga Springs pupfish. (Photo by Michael Mundy)

alone held four million acres of wetlands on the fertile soils of the Tulare Basin and the San Joaquin and Sacramento valleys. These freshwater wetlands have been drained or diked for agricultural use until now fewer than four hundred thousand acres remain (Dennis and Marcus 1983).

Many of these remnant interior wetlands are degraded by an inadequate water supply and by pesticide-laden agricultural runoff. Despite this, they are still a key component of the Pacific flyway for the migratory waterfowl of western North America (Gilmer et al. 1982), as evidenced by the ten to twelve million birds that winter in, or pass through, the Central Valley each year. Most of the still-remaining large inland marsh areas are managed by state or federal agencies to increase their carrying capacity for migrating waterfowl, often at the expense of resident animal and plant communities. If wetlands were not so scarce, areas could be maintained for a suite of plants and animals while still providing waterfowl habitat.

Existing regulations and parks are not adequate to reduce the threats from development and degradation. Losses from land conversion continue, and few wetland acres are being added to preserves each year. Existing preserves also face problems. Water quality problems like the selenium poisoning of birds at Kesterson National Wildlife Refuge are believed to be common in many of the isolated wetlands in the San Joaquin Valley and the Tulare Basin. Guaranteed water availability for wetlands and wildlife refuges continues to be a problem. Of the nine national wildlife refuges in the Central Valley, only three have their future water supply assured (Gilmer et al. 1982).

As with its freshwater interior wetlands, the state's coastal wetlands have been largely destroyed. Considering its long coastline, California has few estuaries or deltas; the shoreline consists mainly of cliffs and beaches, with only a few locales containing coastal salt or brackish wetlands. Coastal wetlands are largely limited to areas where major rivers meet the ocean. These areas are now ports, surrounded by some of California's most industrialized cities: San Diego, Long Beach, Oakland, San Francisco, and Eureka. The wetlands and tidal flats that bordered these great estuaries are now dredged or filled. Where willets, sandpipers, and rails were common we now find barges, oil tankers, houses, and office buildings.

The magnitude and importance of wetland loss in California is neither new nor disputed. Forty years ago, Albert Day (1949) described the prospects for wetlands protection as discouraging. Conservation efforts were localized, focusing on a particular site or region, without evaluating the statewide loss of wetlands or developing statewide policies. Nevertheless, significant actions such as the establishment of wildlife refuges for waterfowl in the Pacific flyway were taken.

Concern over the filling of the San Francisco Bay led, in 1965, to the establishment of the Bay Conservation and Development Commission (BCDC) to regulate filling activities. The BCDC has had significant success in protecting tidal wetlands around the San Francisco Bay and has greatly slowed the amount and rate of wetlands conversion. However, BCDC's jurisdiction is limited to 100 feet above the line of highest tidal action. As a result, nontidal seasonal wetlands have not received the conservation attention comparable to that received by tidal wetlands. In the 1700s, over 200,000 acres of seasonal wetlands fringed San Francisco Bay; 90 percent of this historical coastal wetland acreage has been lost. Between 1975 and 1988, a period characterized by widespread awareness of the value of protecting remaining wetlands, more than 5,000 acres of seasonal wetlands were lost, leaving only 18,500 acres (Granholm et al. 1989), of which 2,000 acres are degraded.

By the mid 1970s, it was evident that wetlands losses were not restricted to small areas, but rather wetlands throughout California and the nation were at risk. California's policy makers began to focus attention on the issues of wetlands loss and protection. Many reports were written documenting wetland loss throughout the state and emphasizing the need for dramatic action. The California Department of Fish and Game was directed by the state legislature to increase the wetland acreage by 50 percent by the year 2,000 (Senate Concurrent Resolution 28, 1979).

Public acquisition of inland and coastal wetlands combined with management and restoration is considered to be the best wetlands protection strategy (CDPR 1988). However, the complex web of regulatory and management agencies and the numerous laws affecting wetlands bog down efforts to implement this strategy. The California Wetlands element of the California Outdoor Recreation Planning Program lists twenty state agencies involved in wetland management or regulation, eight federal laws or policies, and eleven state laws that affect wetlands in California (CDPR 1988). But there is no comprehensive state statute for the preservation of wetlands (or any other habitat type). This regulatory complexity, in conjunction with the difficulty of guaranteeing adequate water supplies, suggests an uncertain future for the wetlands of California.

California's coastal and inland wetlands have been recognized as critically rare habitat types in the state. Numerous efforts are being made to provide protection for these habitats. Acknowledgment of the importance of protecting and restoring these habitats, backed up by regulation, has slowed the loss of wetlands acreages throughout the state. But it takes a long time to implement effective habitat protection regulations, especially in the face of incomplete authority and bureaucratic complexity. Successful protection of the state's wetland habitats, the services they provide, and the species that depend upon them requires profound changes in the way California manages biodiversity.

COASTAL DUNES

Millions of Californians have enjoyed walking in the sand dunes along the beach, but few are aware of the diversity of life found there or of the stresses exerted by Californians on this habitat. Historically, three to four hundred miles (about one-quarter) of the state's coastline contained beach and dune habitats. There were thirteen major dune systems, located at Crescent City, Humboldt Bay, Fort Bragg, Point Arena, Bodega Beach, Dillon Beach, Point Reyes, San Francisco, Monterey, Morro Bay, Nipomo Dunes, Los Angeles, and San Diego Bay. Many of these sites now no longer contain healthy dunes habitat. Those that do are of great value, however, for although healthy coastal dune ecosystems cover a small geographic area of the state, they are home to hundreds of species including six plants and four animals listed under the Endangered Species Act (CDFG 1989*a*), and forty-three plants considered rare or endangered by the California Native Plant Society (CNPS 1988).

Coastal sand dunes are formed when sandy sediments deposited by large rivers are washed ashore and then blown inland by the wind to form dunes of various shapes and sizes. Storms play a major role in determining their size and shape. The foredunes, closest to the beach, have little vegetation and are not well stabilized by vegetation. Further inland, vegetation stabilizes the dunes, forming a hummocky shrubland. Storms, trampling, and vehicles can eliminate the vegetation, causing "blow-outs" of moving sand within the stabilized dune areas. If these open sandy areas are small, the vegetation can recolonize. If the blowout is large or the disturbance continues, the vegetation cannot recolonize, and the open sandy area expands.

Dunes have been damaged and eliminated by development, recreation, and introduced species. The western edges of San Francisco and Los Angeles were built on once extensive dune habitat, leaving only a few small fragments of undisturbed dunes. In other areas of the state, particularly in the large dune complex of the central coast, recreational vehicles have killed and eliminated the vegetation from vast areas of dunes. Two introduced plant species, European beach grass and the

Native and introduced plant species cover the dunes at Pescadero Marsh Natural Preserve. (Photo by Charles Kennard)

South African ice plant, have been planted to stabilize dunes, mainly to reduce blowing sand. These two species are very successful at outcompeting the native species and have taken over large expanses of dunes, forming single-species stands and eliminating native plant species in many areas.

The Nipomo Dunes in San Luis Obispo comprise one of the largest coastal dune areas remaining in California. The area has been the subject of continuing battles between groups who want to protect the dunes and groups who want to use them for off-road vehicles. Aerial photographs taken over several decades have documented that vehicular play areas have denuded the dunes, increased blowing sand areas, and killed nearly all plant and animal life. Restoration efforts to reestablish dune vegetation have been very costly and generally unsuccessful.

Although there are numerous state beaches managed by the Department of Parks and Recreation, few of these provide adequate protection for dunes because beach parks are managed primarily for recreation rather than to protect natural resources. There are some notable exceptions however. The natural dune vegetation at Asilomar State Beach in Monterey is being restored, after extensive damage by disturbance and the introduced ice plant. The Nature Conservancy has invested considerable effort in the acquisition and protection of central coastal dunes in the Nipomo Dunes complex.

Without a commitment to protecting and restoring coastal dune habitats, this portion of the state's biodiversity could easily be completely lost, as it already has been in some regions. As California's population continues to grow along the coast, increasing both development and recreation pressure, the task of protecting and restoring dunes will only become more difficult.

OAK WOODLANDS

For many, rolling golden hills dotted with gnarled oak trees mean California. Oak woodland habitat, covering 7.4 million acres in the Coast Ranges, Peninsular Ranges, and the Sierra foothills, occurs in the regions of the state where most people live and is often in the path of expanding suburban development. Many types of oak forests and woodlands can be found in California. Closed-canopy evergreen oak are typical of the northern coast range, whereas the open-canopy woodlands and the scattered trees and grasslands of oak savannas typify drier areas in the foothills ringing the Central Valley, in the Central Coast Range, and in the Peninsular Range of southern California.

California's oaks are well adapted to the state's Mediterranean climate, characterized by cool, wet winters and hot, dry summers. Deep roots and thick leathery leaves are among the strategies oaks deploy to withstand the absence of rain in summer when growing conditions are otherwise most propitious. Nine different species of oak trees grow in California; nine other oak species are shrubs. Both the blue oak and the valley oak are endemic to the state, and several of the other oaks have the bulk of their geographic range in California. Engelmann oak has the most limited range, found in only 39,000 acres in southern California and Baja. Valley oak woodlands, once more widespread, now cover only 270,000 acres. Oak woodlands and oak forests are home to over two hundred species of vertebrates.

Beneath the oaks, in woodlands and savannas, there once grew a dense coverage of perennial grasses. Now these perennial natives have been almost completely replaced by annual Mediterranean grass species introduced with livestock in the 1800s. It is believed that a combination of factors caused the successful invasion, primarily intensive grazing and fire suppression, which created conditions that favored annual species over perennials. As a result, the species composition of the grass-

An Oregon oak among annual grasses in Marin County. (Photo by David Cavagnaro)

lands of California have been completely changed from a community dominated by perennial grasses to one dominated by the introduced annual grasses. This alteration in the species present has likely been accompanied by a shift in the timing of nutrient flows through the system. Because annual grasses germinate, grow, and die before the summer, all the nutrient capture occurs in the spring. In a perennial grassland, the nutrient capture would be spread out over a longer time period, well into the summer months. Because there are no large areas in the state where the grassland has not been invaded by introduced annual grasses, it is impossible to determine how important the change in dominant grass species has been to the many other species dependent upon grassland habitats.

Oak woodlands have become habitats of concern for two major reasons: the increasing residential development pressures in oak habitats and substantial regeneration problems in several species. Whereas most oak woodlands are still rangeland, some types, like Engelmann oak woodlands, have lost substantial acreage because of expanding urban areas. Development pressure is beginning to affect much of the oak woodland areas in California. Population growth in the coast ranges and residential developments in the Sierra foothills are making substantial inroads into oak habitats. In addition to losses incurred to residential development, in the 1980s many oak trees were felled for commercial firewood.

Three species, valley, Engelmann, and blue oaks, are not successfully reproducing. Although many factors are implicated in the regeneration problems—including grazing, changes in fire frequency, increased competition from introduced grasses, and predation by gophers—no explanation is agreed upon by the experts. Many scientists do agree, however, that the poor reproduction of the oaks shows that current management practices are not sustainable. Attention to sustainable management of oaks is quite new, and the research has not yet been done to provide sound advice to rangeland managers about how to sustainably manage oak woodlands. In fact, in the past ranchers were advised to remove all the oaks from their rangelands to provide more forage. Luckily, times have changed, and contemporary research has shown that oaks provide shade and keep the forage from drying out and dying early in the season. While ranchers and researchers struggle to determine the best means of maintaining viable oak woodlands, pressures to cut oaks are increasing. These two forces in conjunction could spell disaster for several types of oak woodlands in California. In addition, the conversion of oak woodlands is fragmenting the landscape, leading to concern that many of the animals dependent upon oak woodland habitats will suffer population declines and losses.

As cutting of, and development in, oak woodlands has increased, there has been a growing controversy over state regulation of hardwoods. The majority of the land containing oaks is privately held and only small areas are protected in parks or natural areas. At first, the State Board of Forestry declined to consider statewide regulation. Many counties and cities have written their own local ordinances protecting oaks in urban and developing areas. Each local community's ordinance is different, and there are no statewide standards for oak protection or regulation. Concern over the proliferation of conflicting rules has led to a discussion and reconsideration of uniform policy created by the State Board. In addition, several new programs have been initiated to find a nonregulatory approach to the problems facing oak woodlands. In 1986, the California Department of Forestry started a significant ten-year research program, managed by the Forest and Range Resources Assessment Program (FRRAP), designed to increase our understanding of the regeneration problems oaks face and to focus attention on the status of oaks. A new private organization has formed, the

California Oaks Foundation, that is solely concerned with the protection of California's oaks.

Although some of the current trends in oak woodland management and conservation look positive, there is still a long way to go. Sustainable management practices on oak rangelands are critical to their long-term viability. This will require both research and education. Land use planning for development in oak habitats needs to take into account the long-term preservation of these attractive landscapes that exemplify California.

How Is Biodiversity Lost?

Why is biodiversity disappearing? There are three levels at which we can seek answers to this question: threats from human activities, ecological responses to threats, and institutional and other societal barriers to protection.

At the first level, biodiversity is disappearing because it is under attack—it is subject to threats from human activity. Oak woodlands are being degraded by grazing and housing development, wetlands are being polluted and drained, dunes are being damaged, and riparian forests are being cut. We discuss the entire range of threats to California's habitats, species, and genetic diversity in chapter 4.

To scientists concerned with the loss of biodiversity, however, there is more to the story. Not all ecosystems respond to the same threat in the same way. Dune vegetation is highly vulnerable to human foot traffic, whereas the grasses beneath the oak trees in our oak woodlands are not. Moreover, there are a host of ripple effects that can be set in motion when an ecosystem is subject to threats, causing damage in unexpected quarters. For example, removal of riparian forests often results in excess siltation of the nearby stream, and this damage can propagate for miles downstream. Much as medical researchers seek to understand the progression and spread of disease as well as the identity of the causal agent, so conservation biologists strive to learn about the mechanisms by which threats actually wreak their damage and how a cascade of effects occur when a habitat is stressed. At this second level of understanding, there are biological and physical principles that help explain how damage to habitats, species, and gene pools lead to further loss—how damage propagates within and among these three scales of biodiversity—as a result of the ways in which ecosystems are structured. These principles are discussed below.

Then we turn to a third level of understanding, as we deduce from the case studies (and discuss at greater length in chapter 5) the existence of societal barriers to the protection of biodiversity. For example, the multiplicity of threats to California's wetlands are not within the purview of any one local, state, or federal agency, leading to an absence of coordinated policy and poor implementation of existing laws. These barriers have their origin in the social, economic, legal, and political makeup of our society. Although the case studies address only a few of California's habitats, they do provide a useful starting point for introducing some of these major ecological and societal issues.

Lessons from Conservation Biology

Loss of biodiversity at one level is often linked to other losses in the system. Most species such as robins, or foxes, or poppies have many distinct populations in the state. Because populations are genetically differentiated from each other, some genetic diversity is irretrievably lost when a population is lost. Each time an entire population is lost that species is a little closer to extinction. Thus, loss of biodiversity occurs along a continuum, with genetic diversity declining and vulnerability to extinction increasing as each population disappears. Extinction occurs when the last population of a species disappears. As a result, to understand species extinction, factors causing population extinction need to be examined. Species and ecosystems are also linked; ecosystems include a collection of populations of different species interacting with their environment. Loss of species degrades ecosystems, and conversely, factors that diminish ecosystem productivity or that change the patterns of ecosystems in the landscape limit the numbers and abundances of species present.

Conservation biologists recognize five major processes that result in the loss of biological diversity: ecosystem degradation, habitat loss, habitat fragmentation, direct species mortality, and altered species interactions. Although it is possible to identify these distinct causes of loss of biodiversity, rarely does any process act in isolation. Typically several forces work in concert to reduce biodiversity.

ECOSYSTEM DEGRADATION

Ecosystems can be characterized by patterns of environmental influences such as flooding, fires, climate, and nutrient cycles, as well as by functional capabilities, such as water-holding capacity, nutrient availability, or soil retention. These characteristics influence which species live in any particular ecosystem and help shape patterns of community organization and succession.

Ecosystem degradation occurs when human activities such as pollution, physical disturbance, overutilization, or water diversion reduce the functional capacity of the ecosystem or alter ecosystem processes. These effects can be subtle and need not produce a dramatic impact during any one year. When water pollution in an estuary or wetland occurs at low levels, the aquatic life may not die immediately. Pollution can reduce the productivity of the ecosystem, however, by decreasing the growth and reproduction of either the fish or their prey, or by making the fish more vulnerable to diseases. When an ecosystem is degraded, species and genetic diversity decline, reducing the benefits the area can provide.

Many plant communities in California are adapted to the presence of periodic fires. For example, closed-cone pine forests, some types of chaparral, and oak woodlands either require fire to regenerate, or, as in the case of many oak species, benefit from the damage low-intensity fires do to insect pests and other plants competing with the oaks for soil nutrients. Changes in the frequency and distribution of fires can dramatically alter both the ecosystem processes and the resident species. In California, natural fire patterns have been changed through fire suppression, accidental starts, and arson. Ironically, fire suppression controls small fires, allowing fuels to accumulate to levels that result in catastrophic fires that cannot easily be controlled. Catastrophic fires remove most vegetation, which can recover only slowly, and can also cause substantial erosion and nutrient loss during the rainy season. In addition, if wildfires occur more frequently than the recovery time of the system, substantial shifts in species composition of that area will result. In some regions of the state, 90 percent of the wildland fires are started by people (CDF 1986), suggesting fire starts will increase as population grows.

Erosion is a widespread problem and one that frequently causes damage well beyond the immediate site. Logging of forests not only reduces the nutrients available in the soils of the riparian forest, but also increases sedimentation in streams. This sediment may cover gravel beds essential to salmon for spawning, fill-in downstream wetlands eliminating habitat for waterfowl, or fill manmade reservoirs, thereby reducing the useful lifetime of dams.

Clearly ecosystem processes are linked to the ability of the ecosystem to support species. Where degradation is not severe, the number or types of species present may not change, but the number of individuals of each species will be fewer. Because species and ecosystem processes are interdependent, degradation rarely affects only one portion of the system and typically reduces many of the benefits humanity receives from biodiversity.

Unfortunately, because degradation is often gradual, with long-lasting cumulative consequences rather than dramatic, easily evident effects, it is often overlooked. Habitat loss, in contrast, is, indeed, dramatic and at the site of the loss it is impossible to overlook.

HABITAT LOSS

Habitat loss occurs when areas suitable for maintaining a species are eliminated. Because smaller areas can support fewer individuals than larger areas, as the total acreage of a habitat declines so do the number of individuals of each species as well as the total number of species. Hence as the habitat-area shrinks, the number of species present declines. This "species-area" relationship is one of the best documented patterns in ecology.

Habitat loss need not be the complete elimination of habitat for all species; more typically it is the conversion of land from one type of vegetation to another, such as converting oak woodland to grassland. The grassland will support a different group of species than the oak woodland did. River habitats in California have been converted by damming rivers and creating reservoirs. The species that dwell in streams and riffle habitats have been replaced by species that can inhabit lakes or reservoir habitats. As a result, species such as carp, sunfish, and catfish have become much more abundant in California, and trout, chub, and squawfish are less common (Moyle 1986). Some native fish species have had such a large extent of their habitat eliminated by conversion from streams to reservoir aquatic types that they are now in danger of extinction (Shapovalov et al. 1981; Moyle et al. 1989).

As the total area of converted land increases, the cumulative effects of this may result in complete loss of one vegetation type and the concomitant extirpation of species dependent on it. One contemporary example of this phenomenon is the salt marsh harvest mouse, which lives in the coastal salt marshes around San Francisco Bay. As conversion and filling of marshes occurred around the Bay small patches of salt marsh were lost. Eventually, throughout the entire Bay there were only a few sites where the species could be found. It is now endangered and has been listed under the Endangered Species Act.

Removal of a critical micro-habitat feature can also result in habitat loss. Many activities can render an area uninhabitable for a particular species because species have specialized needs. For example, cutting down all the snags and damaged trees that serve as nest sites in a forest could make the area unsuitable for hole nesters such as woodpeckers, although other forest species could still persist.

Habitat loss has two consequences: the decrease in total area of a habitat and the fragmentation of the remaining habitat. Although habitat loss leads to diminished biodiversity directly via lost acreage, it also has effects that are best perceived at the landscape level, where remnants of habitat result in what conservation biologists refer to as a fragmented habitat.

HABITAT FRAGMENTATION

Imagine a large area of deciduous forest, such as that present in the northeastern United States in 1492, and then create a mental picture of farms within this forest. As the farms grow in size and number, the pattern becomes one of a patchwork of forests and farmland. Eventually the farms are more common than the forest and the forest is fragmented into many small pieces, leaving "islands" of forests surrounded by farmland. Although in parts of the northeast the forests are returning, many California habitats—oak woodlands, riparian forests, and Douglas-fir forests, for example—are increasingly fragmented.

The impact of habitat fragmentation on biodiversity exacerbates that due directly to lost acreage. In any fragmented habitat, the remaining undisturbed "islands" will support less wildlife than their combined acreage would suggest, because many of these islands are likely to be too small to support native species. Many species have what is referred to as "minimum area requirements." For a population of a species to be able to persist within the forest, the patch of forest must be of sufficient size. Even for mobile species such as birds, the numbers of species present decreases the longer the patch is isolated and the smaller the patch.

These clear-cuts of old-growth redwood fragmented the landscape, creating isolated patches of mature forest habitat and miles of exposed forest edges. Logging roads have resulted in the dense network of bare soil criss-crossing the cut areas. (Photo by David Swanlund courtesy of the Save-the-Redwoods League)

Many forest patches and woodlots in the eastern United States have been shown to be too small to support the collection of songbirds that are typical of larger patches of these forests (Whitcomb et al. 1981).

In addition, ecosystem patches are functionally smaller than their total area suggests because the edges of the habitat are ecologically different from the interior. In a forest fragment, for example, the edges receive more sunlight, more wind, and typically have earlier succesisional species and more weedy species than the interior of the forest patch. For species that require forest habitat typical of the interior of a forest, these edge areas are not usable, making many forest patches too small to support a viable population.

The second problem with fragmented habitat is that the inhospitable areas between fragments often serve as impassable barriers to species, though the physical distance may not be large. As the distance between fragments increases or the size of the fragment decreases, the chances of a habitat fragment being recolonized after a species is lost declines. Mortality at the edge of the habitat patch also may be very high. Patch edges can also allow predators, parasites, and weedy species entry to the habitat patch, leading to high mortality or competition within the patch. For example, nest parasitism by cowbirds is more frequent in fragmented riparian vegetation, because cowbirds prefer the edges of riparian patches rather than interior riparian forest. The increase in cowbirds has contributed to the decline of the endangered least Bell's vireo.

By looking at a landscape or regional scale, we can understand the consequences of the loss of many individual patches of habitat and expose the fallacy of the frequently heard assertion that cutting down old-growth forest increases diversity. In any single harvested patch, the species of birds, insects, and other organisms will be those adapted to early successional vegetation. Early successional forests typically have more species of vertebrates than late successional stages. However, if all the old growth is cut, on a landscape scale the number of species declines because some species cannot inhabit early successional stages. When all of the forest is at an early successional stage the species dependent upon late successional stages will be locally extinct. In contrast, forests that contain old-growth stands also contain naturally occurring patches of early successional stands in places where fire or tree fall has opened up the dense forest, so the total number of species is higher. The most species-rich forests are those that contain a mixture of stand ages.

Habitat fragmentation is a significant problem in all types of habitats. One of the few California studies of this problem is from San Diego County where the effects of fragmentation of chaparral by urban development have been documented. Housing and roads have created small isolated patches that support lower densities of native species than do larger areas of chaparral. Many of the remnants are too small to support several of the common chaparral bird species. As a result, many populations of wrentit, Bewick's wren, and California quail have been eliminated. In some instances, a narrow wildlife corridor of several meters can be adequate to allow passage of these small chaparral birds from one remaining habitat patch to another, thereby reducing the effective degree of fragmentation of their habitat (Soulé et al. 1988).

In short, fragmenting habitats may lead to extirpation of numerous species from an area because the individual patches of vegetation are too small to support these species although the sum of all the remnants appears adequate. Once the species is lost from a patch, the barriers to movement between patches make recolonization difficult. Increased mortality and decreased recolonization results in a decline in the number of species present in the habitat patch and loss of some species from the region or landscape.

DIRECT SPECIES MORTALITY

Many activities selectively reduce the populations of individual species. The cutting of oak trees for fuel wood exemplifies this, but other activities such as hunting, fishing, or pesticide and herbicide application also cause selective mortality. Although any action that decreases a species population makes the species more vulnerable to extinction, some actions are targeted to eliminate a particular species.

Humankind has proven its ability to cause the extinction or near elimination of a species by a combination of hunting and habitat destruction. Shrinking habitat confines the remaining individuals to smaller and smaller locations where hunting them then becomes easier. For example, this combination of forces led to the extinction of California's populations of the grizzly bear, the state animal of California, in 1922.

In addition to intentional actions that reduce species numbers, species may be unexpectedly vulnerable to particular activities. For example, DDT use not only killed insect pests, but it caused egg-shell thinning in the peregrine falcon and brown pelican whose populations fell to precariously low levels (Anderson et al. 1975, Peakall and Kiff 1988).

For several species, direct mortality is the cause of their endangerment. However, this factor is most likely to reduce biodiversity when combined with other threats causing individual species populations to decline (see chapter 4, "Threats to Biological Diversity").

ALTERED SPECIES INTERACTIONS

Ecosystems are characterized by species interacting with each other through a variety of competitive, predatory, and symbiotic relationships. Loss or addition of an individual species from an ecosystem can have ripple effects due to the changes in species interactions, with dramatic consequences for biodiversity. The case of the sea otter illustrates how predator removal can have such effects. Sea otters were hunted for their fur until they were present in very low numbers along the California coast. In response, sea urchin populations increased greatly, because urchins, an important otter food, were released from predation pressure. The urchins, which eat kelp, caused a serious decline in the kelp beds off the California coast. Kelp is an important commodity and kelp forests are home to numerous marine species. In this case, decline in the population of the predator in the system led to significant ripple effects, with adverse consequences for the other components of the ecosystem and for humans (Duggins et al. 1989). Species that play critical roles in the abundance of many other species in the community are often called keystone species.

Adding a new predator or changing the abundance of predators is just one way to alter species interactions. Changing competitors can also be important. For example, the honey bee, a species introduced from Europe, can successfully outcompete native bees and exclude them from visiting flowers. This not only has an adverse impact on the native bees, but in cases where the honey bees fail to pollinate the plant and instead simply remove the pollen or nectar, the plant produces fewer seeds (Schaffer et al. 1979).

Introduced herbivores such as sheep, rabbits, goats, cattle, and pigs have had dramatic impacts on the native flora in California. Introduced herbivores so reduced the numbers of individuals of the Santa Barbara Island dudleya (*Dudleya traskiae*), a small succulent plant endemic to the island, that it was federally listed as an endangered species. The only thing that saved this plant from extinction was that some populations grow on bluffs too steep for the animals. All the introduced herbivores have been removed from Santa Barbara Island, and the plant is making a slow recovery.

Certain species play critical roles in ecosystem processes such as plants that fix nitrogen, enriching the soil, or beavers that dam streams creating ponds and changing the local hydrology. If these species populations decline, great adjustments in the ecosystem may occur. Similarly, if a species that can alter ecosystem processes is introduced to an area, the ripple effects will be large. The change from perennial to annual grasslands in the oak savannas and grasslands mentioned in the case study is one example.

Why Is Conservation Difficult?

MULTIPLE MECHANISMS AND CREEPING CRISES

All four case studies illustrate that entire habitats are rarely lost as a result of a single threat or in one catastrophic event. Rather, they are subjected to multiple threats and are gradually degraded. Riparian woodland habitat, for example, has been cleared to grow crops, flooded by reservoirs, and cut down for lumber and fuelwood. Wetlands have been poisoned by selenium, filled in to accommodate urban growth, and may eventually be submerged by rising seas due to global warming.

When several threats interact, the effect on biodiversity can far exceed the sum of the individual effects of the threats. For example, pollution may reduce the population numbers making the species vulnerable to other threats, such as habitat fragmentation. This multiplicity of interactions makes it much more difficult to understand or to manage threats to biodiversity. Often, no one agency has responsibility over the multiplicity of threats and so responses from government are uncoordinated. For example, in riparian ecosystems, federal agencies have authority over flood control and hydroelectric development, whereas state agencies regulate the water quality and supply. No entity is responsible for evaluating all the threats and impacts.

The case studies also demonstrate that habitats such as oak woodlands have been disappearing so slowly that it has been hard to detect significant reductions in total remaining area during any one year and yet so continually that most of the original acreage of habitats such as Engelmann oak woodland is now lost forever. Dramatic events, such as large oil spills, easily capture the public's attention and are often thought to be the major reason for concern about ecosystem degradation. But most of the damage to California's ecosystems during the past century is the result of slow, steady nibbling away of habitat, not of easily visualized catastrophic events. Unfortunately, it is exceedingly difficult to mobilize political action around such creeping crises.

CALIFORNIA IS NOT AN ISLAND

Another set of barriers to protecting biodiversity has its source in the linkages between California and the rest of the world. Both physical and political, these linkages make it difficult for California alone to control the fate of the state's biodiversity. In some ways California is physically isolated from neighboring states, with mountains and deserts serving as barriers to the transboundary movement of many species. In addition, since there are few sources of air pollution upwind of the state, most of California's air pollution originates within the state. Indeed, a popular book on the natural history of California is titled "An Island Called California" (Bakker 1984). Yet ecologists are acutely aware of how interconnected is life on our planet. We are not an island, and many of our ecological disasters reflect our ties to the rest of the nation and, indeed, the planet. These ties are exemplified by migratory birds—song birds that nest here but winter in the tropics and shorebirds and waterfowl that winter in California's wetlands and nest in the far north.

Migratory birds illustrate well the conservation implications of California's ties to other regions. Song birds that winter in the tropics are vulnerable to tropical deforestation. Similarly, shorebirds and waterfowl nesting in the far north are vulnerable to the drying up of breeding grounds as a result of global warming, which is predicted to be particularly severe in the Arctic. More immediately, these same populations of water birds are threatened by loss of their wintering grounds, California's inland wetlands. Fish that spawn in our streams but mature in the ocean where oil spills may poison them or harvesting capture them also illustrate California's ties to the wider world. Closer to home, California shares old-growth forest habitat with the states of Oregon and Washington, and thus we share responsibility for protection of old-growth forest species such as the spotted owl, marbled murrelet, fisher, martin, and wolverine.

Organisms do not have to cross the state border for their survival to be linked to activities elsewhere in the world. Water quality in Lake Tahoe suffers from activities in both California and Nevada. The Tijuana Estuary suffers from industrial pollution and municipal waste from

Baja Norte, Mexico. DDT and other pesticides that are banned in the United States are still being sold and used in Mexico, affecting wildlife on both sides of the border. Global warming, stemming from the actions of people around the world, will certainly threaten all of California's habitats. For instance, coastal wetlands are particularly at risk from sea level rise. Similarly, increased ultraviolet radiation from stratospheric ozone depletion will threaten life in California.

Just as California is not ecologically isolated, it is also not a regulatory island, for there is federal as well as state authority over land and water use in the state. Indeed, the federal government manages close to half of California's undeveloped land and some of the state's largest water projects. The need to coordinate the actions of federal, state, and local governments complicates conservation efforts and frequently leads to protracted struggles over authority to regulate water use and aquatic habitat. Clearly, policies made in the nation's capital affect the use and conservation of biodiversity in California.

Not only is California not an island, but the parks and preserves within the state cannot be viewed as isolated protected areas either. Parks and preserves are strongly linked to the nonpark environments surrounding them. This can be an advantage when a small preserve is insufficient to protect an organism but the surrounding area, although unprotected, nevertheless provides congenial habitat. It can be a disadvantage, however, because park boundaries are permeable to pollution and to species that may be threatened by land and water degradation outside the park. The linkage of parks to surrounding lands and waters presents a barrier to "one-step" conservation and necessitates that much more be done in addition to park acquisition and management.

OVERVIEW OF CONSERVATION BARRIERS

We have introduced here some of the barriers to conservation of biodiversity—a government that is ill prepared to deal with multiple mechanisms, a larger society that is deaf and blind to gradual losses of habitat, state borders that are permeable to organisms, pollutants, and regulatory authority, and the inadequacy of parks alone to protect biodiversity. Other barriers exist, as well, including a legacy of land use practices and economic policies that overlook biological processes, and the multifaceted causes of inadequate enforcement and implementation of existing laws. All these barriers to effective conservation are discussed further in chapter 5.

One final lesson from the case studies needs particular emphasis—the role of sheer numbers of people in destroying habitats. Although the lifestyles of Californians and the ways Californians manage resources affect how much impact people have on biodiversity, it is also true that more Californians means more threats to genes, species, and ecosystems. Oak woodlands are disappearing in part because more people want room to build their homes and raise livestock for beef. Coastal wetlands and dunes are disappearing in part because more people want to drive or live along the spectacular coast. The damming of more and more rivers to provide agriculture and a growing population with water and hydropower has contributed to the destruction of riparian and aquatic habitats. If population growth in California continues unabated, our efforts to protect biodiversity will eventually be doomed.

We have seen from the case studies that ecosystems are subject to a variety of threats, that these threats reduce biodiversity through a variety of mechanisms, and that many barriers stand in the way of our preventing this loss. Before a plan of action to protect biodiversity can be formulated, we need to survey California's biodiversity, evaluate the current and impending threats, and understand more systematically the nature of the barriers to effective action. The next three chapters lay this groundwork for the formulation of a viable strategy to protect California's remaining natural heritage.

CHAPTER THREE

The Status of Biological Diversity in California Today

Concern over the loss of species and their habitats in California is certainly not new. Save-the-Redwoods League was founded in 1918, and numerous other campaigns to protect specific areas or resources have been ongoing for decades. Loss of inland wetlands and the resulting impacts on the waterfowl of the Pacific flyway have been written about since the 1940s. And since the mid-sixties, there have been several calls for a statewide approach to protecting California's biological diversity, rather than concern for only individual pieces of the system. *The Destruction of California* is but one example of this more comprehensive concern (Dasmann 1966). More recent is the recognition by many citizens that many species and even entire ecosystems are now on the verge of elimination. The gravity of the problem is due to its omnipresence.

In the late 1980s, two significant studies were completed which summarized current understanding of the status of biological diversity in California: *Sliding Toward Extinction* by Jones and Stokes (1987) and *California's Forests and Rangelands* by the Department of Forestry and Fire Protection's Forest and Range Resource Assessment Program (FRRAP) (CDF 1988). These excellent documents provided a more complete understanding of California's biodiversity than had previously been available and made evident, through their limitations, where information was lacking.

An ideal assessment of the status of biological diversity in California would include an evaluation of the amount of diversity in the state at all levels (genes, species, ecosystems, and landscape), a review of the condition or quality of these resources, an examination of the quantities at risk in comparison to the quantities protected, and an investigation of the trends in loss and protection. Although limited by incomplete data, we attempt such an assessment here. Because the health and acreage of habitats are essential to the maintenance of species, we have put primary attention on the status of California's ecosystems, although we also discuss at some length species and genetic diversity.

Genetic Diversity

Understanding genetic diversity expands our awareness of the richness of California's biological resources. Every individual organism contains a distinct collection of genes that help determine thousands of heritable traits such as height, weight, growth rate, flower color, fur color, or drought tolerance. The different individuals of a region together make up a population, which may be genetically different from other populations of the species. Although many heritable traits affect physiological processes we can't see, some genetic differences between populations of a species are quite noticeable. For example, the California poppies found near the coast are yellow-flowered, unlike the more common bright-orange flowers typical of the interior of the state. The genetic differences we can't see, such as drought tolerance, are also variable and uniquely adapted to the local conditions as those we can easily view. Genetic variety really is the spice of life.

Genetic differences make individuals within a population different from each other and make populations within a species distinct. Genetic variation at both the individual and population level has been shown to provide increased survivorship and productivity in many species. But more diversity is not always better. A portion of the genetic variation in a population is due to natural selection for traits that are well suited to the particular environmental conditions the population experiences. Maintaining locally adapted traits is critical to insuring the local population continues to thrive. Actions that indiscriminately add new gene combinations to a well-adapted population will have a detrimental effect, even though the total genetic diversity is increased.

Adaptive genetic diversity helps individuals grow well under the environmental conditions typical of the natural population. Moving individuals or populations to a new area may result in poor growth because the individuals are not well adapted to the environmental conditions of the new site. Mixing genes, such as by planting seeds from a population living in a moist coastal area with those from a drought tolerant Central Valley population, would increase the genetic diversity of the valley population, but would likely have detrimental effects. Recognizing the importance of local adaptation in forest trees led foresters to identify seed zones—areas of similar elevation and climate. To assure high survivorship and productivity of seedlings, trees replanted after harvest are grown from seeds taken from the same zone.

Patterns of genetic variation are not randomly distributed on the landscape. Many traits that influence survival and growth have been subject to natural selection, and the patterns of genetic variation often reflect environmental gradients. Some genetic variation present in populations and species does not appear to have been caused by past environmental changes or selective pressures. Nonetheless, this variation contributes to the population's ability to respond to future environmental changes or to human disturbances. Genetic diversity enhances the capacity to tolerate and adapt to conditions never before experienced, providing the population with long-term viability. When the degree of local adaptation in a species has not been determined experimentally, most conservation geneticists recommend management actions that maintain the natural patterns of genetic variation.

The maintenance of highly productive agricultural crops, timber species, or commercially important fish species requires wise gene resource management. The importance of gene resource conservation is well recognized in agriculture and is gaining notice in forestry and fisheries management. Similarly, maintaining viable populations of wild species requires attention to maintaining genetic diversity in wild populations.

Evaluating the status of genetic diversity requires answering the questions: what genetic diversity exists in California? what has been lost? what has been protected? and what are the likely future trends? Years of research have provided substantial information on the patterns of genetic variation in many California species. For these species, genetically distinct populations have been identified, and the amount of genetic variation typically found within and between populations is well established. Much is known about particular groups such as coniferous trees, small rodents, salmon and trout, and many species of flowers. Unfortunately, these species represent only a small percentage of the many organisms found in California.

Where data on patterns of genetic variation do exist, there is no single consolidated source of information. Rather the data are in the many papers published by individual investigators, making an evaluation of the status of even a single species difficult. In the early 1980s, the California Gene Resources Program completed statewide assessments and gene resource management plans for several species, including salmonids, Douglas fir, and the strawberry. They found that once the data were assembled for these species, enough information was available to improve significantly the management of genetic resources, even though comprehensive identification of genetically distinct populations had not yet been completed (California Gene Resources Program 1982).

Loss of genetic variation has rarely been documented. Many actions are contributing to the loss of genetic diversity, but with the exception of a few case studies, the magnitudes of the losses are poorly known. Systematic evaluations of loss of genetic diversity have been completed for only a small fraction of the species in the state. However, current patterns of losses of species and populations clearly reduce genetic diversity. Actions that result in the loss of genetic diversity include: loss of genetically significant populations, significant declines in population size, loss of population-level genetic diversity (particularly due to geographically systematic loss of individuals and populations),[1] disrupted patterns of gene exchange between populations through habitat fragmentation, and the neglect of genetics in management practices and conservation planning.

Some of the losses of genetic variation result from the activities that subtly change the genetic composition of wild populations. For example, many salmon species are propagated in hatcheries from eggs taken from wild fish. Hatchery managers catch salmon as they begin returning from the ocean and collect eggs and milt until they have enough to meet the hatchery's annual goal. By choosing the earliest returning fish, the hatchery managers are actively selecting for earlier runs of salmon. Because the timing of returning fish has a genetic basis, the practice of growing numerous hatchery fish from early returning fish and then releasing young hatchery fish back into the streams has changed the timing of the run in some areas to as much as two weeks earlier and shortened the length of the run. In Oregon, early-returning hatchery-raised fish, although advancing the timing of peak spawning, contributed little to the natural fish production of these streams (Nickelson et al. 1986). In many of these management circumstances, simply paying attention to the genetic consequences of different management practices can significantly improve gene resource conservation. Salmonid gene resource management plans are being pursued actively in the Pacific Northwest (Riggs 1986, 1990a) and could be implemented in California.

Conservation of genetic diversity can be accomplished through either maintaining genetic diversity in naturally occurring species in their native habitat, or through making collections of samples such as seeds, sperm, pollen, or whole organisms and maintaining these in appropriate storage facilities. Conservation efforts to protect genetic diversity of species by insuring that healthy populations continue to live in their native habitats are referred to as "in-situ" (on-site) conservation. "Ex-situ" conservation removes samples off-site and stores them in artificial facilities such as seed storage banks, zoological parks, or botanical gardens.

Genetic conservation efforts are increasing, although to date less effort has been made to conserve genetic diversity of wild species than to conserve species or ecosystem diversity. Both in-situ and ex-situ conservation are receiving increasing national and international attention. For wild plants and animals, in-situ gene conservation is considered preferable as it maintains natural evolutionary processes. In addition, there are many practical problems with attempting ex-situ conservation for more than a small number of species.

The Global Biodiversity Strategy produced by a consortium of international organizations includes conservation of genetic diversity as one of its priority actions (World Resources Institute 1992). Nationally there are both government and private ex-situ conservation efforts including the U.S. National Plant Germplasm System and collaborations between zoological parks and botanical gardens to manage collections of high priority endangered species.

In California, several ex-situ conservation programs exist. In 1985, the state established the University of California Gene Resources Conservation Program to "assess the needs for genetic resource conservation, coordinate the various existing efforts, direct new efforts at preservation and collection, increase public awareness of conservation issues, and stimulate new research on topics of conservation biology" (McGuire and Qualset 1986). One of the emphases of this program is the conservation of the genetic resources of the 250 agricultural crops grown in California, mainly through a research grants program. The U.S. Forest Service (USFS) maintains collections of commercial and noncommercial forest tree species at the Institute of Forest Genetics in Placerville. The San Diego Zoo conducts active research and conservation activities for many species of native and exotic endangered animals. In addition, botanical gardens such as the Rancho Santa Ana gardens in Claremont and the Tilden Regional Parks Botanical Garden in Berkeley have made substantial commitments to propagating and maintaining collections of endangered California native plants. All these different efforts would benefit from greater coordination as well as replication of stored material to assure that the conservation of a species is not dependent upon a single storage facility.

Despite the importance of in-situ conservation, genetic diversity is rarely taken into account in land conservation projects. In the past, little or no attention has been paid to the placement of reserves to include the best site for genetic variation, nor has the size of reserves considered genetic processes. Although many parks and natural areas function as gene resource conservation areas, the past emphasis on protecting high elevation mountainous sites assures a biased sample of genetic diversity; only populations adapted to the high-elevation environments are included (Ledig 1988). With the exception of the desert region, many of our low-elevation parks and preserves are too small to adequately protect the genetic diversity of the included populations. Few assessments have even been attempted to discover if the existing parks and natural areas adequately protect the genetic variation of even the commercial species. In contrast to California, Washington has recently established a system of one hundred gene-pool reserves for Douglas fir, recognizing the importance of maintaining genetic diversity of this commercial species to the future productivity of the timber industry (Wilson 1990).

Management practices can greatly affect genetic diversity. One notable example is the planting of nonnative rainbow trout throughout the streams of the Sierra Nevada. Planted fish interbred with the native subspecies and stocks of golden trout, nearly eliminating the native locally adapted populations of golden trout in areas like the upper Kern River. Timber harvest practices can select for diminished forest productivity by removing the best trees and leaving weaker or less well-dimensioned trees to provide seed for the future.

Some land management practices now consider the consequences for genetic diversity and future productivity, but more commonly genetics are overlooked. Many restoration projects occurring today are prone to the same difficulty. In an attempt to repair or mitigate environmental damage, restoration projects are replanting with native species. If no attention is paid to the genetic source of the seeds or plantings, the integrity of the gene pool of the surrounding native vegetation may be at risk. Using local sources of plants for restoration will not only increase the likelihood of a successful project, but will also safeguard the existing population (Millar and Libby 1989).

In summary, although several endeavors are working to conserve genetic resources, we cannot quantitatively evaluate the status of genetic diversity in California today. It is well known that genetic resources are found in different levels: the genes themselves, the individuals of a species, and the races or populations that contain genetic attributes not found uniformly throughout the species. Although we know little about the patterns of genetic variation in most wild species, we can use basic principles to help incorporate genetic conservation into conservation and management actions. Genetic conservation efforts now receive less attention than species or ecosystem conservation even though genetic diversity is critical to species' long-term survival, and many activities are daily contributing to the loss of genetic diversity. Several organizations are making progress by increasing California's ex-situ conservation capacity, but these would benefit from coordination. In-situ efforts are still mainly by chance rather than by design. In wildlands, future management and conservation efforts could contribute greatly to maintaining genetic variation, even by the simple initial action of considering the consequences of various management alternatives on the genetic diversity of wild species and their populations.

Species Diversity

The number of species in an area has long been considered indicative of the region's biodiversity. Although species diversity reflects only a portion of the biodiversity of a region, most of us think of particular species as representative of an area, for example, "Redwood Country." Both the particular species present and the diversity of species in a region provide a means of comparing areas.[2] The total number of species gives an indication of the "richness" of an area, whereas the number of endemic species, those species restricted to a single region, indicates how distinctive the flora and fauna of that region are. By all measures, California has unusually high species diversity. California not only has an unusual number of plants and animals, even for so large a state, but a sizable number of California's species are

Tule Elk were nearly extirpated from California in the 1860s due to hunting for tallow, hides, and meat. This population in Point Reyes National Seashore was reintroduced from the San Luis herd in 1978. (Photo by Charles Kennard)

endemic: that is, they are found nowhere else in the world. This confers both a blessing and an obligation.

California is world renowned for its varied and distinctive flora. Our wildflowers are sought for European gardens and the Monterey pine is a significant timber tree in Australia and other countries. There are an estimated 7,850 vascular[3] plant species in California (Hickman 1989).[4] In comparison, Texas, the next most species-rich state, has 5,500 species and Arizona has approximately 3,400 species, yet even they are considered species-rich states (Smith 1987) (table 3.1).

These numbers are estimates because the exact number of vascular plant species present in California is not known; researchers agree there are still many additional species awaiting discovery. When the last complete guide to the flora of California was published (Munz and Keck 1968), 6,633 native plants and 1,013 introduced plants were known to occur in the state (Howell 1972).[5] In the twenty years that followed, over two hundred new native plant species were discovered and described in California (Shevock and Taylor 1987).

Table 3.1. *Numbers of Native and Non-native Plants and Vertebrates in California*

	Vascular Plants		
	Species	*Subspecies*	*Total*
Native	5,143	1,709	6,852
Non-native			1,000 approximately
Total			7,850

	Vertebrate Species					
	Mammals	*Amphibians*	*Reptiles*	*Birds*	*Fish*	*Total*
Native	193	46	82	446	66	833
Non-native	21	3	5	15	47	91
Subtotals	214	49	87	461	113	924

California also harbors the largest number of endemic plant species of any state except Hawaii. Over 1,600 full species of California native plants are found nowhere else in the world, and many of the subspecies are also endemic (Raven and Axelrod 1978, Shevock and Taylor 1987). Nearly half (48 percent) the species found west of the California deserts are endemic. This high endemism, which is very unusual for a continental area, is due in part to the Sierras, which create a wall barring migration and encouraging the evolution of new species. When the flora of the entire state is viewed, one-third (32 percent) of California's native plants are found nowhere else in the world (Raven and Axelrod 1978).

California's unusual plant species diversity results from the many factors that increase habitat complexity; these factors work in concert to create many different niches for plants. Mediterranean climates, with cool, wet winters and hot, dry summers, are found in only five parts of the world: California, Chile, southwestern South Africa, the Mediterranean, and western Australia. All five areas are noted for their diverse and unusual floras (Stebbins 1978). California's climate has more extremes than most of these areas (58 inches of rain annually in Happy Camp, Siskiyou County and 3 inches of rain annually in Blythe, Riverside County (Hornbeck 1983)). Complex geology has created varied topography with several distinct mountain ranges, major valleys, local features such as springs, and unusual substrates such as serpentine and limestone. In conjunction with the varied climate, these geological features present a complex array of plant habitats. In some groups, genetic diversity and a diversity of habitats have led to the evolution of many new species within a single genus. In addition, California has a rich and varied climatological history, so that some of our species are relicts of past, cooler climates (Axelrod 1977). All these contribute to the evolution of a flora that is extremely diverse.

California is also home to one-quarter of the 2,300 vertebrates found in the United States (The Nature Conservancy 1989). The array of plant life, topography, and climate provide a diverse landscape for California's 833 different full species of furred, feathered, finned, and scaled native wildlife[6] (Moyle et al. 1989, Laudenslayer et al. 1991). Although 583 bird species have been sighted in California (Laudenslayer et al. 1991), 454 birds regularly occur in California, and 285 regularly breed in the state, (Bailey 1992). Only one full species of birds is endemic to California, the yellow-billed magpie, although in recent times, the California condor has also been restricted to California. Many subspecies of birds are restricted to the state. These endemic subspecies of birds are particularly common in oak woodlands and chaparral. Miller speculates that the plants and birds were "closely associated in their evolution" dating back to the Pleistocene (Miller 1951). Unlike California's flora, which has assimilated an enormous number of nonnative species, the avifauna includes relatively few permanent introductions. Only eight introduced birds have well-established breeding populations (DeSante and Pyle 1986), although 7 other species including several parrots are common escapees and may become established in southern California (Laudenslayer et al. 1991). Two of these introduced species, the European house sparrow and the starling, are found virtually throughout California.

Bears, deer, bobcats, coyotes, and squirrels are but a few of the 214 different mammals in California. In addition to terrestrial mammals, 37 species of whales, dolphins, porpoises and seals are included on this list. Only 19 mammals are found only in California (Jones and Stokes 1987), whereas 21 species of mammals, including burros, feral pigs, and Norway rats are introduced species (Laudenslayer et al. 1991). Many subspecies of mammals have been identified in the state, and endemic subspecies are particularly common among the small mammals of California.

The proportion of endemic and introduced species varies among the vertebrates. Of the 136 species of turtles, frogs, salamanders, lizards, and other reptiles and amphibians found in California, 17 are endemic and 8 are not native (Jennings 1987). In marked contrast, 40 percent of the 66 full species of native freshwater fish are found only in California and 47 non-native species including carp, mosquito fish, and striped bass have been introduced (Moyle et al. 1989, Moyle 1992).

Insects and other invertebrates comprise the largest group of organisms in California. Butterflies are the best known of the insects, but among the estimated 28,000 California insect species (Powell and Hogue 1979), there are also bees, flies, beetles, grasshoppers, crickets, aphids, dragonflies, ants, and others. Neither the numbers of endemic insects nor an estimate of how many insects have been introduced to the state is available. Sailer (1978) estimates that 1.3 percent of the insect fauna of the United States are introduced. California may have a higher percent of introductions, as the state appears to be fairly vulnerable to the successful establishment of new species (Mooney et al. 1986). Some non-native insect species have been introduced to the state with little consequence, whereas tremendous efforts are waged to assure that some introduced agricultural pests, like the Mediterranean fruit fly, or forest pests, like the gypsy moth, do not become permanent residents.

There are many other types of invertebrates in addition to insects that contribute to California's diversity and to the healthy functioning of natural ecosystems. There are few estimates of how many of these less well-known but quite important organisms are found in the state. A recent study of the H. J. Andrews Experimental Forest in Oregon found 3,402 species of insects and other arthropods just on that one site (Parsons et al. 1991). The invertebrates in California include arachnids (spiders and their allies), crustaceans (such as crabs, crayfish, and shrimp), and molluscs (for example abalone, oysters, and snails). There is also a tremendously diverse group of worms and nematodes, which are crucial to maintaining ecosystem functions such as soil fertility. Anyone who has seen a tidepool realizes that intertidal regions contain a remarkable array of invertebrates. The crustaceans and molluscs are essential links in aquatic food webs in freshwater, estuarine, and marine systems.

In addition, many organisms that seem obscure to all but professional biologists in fact add significantly to the biodiversity of California and the health and well-being of the state's ecosystems. The many exotic wild mushrooms found in specialty food stores give only a glimpse of these riches. Plankton, diatoms, and other one-celled organisms make up the base of aquatic food webs, and perhaps 1,000–1,200 species of lichens, 4,000–5,000 kinds of gilled fungi, 300–400 types of slime molds, and 660 species of mosses and liverworts contribute to the functioning of California's ecosystems (Jones and Stokes 1987).

WHAT HAS BEEN LOST? TRENDS IN SPECIES ENDANGERMENT

Although the California condor is probably the most famous California species in danger of extinction, it is not the first. We have ample evidence that the native species diversity of the state is declining. In fact, seventy plants and animals are known to have been lost from California. The grizzly bear, the gray wolf, the Tecopa pupfish, and the Santa Barbara song sparrow are four of the thirty-eight animals that have been eliminated (Jones and Stokes 1987, Steinhart 1990) (table 3.2). Although eight of these animals, like the wolf and the jaguar, are still found outside California, twenty-one animals are extinct. In addition, several species of birds used to breed regularly in California and now no longer breed in the state, though they are still regular visitors. Thirty-four plant species and subspecies (table 3.3), including the single-flowered mariposa lily and the Point Reyes Indian paintbrush, are presumed extinct in California (Smith and Berg 1988, Bittman 1992).

Extinction is only one measure of lost species diversity. When a single population is lost some biological diversity is lost, because each population contains a unique collection of genetic traits. In the long term, loss of these heritable traits may reduce the species' ability to respond to environmental changes. In the short term, the loss of any one population does not usually result in extinction, although it does bring that species closer to the edge. Too often we pay attention only when the last population is threatened or endangered, ignoring the first populations lost. Attention to the last populations sometimes produces good news; for example, five plants believed extinct have been rediscovered since 1988.[7] However, the news isn't always positive. An additional six to ten plants have not been found in the past thirty years, despite field searches by botanists. They may join our list of extinct plants.

To understand the current status of species diversity, we need to know not only which species have already been lost, but also how many are at risk today. Species are at risk when they become very rare, through either loss of populations or loss of individuals. Evaluating the numbers of species at risk, therefore, requires detailed information on the rarity

Table 3.2. *Animals Extinct or Extirpated from California*

Extinct Animal Species and Subspecies

Long-eared kit fox   *Vulpes macrotis macrotis*
San Clemente Bewick's wren   *Thryomanes bewickii leucophrys*
Santa Barbara song sparrow   *Melospiza melodia graminea*
Tecopa pupfish   *Cyprinodon nevadensis calidae*
Clear Lake splittail   *Pogonichthys ciscoides*
Thick-tail chub   *Gila crassicauda*
Pasadena freshwater shrimp   *Syncaris pasadenae*
Sooty crayfish   *Pacifasticus nigrescens*
Antioch shield-back katydid   *Neduba extincta*
Oblivious tiger beetle   *Cicindela latesignata obliviosa*
San Joaquin Valley tiger beetle   *Cicindela tranquebarica* spp.
Mono Lake hygrotus diving beetle   *Hygrotus artus*
Strohbeen's parnassian butterfly   *Parnassius clodius strohbeeni*
Sthenele satyr butterfly   *Cercyonis sthenele sthenele*
Atossa fritillary butterfly   *Speyeria adiaste atossa*
Xerces blue butterfly   *Glaucopsyche xerces*
El Segundo flower-loving fly   *Raphiomydas terminatus terminatus*
Valley flower-loving fly   *Raphiomydas trochilus*
Antioch robber fly   *Cophura hurdi*
Antioch specid wasp   *Philanthus nasalis*
Yellow-banded andrenid bee   *Perdita hirticeps luteocincta*

Species Extirpated or No Longer Breeding in California, but Surviving Elsewhere

Gray wolf   *Canis lupus*
Grizzly bear   *Ursus arctos*
Mexican jaguar   *Felis onca*
White-tailed deer   *Odocoileus virginianus*
Bison   *Bison bison*
Common loon   *Gavia immer*
Barrow's goldeneye   *Bucephala islandica*
Harlequin duck   *Histrionicus histrionicus*
Harris' hawk   *Parabuteo unicinctus*
Sharp-tailed grouse   *Tympanuchus phasianellus*
Yellow rail   *Coturnicops noveboracensis*
Sonoran mud turtle   *Kinosternon sonoriense*
Bull trout   *Salvelinus confluentus*
Bonytail   *Gila elegans*
Colorado squawfish   *Ptychocheilus lucius*
Flannelmouthsucker   *Catostomus latipinnis*
Largescale sucker   *Catostomus snyderi*

SOURCES: Jennings 1987, Steinhart 1990.

The endangered salt marsh harvest mouse encounters a researcher at an Alviso marsh, near San Jose. (Photo by Charles Kennard)

of each species, and the threats each species faces. Not surprisingly, compiling these data for all the species in California is a very large task. Researchers in California have been compiling these data for over twenty years; the estimates of species at risk are increasingly detailed despite the magnitude of the task and the rapid changes in California that are affecting wild populations of plants and animals.

The number of species on either the California or Federal Endangered Species lists is one approximation of the numbers of species at risk in California. Listed species have been recognized by the government as being on the brink of extinction. By definition, an endangered species is "in danger of extinction throughout all or a significant portion of its range" (16 U.S.C. sec. 1532(6)). Threatened species are those "likely to become an endangered species within the foreseeable future throughout all or a significant portion of its range" (16 U.S.C. sec. 1532(20)). In the fall of 1991, 150 plants and 106 animals in California were listed as threatened or endangered by the federal or state government;[8] an additional 66 plants were listed as rare (CDFG 1991*a*, 1991*b*). Rare species have so few populations or individuals that they are intrinsically vulnerable to threats.[9]

Table 3.3. *Plants Extinct in California*

Laurel Hill manzanita   *Arctostaphylos hookeri ssp. franciscana*
Curved-pod Mohave milk-vetch   *Astragalus mohavensis var. hemigyrus*
Ventura marsh milk-vetch   *Astragalus pycnostachyus var. lanosissimus*
Oregon moonwort fern   *Botrychium pumicola*
Single-flowered mariposa lily   *Calochortus monanthus*
Livid sedge   *Carex livida*
Pt. Reyes indian paintbrush   *Castilleja leschkeana*
San Fernando Valley spineflower   *Chorizanthe parryi var. fernandina*
Mosquin's clarkia   *Clarkia mosquinii ssp. mosquinii*
Enterprise clarkia   *Clarkia mosquinii ssp. xerophila*
California dissanthelium grass   *Dissanthelium californicum*
Mt. Diablo buckwheat   *Eriogonum truncatum*
Los Angeles sunflower   *Helianthus nuttallii ssp. parishii*
Mojave tarplant   *Hemizonia mohavensis*
Howellia   *Howellia aquatilis*
Santa Catalina Island desert-thorn   *Lycium hassei*
San Nicholas Island box-thorn   *Lycium verrucosum*
Mendocino bush mallow   *Malacothamnus mendocinensis*
Santa Cruz Island monkeyflower   *Mimulus brandegei*
Santa Catalina Island monkeyflower   *Mimulus traskiae*
Whipple's monkeyflower   *Mimulus whipplei*
Veiny monardella   *Monardella douglasii var. venosa*
Merced monardella   *Monardella leucocephala*
Pringle's monardella   *Monardella pringlei*
Adder's-tongue fern   *Ophioglossum vulgatum*
Shasta owl's clover   *Orthocarpus pachystachyus*
Saline Valley phacelia   *Phacelia amabilis*
Ashy phacelia   *Phacelia cinerea*
San Francisco popcornflower   *Plagiobothrys diffusus*
Petaluma popcornflower   *Plagiobothrys mollis var. vestitus*
Ballona cinquefoil   *Potentilla multijuga*
Keck's checkerbloom   *Sidalcea keckii*
Showy Indian clover   *Trifolium amoenum*
Caper-fruited tropidocarpum   *Tropidocarpum capparideum*

SOURCES: Smith and Berg 1988; M. Skinner 1992.

The list of endangered species vastly understates the numbers of species at risk. Many species meet the scientific criteria for listing but the administrative process has not been completed. Increasingly, political controversies are obstructing listing of species that scientists agree are endangered. Often the controversies surrounding the listing process are arguments about the actions necessary to save the species, rather than evaluations of whether the species is in trouble.

Official lists of candidates for listing under the Endangered Species Act or species of concern lists held by the U.S. Fish and Wildlife Service or the California Department of Fish and Game indicate that 215 animal species and subspecies may be in trouble (CDFG 1991c). The number of plant species and subspecies at risk in California is considerably larger. The California Native Plant Society's *Inventory of Rare and Endangered Vascular Plants of California* includes 383 plants which merit listing as threatened or endangered but are not yet listed by the state (Smith and Berg 1988, Skinner 1992). *In short, 599 plants (9 percent of the native species and subspecies) and 306 vertebrates (30 percent of the full species of natives)* [10] *are documented to be declining or seriously at risk of extinction, yet only a small portion of this group has received the minimal protection afforded by the state and federal endangered species acts.*

Unless conditions change, these species will not simply hang on at low numbers into the indefinite future while society decides whether or not to act. The Center for Plant Conservation recently estimated that if current trends continue 680 plants will become extinct in the United States by the end of the century. California is home to 129 of these species (Shabecoff 1988). The numbers of plants at risk in California are even more significant nationally because so many of these species are found nowhere else. If they are lost here, they are lost to the world.

Many other species are declining, but are not yet so diminished in numbers and geographic range to qualify as threatened or endangered species. Some of these are major commercial species like the crab, striped bass, and abalone. Others are species hunted for sport, such as the numerous species of waterfowl whose numbers have declined so dramatically. In addition, many common species' numbers and ranges have declined in response to the many activities threatening species in California. Although these species are not in imminent danger of extinction, the decline in their numbers represents a loss of genetic diversity nonetheless.

The history of the winter-run Chinook salmon shows that the declining commercial species of today may be the endangered species of tomorrow. The world's population of winter-run Chinook spawn in California, virtually all of them in the Sacramento River system.[11] Annual runs numbered from 60,000 to 120,000 individuals in the late 1960s; in 1988 the annual run had only 2,000 fish (Moyle et al. 1989). The Department of Fish and Game (CDFG) has concluded that water diversions and dams are responsible for the precipitous decline of the winter-run chinook. The Red Bluff dam is a major impediment to spawning, and changes in the gravel beds downstream have diminished the spawning areas below the dam. The dam, water flow management, and drought continue to threaten the winter-run chinook salmon, which was listed as endangered by the Fish and Game Commission in 1989. Listing did not end the controversy, however. Fights over appropriate actions to recover the species continue while numbers decline. The run in 1992 contained only 191 fish (Diringer 1992).

Declining species may be indicators of the poor health of an ecosystem; when individual species can no longer be sustained by the system, something is amiss. In addition, because species are dependent upon others in the food-web, through predator-prey relationships and through cooperative relationships as between plants and their pollinators, when one species declines others will feel the effects. Loss of critical or keystone species in an ecosystem can result in a cascade of extinctions of other species that are linked together (Terborgh and Winter 1980). Linked species losses have been documented in the Pacific Northwest, where the removal of a single predator species resulted in the local loss of many other species in the marine intertidal ecosystem (Paine 1966).

SPECIES PROTECTION

Species can be protected by protecting their habitat, by regulating their take and harvest, or by a combination of habitat protection and regulations. Two laws, the California Endangered Species Act (CESA) and the Federal Endangered Species Act (ESA), are designed to protect animals from actions that would harm individuals or their habitat.[12] Plants receive less protection under these laws. Furthermore, the protection offered by the ESA, as measured by the population trends of listed species, appears ineffective. Nearly 75 percent of listed plant species and 58 percent of listed animal species are still declining, despite their listing under the CESA (CDFG 1991d). Clearly, listing alone does not protect species. Many other laws regulate the harvest of species for commercial and recreational reasons. As these laws, unlike the ESAs, govern only harvest of species, they cannot protect species from other threats such as pollution or habitat loss. For most endangered organisms, regulating loss is not enough to prevent extinction. By the time a species is eligible for listing, affirmative actions are needed to ensure recovery.

Protection of habitat is widely recognized as the most effective way to protect species. Many people advocate establishing a system of parks or protected areas to protect representative habitats of all the species in the state. To evaluate our progress on this front, we must look at the status of ecosystem diversity in the state.

Terrestrial Ecosystem Diversity

Ecosystem diversity encompasses the variety of different systems in which plants, animals, and microorganisms interact with the nonliving environment. Although ecosystem diversity is the largest scale of biodiversity, we can think of many different scales within ecosystem diversity. The largest is *biome,* which is a community characteristic of a broad global climatic region, such as the boreal forest found in Canada, Siberia, and other high-latitude areas of the Northern Hemisphere. The next smaller scale is the *habitat-type,* a repeating assemblage of plants and animals characteristic of the environmental constraints of a region or locale, such as the familiar oak woodlands, redwood forests, Sierran trout streams, or coastal dunes. The smallest scale is the *micro-habitat.* Examples include the deep pools trout live in, or the fallen logs in the redwood forest under which salamanders dwell.

The best scale at which to evaluate ecosystem diversity in California is the habitat-type. The names alone evoke images exemplifying California: valley oak woodland, Joshua tree desert-woodland, or mixed conifer forest. Evaluating the status of terrestrial ecosystem diversity requires knowing how many habitat-types there are, how much area each one covers, what has been lost, the current condition of California's habitat-types, and what has been protected. This section addresses these questions first for terrestrial habitats, and second for aquatic habitats.

Like many other researchers, we use dominant vegetation as an indicator of terrestrial habitat-type. This is for both theoretical and pragmatic reasons. The geographic distributions of the dominant plant species are generally well correlated with climate, so vegetation is considered indicative of the climate and other environmental variables. In addition, the dominant vegetation has a profound effect on the resources available at a site and influences which other species will be found. For example, little sunlight reaches the forest floor underneath a tall forest, constraining which species can grow there. Finally, different types of vegetation provide different homes or habitats for wildlife. Hawks that nest in tall trees won't make their home in chaparral. So vegetation diversity indicates habitat-type diversity. Vegetation types are distinct, identifiable, recurring assemblages of organisms and environmental features that incorporate a significant portion of a region's biodiversity. In addition, inventorying the existing vegetation of an area is a relatively straightforward task, although for a region the size of California a time-consuming and expensive task, and hence has not yet been accomplished.

To review the status of California's habitat diversity, we must have units or categories of analysis. However, unlike species diversity, no scientific consensus exists on how to identify units or subunits of habitats that can be counted or evaluated. Each different vegetation classification system has been designed to meet a particular goal—identifying wildlife habitat, identifying highly productive timber types, or identifying units of plant diversity. Since agencies and researchers organize data for their own purposes it is frequently quite difficult to synthesize information from different sources. Although there are published efforts to translate between different systems (e.g., de Becker and Sweet 1988), the proliferation of specialized classification systems makes the comparison of classifications awkward at best and results in incompatible data sets (table 3.4). The assortment of approaches to habitat-type classification does not decrease the importance of assessing the status of habitat diversity in California; it simply makes the task more challenging.

California's habitat-type diversity is very rich, corresponding to the notable species diversity. The Department of Fish and Game's Natural Diversity Data Base (NDDB) is the best single source of information on the status of rare species and rare habitats in the state. Unlike most habitat classification systems, NDDB's list is designed with the purpose of documenting California's biodiversity. The NDDB list of natural communities identifies 273 terrestrial communities in California (Holland 1986). Unfortunately the NDDB program does not have estimates of either current or historic acreages for the majority of the com-

Table 3.4. *An Example of 5 Different Habitat Classification Systems, Designed for Five Different Purposes* *

	Number of Habitats				
	WHR	*FRRAP*	*NDDB*	*CALVEG*	*KUCHLER*
Terrestrial and Wetland habitats	45	31	273	125	54
Aquatic habitats	4	1	123	0	0
Other (urban or crops)	3	1	0	0	0
Total	52	33	396	125	54
Distribution of Terrestrial Habitat Types by Biome					
Forest and woodland types	27	16	116	73	32
Scrub types	12	10	93	45	13
Herbaceous types	6	4	41	7	7
Other types	3	3	23**	0	2

SOURCES:
WHR = Mayer and Laudenslayer 1988
FRRAP = CDF 1988
NDDB = Holland 1986 and Ellison 1984
CALVEG = Parker and Matyas 1981
KUCHLER = Kuchler 1977
* Note the variation in the numbers of types of habitats described by each.
** The number of "other" types in the NDDB classification system includes no urban or agricultural types.

munity types it identifies. No statistics are available to show how widespread each of the 273 types are. The only source of statewide data on current acreages of habitat-types in California is the Department of Forestry's Forest and Range Resource Assessment Program (FRRAP). However, this program uses one of the most generalized classification systems in California, lumping many different habitat-types together. The FRRAP assessment collects information on the acreage of 31 terrestrial habitat-types plus water areas and urban/agricultural areas (CDF 1988). For example, FRRAP identifies only 10 different types of shrub vegetation whereas NDDB identifies 93 types; and although NDDB identifies 123 different types of aquatic habitat, FRRAP lumps everything into one category—water.

Although FRRAP's system does not adequately represent the diversity of habitat-types in California, it is the only comprehensive collection of acreage estimates for the entire state. Simplifying California into thirty-one different habitat-types streamlines the inventory task, allowing broad statistics to be compiled. Unfortunately, this broad-brush approach suggests that everything with the same name is the same ecosystem. Over-aggregation encourages people to forget that the foothill hardwood habitat-types of Tehama County are different from those of Kern County or San Diego County. The soils, dominant oak species, and many of the resident animals are different between these three areas.

A second problem with broad categories for inventorying habitat-type diversity is that some special habitat-types are overlooked because they are small or occur infrequently. Vernal pools and desert oases are two examples of habitat-types that are very important to wildlife, but because they are found as small dots on the landscape they are not included in a statewide mapping effort. As a result, small habitat-types are not included in the broad list of habitat-types or in the statistics. Visually, on a map of the state's habitat-types, in the area painted tan for the desert, oases will also be painted tan, rather than blue for a watery area. Vernal pools will be painted green for the grassland matrix in which they occur, instead of blue for a wetland.

Community types that occur infrequently are also omitted from the broad-brush approach to habitat-type inventorying. For example, serpentine soil areas, though not necessarily small, are relatively uncommon in the state. Serpentine soils have unusual chemistry due to the minerals in the rocks on which they occur. The characteristic soils make it difficult for most plants to grow. As a result, serpentine areas often have unusual vegetation and many endemic species. Not only do serpentine areas occur infrequently around the state, some areas are covered with herbaceous species, others with shrubs, and others with trees. Serpentine areas and other infrequent habitat-types are difficult to include in a broad-brush inventory, even though they contribute significantly to California's ecosystem diversity. In a map, they are also painted the same color as the surrounding habitat-type.

Despite the limits of the FRRAP inventory, it is the best available, and it is the first such comprehensive analysis. Mapping and inventorying at a detailed scale is a large and difficult endeavor. New efforts are progressing to produce a more detailed analysis of the vegetation of California, both through collaborations among state agencies and through innovative work being done using remote sensing data and field work to combine habitat data in a geographic information system at University of California, Santa Barbara. Our knowledge will improve as these efforts come to fruition.

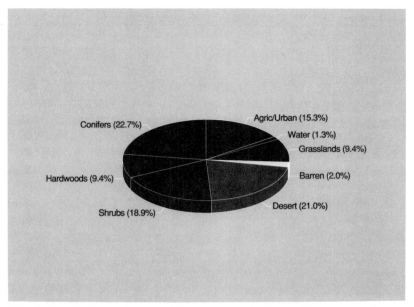

3.1. California biomes. Percent of the state's area by biome (CDF 1988). The total area of the state is 101 million acres. These figures do not include 2 million acres of unirrigated agricultural land in California.

A broad overview of land patterns shows that the majority (83 percent) of California's 101 million acres are wildlands. Densely populated urban areas and agricultural areas cover 15 percent of the state [13] and 1 percent is covered by water (figure 3.1). Dividing California's area into biomes, conifers cover 23 percent and are typical of the mountains of northwestern California and the Sierra Nevada. (Conifers also occur in the mountains of the South Coast and Peninsular Ranges and on several high mountain peaks in the desert.) Hardwoods (e.g., oak woodlands) cover about 9 percent and are most prevalent in the Central Coast Ranges and the Central Valley where they form a mid-elevation band. Shrublands including chaparral, coastal scrub, and sagebrush cover 19 percent, spanning elevations from high to low. Grasslands and other herbaceous types cover 9 percent of the state, mainly in the Central Valley, Central Coast Ranges, and Sierran foothill regions. Over one-fifth of California (21 percent) is desert, including a great variety of shrub and cactus habitat-types. The high peaks and other extremely rocky areas comprise the last 2 percent of the area: alpine barrens or

Table 3.5. *Acreages of Major Vegetation Types (Includes 31 Types)*

Habitat-type	Acres	% of State
Closed-cone pine/cypress	78,000	0.08
Ponderosa pine	2,651,000	2.62
Mixed conifer	9,268,000	9.18
Douglas fir	1,772,000	1.75
Redwood	1,570,000	1.55
Red fir	1,906,000	1.89
Jeffrey pine	700,000	0.69
Lodgepole pine	752,000	0.74
Subalpine conifer	228,000	0.23
Pinyon-juniper	1,463,000	1.45
Juniper	1,469,000	1.45
Montane hardwood-conifer	1,156,000	1.14
Montane hardwood	2,049,000	2.03
Valley-foothill hardwood	7,363,000	7.29
Valley riparian	49,000	0.05
Montane riparian	86,000	0.09
Coastal scrub	2,507,000	2.48
Chamise-red shank	4,808,000	4.76
Mixed chaparral	2,954,000	2.92
Montane chaparral	1,039,000	1.03
Alpine dwarf scrub	206,000	0.20
Sagebrush	6,549,000	6.48
Bitterbrush	581,000	0.58
Low sagebrush	507,000	0.50
Annual grassland	8,653,000	8.57
Perennial grassland	90,000	0.09
Fresh emergent wetland	576,000	0.57
Wet meadow	238,000	0.24
Alkali scrub	1,299,000	1.29
Other desert	19,979,000	19.78
Alpine barren and rock	2,120,000	2.10
Total Forest and Rangeland	84,666,000	83.83
Urban, Agriculture, and Water	16,334,000	16.17
Total	101,000,000	100.00

SOURCE: Adapted from CDF 1988.
NOTE: Agricultural acres include only irrigated lands. AFT 1986 reports an additional 2 million acres are dryland farmed.

rock (figure 3.1). Table 3.5 lists the acreages of each of the thirty-one habitat types assessed by FRRAP.

LOSSES OF TERRESTRIAL ECOSYSTEMS IN CALIFORNIA

Since European settlers first arrived in California, over 17 million acres have been converted from natural habitat to urban or agricultural uses.[14] Although these processes began three hundred years ago, much of the habitat loss has occurred recently, and the pace has been increasing. Nearly 5 million acres were converted between 1950 and 1980, approximately 3.8 million to agricultural land and 1 million to urban uses (CDF 1988). Five major habitat-types have lost significant acreages in this thirty-year period: grasslands, coastal scrub, foothill oak woodland, closed-cone pine-cypress, and redwood forests (table 3.6). Although these habitat-types are not usually thought of as being in danger, significant losses over such a short period guarantee that the species dependent upon these habitat-types, and the ecological services these habitat-types provide, have been greatly diminished in some parts of California.

For many of the 10 million acres converted from native ecosystems to agriculture or urban uses prior to 1950 we will never know what habitat-types were lost. Some habitat-types, like interior wetlands and Central Valley riparian forests, have lost over 80 percent of their historic acreage. However, for certain regions, like the southern San Joaquin Valley which is now almost entirely irrigated agriculture, the original vegetation remains a mystery. Only a few tiny fragments of native vegetation remain to provide clues as to the nature and extent of the original vegetation. The Valley's saltbush scrub, vernal pools, and grasslands are home to blunt-nosed leopard lizards and giant kangaroo rats, both of which are endangered species persisting in the remnants of these habitats; researchers can only speculate on how much of each habitat-type was previously found in the Valley.

Conversion of land to more intensive uses has not occurred evenly across habitat types. In general, habitats associated with water—wetlands, vernal pools, and riparian vegetation—have lost proportionally more acreage than other types. Any habitat-type found only along the central and south coast is also likely to be subject to significant habitat loss from urban development. For example, the coastal sage scrub in San Diego and Orange counties has been reduced to only a fraction of

Table 3.6. *Habitat Acreage Lost Through Conversion to Urban and Agricultural Land*

Recent Conversions: Between 1950 and 1980		
	Acres Converted	% of Total Acreage Converted 1950–1980
Redwood	62,000	4
Douglas fir	2,000	<1
Red fir	1,000	<1
Ponderosa-Jeffrey pine	80,000	2
Mixed conifer	42,000	<1
Lodgepole pine	1,000	<1
Juniper-pinyon	29,000	1
Closed-cone pine-cypress	4,000	5
Montane hardwood-conifer	27,000	1
Valley foothill hardwood	590,000	7
Chaparral	203,000	2
Sagebrush	217,000	3
Coastal scrub	294,000	11
Grassland	2,995,000	26
Desert	300,000	1
Subtotal	4,847,000	

Habitat Conversion over Longer Time Span		
		% of Total Converted
Valley riparian	81,100	89
Valley wetlands	3,800,000	94
Coastal wetlands	200,000	80
Valley vernal pools	2,800,000	56
Subtotal	6,881,100	

Total acreage converted where habitat-type lost is known = 11,728,100.
Total acreage urban area or irrigated agriculture today = 15,211,000.
(AFT 1986 reports an additional 2 million acres are dryland farmed.)

SOURCES: Katibah 1984, CDF 1988, CDPR 1988, Airola 1989.

Few low elevation landscapes look as they did when European settlers first arrived in California. Here introduced annuals dominate where native perennial grasses were once common. (Photo by David Cavagnaro)

its historic acreage (Westman 1987), and losses are continuing. One result has been the decline of several species dependent on coastal sage scrub, including the California gnatcatcher and the coastal cactus wren, both of which have been proposed for listing under the state and federal Endangered Species Acts. Land use patterns in adjacent parts of Mexico are also greatly impacting the coastal sage scrub and its resident species.

Land conversion figures compiled by FRRAP refer only to conversion from native vegetation to agricultural use or urban use. Areas where the vegetation was manipulated for low-intensity rural purposes, such as converting a brushfield to grassland for grazing, represent additional habitat losses and are not documented by FRRAP. Nor is land subjected to rural or low-density residential development reflected in the figures of acreage converted, despite dramatic increases in this growth pattern in the foothills and some areas of southern California and the desert. Both of these "uncounted" conversions result in habitat loss and fragmentation. Small patches within larger areas are paved or built upon, leaving the landscape as a whole with less wildland. But data are not available to evaluate which habitats have been most affected by habitat-type conversions or rural/"ranchette" development.

CURRENT CONDITIONS AND FUTURE TRENDS

What is the health of the acres that have not been converted for agricultural or urban uses? Determining the condition of California's ecosystem diversity is at the heart of evaluating the status of biodiversity and of predicting future trends. If the habitats are healthy and can successfully provide ecosystem services and maintain viable populations of all species, then we can expect biodiversity to fare well (although not in those habitats that have lost tremendous acreage). Conversely, if many habitats are degraded, the future is likely to include additional losses of biodiversity unless the practices causing degradation are altered. Current and future threats to biodiversity are discussed in depth in chapter 4; only a few points, focused on specific habitats, will be mentioned here.

Information on condition or habitat quality is available for only a few terrestrial habitat-types and these data are disturbing. Many habitat-types are known to be threatened by existing land management practices, pollution, and water use and diversions. For example, nearly 18 million acres of California are privately owned grazing land. Most of this grazing land is either annual grassland, or valley foothill woodland. The U.S. Soil Conservation Service documented surface erosion problems on 6.9 million acres of nonfederal grazing land in California (USDA 1984). Thus a significant percentage of the private rangelands are experiencing excessive surface soil erosion. Soil erosion contributes to decreased ecosystem services through nutrient loss from the soils, soil degradation, and water quality problems.

The condition of an ecosystem may change, making it less suitable for wild plants and animals, while still providing some goods and services. The California grasslands long ago were converted from a grassland dominated by native perennial grasses to one dominated by annual species introduced from the Mediterranean (Heady 1977). This complete shift in the dominant species from natives to nonnatives has likely had an adverse effect on many native species, but the grasslands remain productive rangelands. Introduced grasses provide good forage, and although they compete with the natives for water, nutrients, and space there is no conclusive evidence that the introduced grasses alone have caused the extinction of any native species. In contrast, several introduced species are serious range weeds. For example, yellow star thistle from Europe is now a problem in twenty-eight counties because it is unpalatable to livestock. Probably one million acres of rangeland have been made less productive by this species (Thompsen 1985, cited in CDF 1988).

Desert habitats seem hardy to the casual observer because of the harsh climates they endure, but they are very vulnerable to damage from off-road vehicles and military maneuvers. The desert has become increasingly accessible as a recreation area for California's growing population. More than 35,000 miles of roads and trails crisscross the desert. Off-road travel in the desert breaks open the protective cover of desert pavement and native plant growth, exposing the surface to wind erosion and leaving scars that take decades or even centuries to heal (Stebbins 1990). Desert soils are particularly vulnerable to compaction and damage, and the harsh conditions makes recovery slow (Webb and Wilshire 1983). In 1980, the Bureau of Land Management estimated that 47,900 acres were disturbed by motorized vehicles, but researchers at the University of California estimated that significant disturbance had occurred in ten times this area, and impacts of unrated severity had occurred in perhaps twenty times this area (Wake 1980).

Although the condition of California's habitats may be the best indicator of the status of biodiversity, it is also the most difficult to evaluate. Too often it is assumed that so long as some vegetation is standing, and some animals are present, all is well. Unfortunately, this is not the case; where data are available, they show that many diverse activities are decreasing the health of habitat types.

PROTECTION OF TERRESTRIAL ECOSYSTEMS

Land acquisition is one of the most important tools in the protection of biodiversity. Today 12 percent of California is in some type of protected area; but only half of this area, or 6 percent of the state, is managed primarily for the protection of biodiversity. The remainder serves several purposes. Is this enough to protect biodiversity? To answer this question, we must know whether the existing system of protected areas includes representative examples of California's biodiversity, and whether these areas are managed to adequately protect biodiversity.

Before evaluating whether California's parks and protected areas are adequate to protect biodiversity, first ask the question, Should parks be expected to do all that is needed? The answer is a resounding, No! Conservation planners all over the world recommend a multifaceted approach to habitat protection, starting with a system of protected areas that include key sites where the land is dedicated to conservation. These "core" areas provide safe sites for species and ecosystems. Land surrounding the core, when managed sustainably for multiple uses, provides both economic return from the land and habitat for many different species. These multiple-use lands can act as "buffer areas" between preserves and areas away from the core that have little habitat value for biological diversity. In addition to land preservation, laws and regulations to protect critical habitats and species and to guarantee that lands are not degraded are necessary components of a conservation program.

Although many acknowledge that parks alone are not enough, all agree that parks are essential to the protection of biodiversity (for example: Harris 1984, McNeeley and Miller 1984, Jensen 1987a, Western and Pearl 1989). Parks protect populations of species from land conversion and habitat loss, and maintain gene pools for wild species. As large areas of California are used more intensively, many species will only be able to persist in parks and protected areas. But more importantly, parks allow the ecosystem processes to continue. Functioning, productive ecosystems change over time, and the species living within these ecosystems evolve in response to changing environmental conditions.

An ideal system of protected areas in California would contain representative stands of all the habitat-types in the state. Each protected area would be designed to incorporate the patterns and variety found at a landscape scale to assure that successional sequences and wildlife corridors are included. The system would also contain duplication so that the geographic range of each habitat was represented. Widespread habitat-types, such as white fir forest, found from the Warner Mountains of Modoc County, south along the Sierra Nevada, to some of the high desert ranges, should be included in more than one preserved area to encompass the full range of species present within that habitat-type, as well as the genetic variation between the different populations of the wide-ranging species. To the extent that different locations of the white fir habitat-type vary in their species composition, ecological interactions, and genetic makeup, duplication actually provides completeness to the reserve system. To the extent that different examples of white fir habitats are similar, duplication provides redundancy and thereby safeguards the system against loss of one site from a catastrophic event like fire. This strategy for designing a system of natural areas is used by the U.S. Forest Service for the identification and establishment of Research Natural Areas (RNAs) in California. Their goal is to have one RNA of each forest type within each province of California (see figure 3.2). California Department of Parks and Recreation (DPR) and the University of California's Natural Reserve System have similar goals of protecting representative examples of the state's ecosystems.

Habitat-types are very unevenly included within the parks and protected areas of California. Although 12 percent of California is in some type of protected area, 12 percent of each habitat-type is not; a few habitat-types are much better represented (figure 3.3). Of the twenty-five types of habitats evaluated by FRRAP, two (alpine dwarf scrub and subalpine conifer forests) have over 90 percent of their acreage in protected areas (CDF 1988). They will fare well unless threats from outside affect their survival in parks. Other habitats are also over-represented. Conifer forests cover 23 percent of California, but comprise 38 percent of the land in protected areas. Both of these patterns reflect the large acreages of the Forest Service Wilderness Areas and the National Parks in the high Sierra. Other habitat types, like valley riparian forest and perennial grasslands, are dramatically under-represented; less than 2 percent of their area is within protected areas (table 3.7). Unfortunately, the habitats that are poorly represented include some of those that are highly threatened.

The parks and protected areas of California are also unevenly distributed geographically. Although 29 percent of the land east of the Sierra is in some type of reserved status, only 3 percent of the Sacramento Valley region is reserved. This pattern reflects both land ownership and regional history. Regions that are major agricultural areas or are primarily under private ownership have fewer reserved acres. The risk posed by the skewed regional distribution of preserves is that species found only in those regions with few reserves are less well protected, and only a small portion of the genetic diversity of wide-ranging species is protected.

Many land management agencies in California have a goal of protecting representative examples of the state's habitat-types in each province, but progress toward this goal is uneven. This is in part due to a lack of detailed information about which habitats occur within the existing parks and preserves of California (Jensen 1983). Without a fairly detailed understanding of which habitat-types already occur within parks

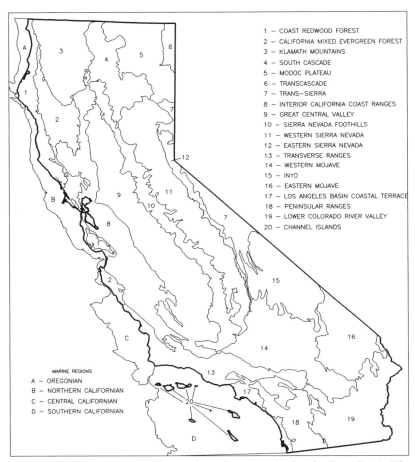

1 – COAST REDWOOD FOREST
2 – CALIFORNIA MIXED EVERGREEN FOREST
3 – KLAMATH MOUNTAINS
4 – SOUTH CASCADE
5 – MODOC PLATEAU
6 – TRANSCASCADE
7 – TRANS–SIERRA
8 – INTERIOR CALIFORNIA COAST RANGES
9 – GREAT CENTRAL VALLEY
10 – SIERRA NEVADA FOOTHILLS
11 – WESTERN SIERRA NEVADA
12 – EASTERN SIERRA NEVADA
13 – TRANSVERSE RANGES
14 – WESTERN MOJAVE
15 – INYO
16 – EASTERN MOJAVE
17 – LOS ANGELES BASIN COASTAL TERRACE
18 – PENINSULAR RANGES
19 – LOWER COLORADO RIVER VALLEY
20 – CHANNEL ISLANDS

MARINE REGIONS
A – OREGONIAN
B – NORTHERN CALIFORNIAN
C – CENTRAL CALIFORNIAN
D – SOUTHERN CALIFORNIAN

3.2. Ecological regions of California (from the Natural Diversity Data Base). The USFS uses a similar but more simplified map of provinces.

and preserves, it is difficult to efficiently improve protection. Gaps in the reserve system need to be identified and then filled by new acquisitions.

Sufficient data already exist to fill some of the obvious gaps in the reserve system while the data bases are improving. FRRAP has made a first-cut estimate using a fairly coarse analysis. In the fall of 1989, the DPR began an inventory of the vegetation types found on its 1.2 million acres (Roye 1989). The Forest Service is currently evaluating its target system to ascertain if representative examples of forest types are,

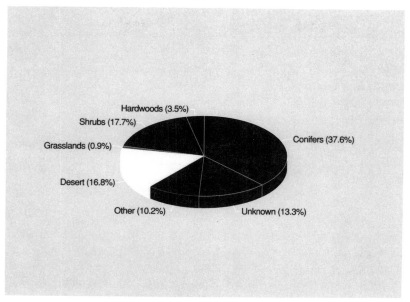

Hardwoods (3.5%)
Shrubs (17.7%)
Grasslands (0.9%)
Conifers (37.6%)
Desert (16.8%)
Other (10.2%)
Unknown (13.3%)

3.3. Vegetative cover of California's protected areas. Total acreage in protected areas is approximately 12 million acres (CDF 1988).

or will be, included in their RNAs. But some of the federal agencies have made little progress in designating protected areas and others do not have a plan to protect representative habitats.

Recognizing the importance of evaluating the gaps in protection provided by reserve systems, the U.S. Fish and Wildlife Service (USFWS) has begun a study of the protection status of vegetation types and vertebrate species. Using geographic information systems, they can overlay the boundaries of parks and reserves over the distributions of vegetation and vertebrate species ranges and get a coarse-scale overview of the gaps in habitat and species protection. The work will identify landscapes that contain large numbers of potentially unprotected vegetation types and species. Such areas may be most desirable for future preserve establishment and can be the focus of intensive field investigations.

These projects are referred to as "gaps analyses." The California "gaps" project is jointly funded by the National Fish and Wildlife Foundation and Southern California Edison Company and is being completed at University of California, Santa Barbara (Davis et al. 1991). The project necessarily includes many collaborators, including the U.S. Fish and

Table 3.7. *Acreage of Habitat-types in California and Acres Protected*
(*In Thousands of Acres*)

Habitat	Total Acres	% of State	Acres Reserved	% Habitat Reserved
Closed-cone pine-cypress	78	0.1	10.14	13
Ponderosa pine	2,651	2.6	212.08	8
Montane hardwood	2,049	2.0	143.43	7
Montane hardwood-conifer	1,156	1.1	69.36	6
Mixed conifer	9,268	9.2	1,112.16	12
Douglas-fir	1,772	1.8	177.2	10
Redwood	1,570	1.6	172.7	11
Red fir	1,906	1.9	933.94	49
Jeffrey pine	700	0.7	112	16
Lodgepole pine	752	0.7	624.16	83
Subalpine conifer	228	0.2	207.48	91
Coastal scrub	2,507	2.4	150.42	6
Valley-foothill hardwood	7,363	7.3	294.52	4
Valley riparian	49	0.1	0.98	2
Montane riparian	86	0.1		
Pinyon-Juniper	1,463	1.5	131.67	9
Juniper	1,469	1.5	161.59	11
Chamise-red shank	4,808	4.8	432.72	9
Mixed chaparral	2,954	2.9	324.94	11
Montane chaparral	1,039	1.0	249.36	24
Alpine dwarf scrub	206	0.2	185.4	9
Sagebrush	6,549	6.5	982.35	15
Bitterbrush	581	0.6		
Low sagebrush	507	0.5		
Annual grassland	8,653	8.6	173.06	2
Perennial grassland	90	0.1	1.8	2
Fresh emergent wetland	576	0.6		
Other desert	19,979	19.7	1,798.11	9
Alkali scrub	1,299	1.3	298.77	23
Wet meadow	238	0.2		
Alpine barren and rock	2,120	2.1		
Urban agriculture	15,211	15.0		
Water	1,348	1.3		
Unknown			1,500	
Totals	101,225	100	10,460.34	

SOURCE: Adapted from CDF 1988.
NOTE: These acreages are from a geographic analysis. The total acreages in table 3.8, which come from records of land ownership of the listed organization, are larger.

Wildlife Service, the California Department of Fish and Game, the California Department of Forestry, the California Nature Conservancy, and many others. The initial phase of the California gaps analysis is being conducted for Southern California. The anticipated products include a new vegetation map for California, digital information on the distribution of vertebrates, and an analysis of the vertebrates and vegetation included within existing protected areas. This research is likely just the first low-resolution compilation of information, but it will facilitate more detailed regional studies. Gaps analyses are being conducted in all the western states and are planned for all the states in the country. When complete, it should be possible for the first time to identify gaps (or redundancies) in systems of parks and protected areas across state boundaries.

Knowledge of what areas need additional attention is a necessary but not sufficient condition for successful conservation. Often important biological areas are sites including several land owners, and only cooperative projects can succeed. Collaborations between agencies have been sporadic in the past. Now a collaborative effort called the Interagency Natural Areas Coordinating Committee (INACC) is encouraging agencies to work together on conservation activities at the regional level. INACC, a program initiated by CDFG, was started by agreement of the heads of the major state, federal, and private land management organizations in California. After several years of meetings at the statewide level, regional committees were formed. Both the magnitude of the task and the need for local coordination motivated the groups to meet to discuss land management and protection issues specific to each region. Although regional INACC committees have not yet been formed in each region of the state, those already started are proving to be one of the more successful ways of establishing contact between the various agencies involved in biodiversity management. Individuals living and working within the same region are able to share information on management problems and solutions and can work toward more complete regional representation of biodiversity within their area by looking across jurisdictional boundaries.

There are many types of protected areas and managed areas in California, not all of which are "core" areas where biodiversity protection is the highest priority. Each designated category of reserved land has different objectives and substantially different constraints on the types of activities permissible (Cochrane 1986). Approximately 6.4 million acres in California have been set aside primarily for the protection and maintenance of ecological processes and the species dependent upon these processes. These lands are designated as parks, nature reserves, research natural areas, and other similar categories. Another 5.5 million acres of reserves are used for a combination of purposes, such as recreation and commodity production in addition to the conservation of species and ecological processes. Wilderness areas, wildlife refuges, and recreation areas are some of the designations of these protected areas.

Different levels of protection are afforded by the different categories of protected area. Some areas are managed primarily for the production of waterfowl or deer, whereas others are open for use as all-terrain vehicle recreation areas. Some areas are subject to fire suppression, others to prescribed burning, and some managed areas are grazed by livestock. These different goals and management practices make it difficult to ascertain whether a given area is "protecting" all of the components of biological diversity. As a rough estimate, only about half of the lands in reserved status, or about 6 percent of California, are managed primarily for the protection and maintenance of ecological processes and all native species present in these areas (table 3.8).

Conflicts regarding the appropriate management of California's state parklands are becoming more common. Many believe that state parks are not functioning as "core" areas of California's conservation efforts, safe from practices that have adverse impacts on biodiversity. The purpose of state parks, run by the California Department of Parks and Recreation, "shall be to preserve outstanding natural, scenic, and cultural values, indigenous aquatic and terrestrial fauna and flora" (Public Resources Code 5019.53). Despite this mandate many state parks are embroiled in management controversies because grazing is permitted in park lands, and because of proposals to remove non-native vegetation such as eucalyptus.[15] Not all lands managed by DPR have nature conservation as their primary goal. Nearly one-fifth of the lands managed by the DPR are state recreation areas which "consist of areas selected, developed and operated to provide outdoor recreational opportunities" (PRC 5019.56). These areas include state recreation areas and state beaches. In these areas, recreation has primary importance, resulting in adverse impacts to threatened habitats like coastal dunes. However, because these are recreation areas, such uses—even those with adverse impacts—are permitted and are not inconsistent with the goals of these areas. Many of the Department of Fish and Game's wildlife refuges have management prescriptions that increase waterfowl production, certainly a worthy goal. Some waterfowl areas are also grazed,

Table 3.8. *Protection Status of Preserved Areas*

	Mixed Goals	Biodiversity Goal
U.S. Forest Service		
Wilderness areas	3,101	880
Research natural areas		25.8
Special interest areas		29
Bureau of Land Management		
Research natural areas		79.9
Areas of critical environmental concern	722.7	
Outstanding natural areas		111.7
National Park Service		
Parks, monuments, seashores, recreation areas		4,990
U.S. Fish and Wildlife Service		
National wildlife refuges	293	
California Fish and Game		
Ecological reserves		53.6
Wildlife areas	305.7	
California Parks and Recreation		
State beach	24.5	
State parks	977.8	
State preserves		33.2
State historic park	10.4	
State recreation area	181.9	
State vehicular recreation area	41.8	
UC Natural Reserve System		85
The Nature Conservancy		120
Other private conservation groups		10.7
Subtotal	5,658.8	6,418.9
Percent of state	5.6%	6.3%
Total acreage reserved	12,077.7	

SOURCES: Cochrane 1986; Jones and Stokes 1987; PCL 1990.
NOTE: Some parks and protected areas are managed primarily for the protection of bio-diversity, others have a mixed-management mandate. Acreage figures (in thousands of acres), are listed by land management agency.

which may be compatible with waterfowl production, yet contributes to the loss of sensitive species such as the sandhill crane (Cohen 1989*b*). Focus on selected species results in decisions that can adversely affect other plants and animals living in the refuge.[16] Because conservation dollars are limited, reconsideration of management goals for some reserved areas may be appropriate and has occurred on some sand dune sites.

The promise of protection in reserved areas versus the reality of management practices is even more controversial on federal lands than on state park land or wildlife areas because of the large acreages involved. Ten million acres of federal land are designated as parks, wildernesses, or recreation areas in California. These lands are 85 percent of the protected area acreage in California, making their management crucial to protecting biodiversity. Unless federal protected areas are in good condition, and co-occurring uses are compatible with biodiversity, the acreage figures exaggerate their conservation value.

Wilderness areas contain the most acreage of any category of protected area in California. Most of the wilderness areas were set up by act of Congress. In the process of designating wilderness, Congress authorized the continuation of numerous nonconforming uses such as mining, water development, fire control, and livestock grazing (McClaran 1990). The goals and objectives in wilderness areas are thereby often conflicting, and no data are available on the impact of these nonconforming uses on the protection of species and ecosystems. For other categories of protected areas, congressional direction is clear, but the appropriateness of current practices are controversial. For example, the desirability of allowing grazing on research natural areas, which are set aside as baseline areas for scientific research and educational purposes, is being debated.

In addition to the ten million acres of various categories of protected areas in California, the federal government owns and manages thirty-five million acres with a multiple-use mandate under the Federal Land Management Planning Act of 1976 and the National Forest Management Act of 1976 (figure 3.4). Much of the rangelands and commercial timberlands in California are managed by the federal government. These nonreserved areas (mainly U.S. Forest Service lands and Bureau of Land Management lands) are also important for the maintenance and conservation of the state's biological diversity.[17] Conceptually, these lands could be the "buffer areas" of the idealized conservation strategy discussed above. If managed properly, they should be able to provide both commodities and habitat.

The fight over the northern spotted owl is a key example of the difficulty of managing multiple uses in national forests while simultaneously maintaining species and habitat-types. The declining owl populations indicate that past forest management practices, particularly the

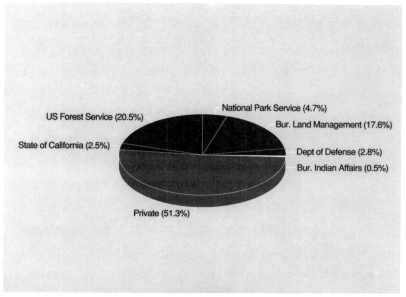

3.4. Land ownership in California. Total area of the state is 101 million acres.

harvest rate, were incompatible with the continued presence of owl populations. Because the northern spotted owl is found in Washington, Oregon, and California, some argue that there is no need to maintain the owl throughout its range, that management should be allowed to eliminate the owl in some areas. Others argue that the real concern is the old-growth forests that owls inhabit, and that the old-growth forests should be protected in all three states. The long-term outcome of the old-growth/spotted owl controversy cannot be predicted. However, it is easy to predict that there will be other conflicts over the appropriate intensity of use of federal multiple-use lands. Because of the continuing conflicts over appropriate management of multiple-use lands, they cannot be considered protected areas.

Conflicting management goals for various categories of public lands are only one of the factors lessening the value of these areas for protection of biodiversity. As documented in chapter 4, there are numerous threats to biological resources in California. Many of these threats, such as air pollution or water diversions, cannot be constrained by property lines. As a result even if a preserve is designed and dedicated to protecting all the species and vegetation types present, success may depend upon actions outside the jurisdiction of park managers. For this reason, where regulatory control of the threats that cross boundaries is inadequate, species and ecosystems in parks are still at risk. For example, air pollution from the Central Valley has been documented to be a problem in Sequoia National Park (CARB 1988), and selenium-contaminated water forced the closing of Kesterson National Wildlife Refuge.

Parks and protected areas are the centerpiece of protecting biodiversity. But buying or setting aside land is simply the first step. Managing the parks and preserves, and protecting them from the many diverse threats, are also critical components of a conservation strategy.

Aquatic Ecosystem Diversity

Aquatic habitats in California contain a rich array of water-dependent species and provide essential seasonal habitat to many terrestrial species in California during the long, dry summers. Unfortunately aquatic habitats throughout the state have been substantially changed and damaged in the past 150 years. Despite an increasing awareness of the importance and the vulnerability of aquatic habitats, few actions are being taken to protect these vital components of California's biodiversity.

WHAT AQUATIC DIVERSITY DOES CALIFORNIA HAVE?

California contains seven major drainage systems, each with its own subsystems: the Klamath River, Sacramento-San Joaquin, North/Central Coast, Lahontan, Death Valley (sometimes separated into the Owens/Mojave and Amargosa units), South Coast, and Colorado River systems (sometimes separated into the Salton Sea and Colorado River units). These systems are defined by major rivers and their associated drainage basins. Although the majority of interior streams and lakes drain eventually into the large rivers, many of the coastal streams drain directly into the ocean. Separated in a past geologic era, each drainage system now contains a distinctive fish (and invertebrate) fauna. The Natural Diversity Data Base identifies 123 different aquatic habitat-types in California, based on fauna (Ellison 1984);[18] of these, 78 are stream habitat-types.

Riparian forest in Tulare County—less than 5 percent of this type of habitat remain in California. (Photo courtesy Walt Anderson)

The mean annual runoff from California's rivers and streams is 71 million acre-feet (MAF)[19] of which 31 MAF flow from the Sacramento-San Joaquin River system (DWR 1987). Water is unevenly distributed around the state; most of the rainfall occurs in the North Coast region and in the Sierra. As a result 40 percent of all the state's runoff is from the North Coast and 44 percent is from the Sacramento-San Joaquin system. The remaining 16 percent (less than 12 MAF) is the runoff from the east side of the Sierra, the vast desert regions, the Central Coast ranges, and southern California (DWR 1983). People are distributed in a pattern that is almost a reverse image of rainfall; more than half the state's population lives in the Central Coast ranges and southern California.

California contains both natural lakes and manmade reservoirs. Reservoirs are included as lakes in classifications of aquatic habitats because these impoundments of streams and rivers often support populations of fish and other organisms that are characteristic of lakes. The major natural lakes in California are Lake Tahoe, Clear Lake (the largest freshwater lake completely within California), Eagle Lake, Goose Lake, and the saline Mono Lake. Numerous smaller lakes are found throughout the Sierra Nevada especially in the southern Sierra. The largest inland body of water within California is the saline Salton Sea. Dry until the Colorado River filled it in 1904, the Salton Sea now receives inflows of Imperial Valley irrigation water. NDDB's aquatic classification lists forty-six different types of lake and pond habitats in California (Ellison 1984).

The interconnections between terrestrial and aquatic communities are nowhere so evident as in an estuary. An estuary is a marine bay with freshwater inflows at one end, creating a salinity gradient between the coastal side and the freshwater inflow (Goldman and Horne 1983). The shores of estuaries have been the sites of human habitation throughout history. Estuaries are known to be important nurseries for the fisheries of the world and are renowned for their productivity. Both freshwater and salt marshes are found on their edges. California contained approximately 552,000 acres of coastal estuary in 1967[20] (Ringold and Clark 1980).

Freshwater wetlands occur inland from salt and brackish marshes, as well as in the interior of California. There are approximately 93,000 acres of salt, brackish, and freshwater marsh in coastal California and 374,000 acres of freshwater wetlands remain in the Central Valley (DPR 1988). Additional acreage occurs in the Modoc Plateau region.

California has 1,827 miles of shoreline as measured by the U.S. Corps of Engineers (cited in Ringold and Clark 1980). This shoreline contains 412 miles of beach; the remainder is primarily rocky shoreline. The intertidal and splash zone communities contain a distinctive and diverse array of species. NDDB lists sixteen different intertidal and splash zone communities, found on various types of substrates from Del Norte County to San Diego (Ellison 1984).

HISTORIC THREATS AND LOSSES OF
AQUATIC HABITATS

Aquatic habitats are the most dramatically and completely altered biotic communities in California. A significant proportion of the natural aquatic habitats of California has been severely altered and degraded, endangering the species dependent upon these habitats (see for example figure 3.5). The Natural Diversity Data Base lists 34 percent of the lake and pond habitat-types and 50 percent of the stream habitat-types as rare or endangered.

Significant changes to aquatic habitats have occurred since the middle of the nineteenth century, when gold miners dug up stream beds, and since the turn of the century, when brook trout and rainbow trout were introduced to previously fishless high Sierra lakes and streams. Dr. Peter Moyle, the leading expert on California's native fish, is blunt about the changes to California's major inland waterways:

The once turbulent and muddy lower Colorado River is now a giant, dammed irrigation ditch and drain. . . . The giant lakes of the San Joaquin Valley are today vast grain farms. The Sacramento-San Joaquin Delta, once an enormous tule marsh dissected by meandering river channels, has been transformed into islands of farmland protected by high levees from the water that flows in straight, dredged channels. (1976, p. 46)

The period of large dam and reservoir construction in California took off with the Central Valley Project in the 1950s, although the first dams were built much earlier. In 1860, no streams were dammed. By 1920, there were 14 reservoirs, each with holding capacities of over 50,000 acre-feet. Most of these had been built by local water agencies or local governments. In 1949, 37 such reservoirs existed (Hornbeck 1983). By 1988, there were 102 major reservoirs;[21] 27 of them Federal. There are now more than 1,200 reservoirs in California with a combined storage capacity of over 43 million acre-feet (California Department of Finance 1988).

Although the numbers and surface area of "lake habitats" have increased greatly in the last seventy years, reservoirs have been added at great loss of river and stream habitats and their dependent species. Natural lakes have also been lost. Historically, the Tulare Basin of the Central Valley contained two huge lakes: Tulare and Buena Vista. These have been drained and converted to irrigated agriculture.

Threats to freshwater aquatic communities are often evaluated in terms of their effects on fish fauna. Because fish are incapable of avoiding many of the impacts to their habitat, they serve well as indicators of the condition of the entire aquatic ecosystem. The very large numbers of endangered fish in California suggest that the aquatic habitats where these fish reside are undergoing profound modifications. Seventy-two percent of the native freshwater fish in California are either listed or likely candidates for listing as threatened or endangered, or are extinct (Moyle et al. 1989).

Moyle (1976) discusses three basic causes of the historic decline of inland native fish fauna: habitat change (which includes both habitat loss and habitat degradation), introductions of non-native species, and fishing. Although the best-documented examples are for fish, these forces have also changed the diversity and abundance of other types of aquatic organisms.

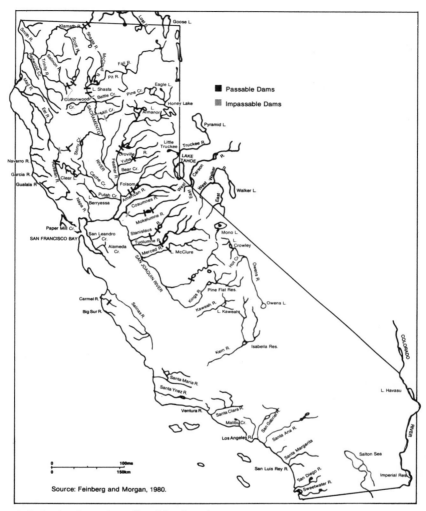

3.5. Major dams that affect fish migration.

Nearly every aquatic system in California has been subjected to some type of habitat alteration. The habitat changes have included modifications of the aquatic habitat itself, such as stream channel alterations (straightening and dredging) which have destroyed fish spawning areas and altered the stability and vegetation of the banks; dams and reservoirs, which have impeded and altered natural streamflows; and dewatering (diversion), which has removed water for irrigation, power generation, or industrial and municipal consumption and thereby affected spawning grounds, stream flows, and riparian vegetation growth patterns. In Eagle Lake, for example, diversion for irrigation reduced creekflow into the lake, resulting in decreased survivorship of trout eggs and fry.

The second cause of decline in native fish fauna has been the introduction of non-native species. Forty percent of the inland fish in California are introduced species. Especially in combination with human modification of aquatic habitats, introduced fish and molluscs have increased in abundance at the expense of native fish such as the Sacramento perch. Some of the introduced fish are predatory and have become pests, devouring the juveniles of other species. For example, white bass, which were introduced into Lake Nacimiento in the mid-1960s, escaped into the San Joaquin River system in the early 1980s. The Department of Fish and Game (which had introduced these fish) then had to undertake a major eradication program to eliminate the white bass to prevent damage to the San Joaquin River fishery (CDFG 1987). Introduced centrarchid fish (sunfish) and bullfrogs have been hypothesized as one cause of the decline of amphibians in California (Hayes and Jennings 1986).

Fishing, both sport and commercial, and management practices that favor fishable species at the expense of any others, have a major effect on native fish fauna. The Pacific sardine fishery reached its peak between 1934 and 1944 when 800 million pounds of sardines were landed each year. The entire fishery began a rapid decline after 1944, due to a combination of fishing pressure and weather patterns. The northern stocks were particularly hard hit; San Francisco has not had a commercial sardine fishery since 1951 (Skinner 1962). The sturgeon fishery lasted for only a brief flurry and then underwent a dramatic decline. The largest freshwater fish, sturgeon was scorned as a commercial fish in the mid-1800s. As the state's population grew with the influx of easterners, demand for sturgeon and caviar soared. The first commercial catch records are from 1875. By 1885 the catch was 1,658,000 pounds and by 1901 the fishery was closed and the fish was believed to be on the verge of extinction (Skinner 1962).

One major threat to lakes that is not common in riverine systems in California is eutrophication from overfertilization with nutrients. Several lakes in California including Clear Lake, Lake Tahoe, and many smaller lakes have suffered from increased algal growth from sources such as fertilizer and sewage. The algal growth decreases oxygen levels in the lakes, harming animal life. At Lake Tahoe, increases in algal growth over the last thirty years were caused by basin development on erosive soils. Streams carrying nutrients and natural organic compounds from erosion are the most important source of nutrients responsible for increased algal growth in the lake (Goldman and Byron 1986). Disturbances to the soils in the watershed increase nutrient release from streams into the lake.

Many forces have contributed to the alteration and degradation of coastal estuaries and their associated wetlands. The largest threats to estuaries are habitat loss from filling and dredging, pollution, sedimentation, logging, and harbor development. Estuaries along the South Coast receive additional pressures from oil production. Changes in the species resident in estuaries are the results of the introduction of nonnative species, overfishing, sedimentation from hydraulic mining, water diversions, point and non-point source pollution, toxic wastes, and possibly synergies between these factors (Nichols et al. 1986). Despite years of research, debate continues as to the causes and degree of change to San Francisco Bay. This is in part because there are numerous different threats to the Bay's biological resources, and the relative effect of each stress is difficult to determine. In other estuaries of California, threats are similar to those acting in San Francisco Bay, especially pollution, sedimentation, and the dredging and filling for ports and harbors (Dennis and Marcus 1983).

Between 1947 and 1967, 255,800 acres, or 53 percent, of the total statewide coastal estuarine and wetland acreage was lost by filling and dredging. This is over four times the acreage lost anywhere else in the United States. Over half of this area was in the San Francisco Bay-Delta system. Between 1950 and 1967, San Francisco and Suisun bays lost 192,000 out of a total of 294,000 estuarine and wetland acres, until filling was virtually stopped by state action in the 1970s after the establishment of the Bay Conservation and Development Commission (Ringold and Clark 1980). This 65 percent loss within the San Francisco Bay-Delta system represented the greatest decrease of habitat in any single estuary in the United States at that time. Extensive use of the watersheds for off-road vehicle recreation, agriculture, and urban development has caused erosion and thus sedimentation of south coastal waters. With the enormous population expansion and accompanying urban development, the coastal wetlands of southern California have experienced a 75 percent reduction (Dennis and Marcus 1983). In recent years the loss has been slowed down, in part due to the California

Coastal Commission and numerous laws to protect coastal and interior wetlands.

Threats to shoreline and intertidal habitats include development, offshore drilling, oil spills and other forms of pollution, excessive collection of tidepool organisms, and overfishing. Dramatic oil spills in Santa Barbara brought the problem to people's attention, and many emergency response efforts were designed. These actions lessen but do not eliminate the threat oil spills pose to shore and intertidal habitats. Although recreational and commercial divers have depleted abalone populations, the major threat to most intertidal species is pollution. Sedimentation of coastal waters, from erosion, is the most widespread type of pollution. Erosion is a natural hazard, but activities such as agriculture and urban development accelerate the process.

PROTECTION OF AQUATIC HABITATS

Attitudes regarding the uses of rivers have begun to change in recent years, from emphasizing human use of the river toward protection of the river for the river's sake. Preservation of parts of rivers and streams has often resulted from the actions of local citizens (Palmer 1986). Federal protection of California's streams and rivers has been granted since 1968 through the Wild and Scenic Rivers Act, which prohibits dams, reservoirs, or other impoundments on designated rivers. State wild and scenic designation, first granted in 1972, offers the same protection as federal, except that it does not preclude projects permitted by the federal government. Reaches of thirteen rivers in California are designated wild and scenic rivers: American, Eel, Feather, Kern, Kings, Klamath, Merced, Salmon, Scott, Smith, Trinity, Tuolomne, and Van Duzen.

Protection of aquatic ecosystems will require assuring adequate water quantities as well as water quality in the streams and rivers of the state. To date, the existing system for regulating water use and water quality does not assure the protection of aquatic biodiversity. California has an administrative system for allocating rights to use water. The State Water Resources Control Board (SWRCB) has the task of permitting water use rights throughout the state and of setting water quality standards. Under the existing system it is impossible to buy water or own rights for instream flow; rather, rights are granted for the diversion and off-stream use of water. The SWRCB can, however, establish standards for the minimum flows and water quality necessary to protect fish and wildlife. Not surprisingly, this process is extremely controversial. In some watersheds in California, use of all the water has already been allocated, without determining the instream flows needed to maintain aquatic biodiversity. In overallocated watersheds the SWRCB can choose to meet the needs of fish and wildlife—but water must then be taken away from an existing permit holder to provide for the needed minimum flows. For example, if through the politically volatile Bay-Delta hearings, the SWRCB determines that additional flows are needed to maintain water quality for the San Francisco Bay and the Delta region, the number of acre-feet that other users can withdraw will have to be reduced. It is clear that the existing permit holders have a large incentive to influence the decision-making process against more flows to fish and wildlife.

To date, the existing water appropriation system provides little protection to aquatic ecosystems, whereas price subsidies discourage water conservation. Creative managers and environmentalists are finding ways to buy water at one end of a drainage system and sell it to an offstream user at the other end of the drainage system in order to have water flowing *through* the system at a critical time of the year. Clearly, the water appropriation system is not designed for the protection of biodiversity; in fact, it contributes to the endangerment of aquatic habitats (see chapter 4).

There are many waterfowl refuges throughout California managed by either the Department of Fish and Game or the U.S. Fish and Wildlife Service. Many of these contain fresh- or saltwater wetlands. Although these are extremely important protected areas—because 80 to 95 percent of historical wetland acreage has been eliminated—there are many flaws that limit the ability of these refuges to adequately protect aquatic diversity. Few wetland refuges have dedicated water rights, so they may not receive water in times of drought (Gilmer et al. 1982).

Certain forms of protection have been given to shoreline communities. Six of the twenty-one National Wildlife Refuges in California are coastal refuges containing 17,000 acres of estuaries and wetlands. Elkhorn Slough, located near Monterey Bay, is the second largest estuary in the state (San Francisco Bay is the largest). It is now a national estuarine sanctuary. Offshore, several federal marine refuges have been established to protect certain areas for fishing or to protect critical bird nesting areas. These national marine sanctuaries include Cordell Bank, the Gulf of the Farallones Islands, Monterey Bay, and the Channel Islands. Efforts to withdraw these areas from offshore oil drilling have been quite controversial, but are essential to their protection.

Although 42 percent of the coastline is in public ownership, it is difficult to determine its protection status. Approximately one-fifth of the coast is federally owned, in both national seashores and military bases. State beaches managed by DPR, the remainder of the publicly owned shoreline, get a tremendous amount of recreational use. One-third of the coast is used for either public or private recreational uses (USGS 1971, cited in Ringold and Clark 1980). This may have a detrimental effect on the nearshore intertidal communities. A substantial portion of the undeveloped shoreline is partially protected simply because it is inaccessible due to steep cliffs and erosive slopes.

Many of the historic threats to aquatic habitats such as water diversion and reduced water quality have not greatly diminished. Although the rate of habitat alteration has slowed, the direction has not. Water diversions and declining water quality continue to pose substantial threats to California's aquatic systems. In addition, new threats such as pollution, acid deposition, and sedimentation threaten streams and rivers, and land use changes threaten seasonal wetlands, low-elevation ponds, and desert aquatic habitats. As a result many streams, rivers, lakes, ponds, and estuaries are subject to a multitude of different stresses. Protection of aquatic habitats must include both the designation of protected areas and assuring adequate water flows and water quality. Because identification and protection of aquatic habitats is not a priority for any state entity in California, future trends do not look promising for aquatic biodiversity.

What Do These Trends Portend for the Future?

California is endowed with a wondrous assortment of species and ecosystems that comprise the state's biodiversity and provide us with a host of benefits. But human activities are beginning to overtax the regenerative abilities of natural systems.

The loss of, and damage to, ecosystem diversity in California is evidenced by the decline and degradation of many of the state's habitat-types. On a statewide basis several terrestrial habitats have lost more than 50 percent of their historic acreages. The majority of the aquatic habitats are altered or in poor condition. If this loss were evenly distributed across California, perhaps the species dependent upon these habitats would simply have suffered declines in their populations. But in fact, the habitat losses have been very unevenly distributed, with great losses in the Central Valley and coastal California. For species dependent upon habitats that once occurred in these regions and which have now been replaced by agriculture or urban land uses, entire populations have been lost, and in some instances, species have gone extinct. Although we have data on the past and present *acreages* for some habitats, we have little information on the *condition* of these habitats. Many human activities degrade natural systems diminishing their productive capacity. Even without decreases in acreages, degraded areas can no longer sustain high populations of the native species resident there.

Ecological theory can be used to predict the species losses that will occur from continued loss of habitat. As the area of habitat increases, the number of species present increases, following a regular pattern predicted by island biogeography theory (MacArthur and Wilson 1967). This pattern can also predict how many species will be lost when the acreage of habitat decreases. However, the rate of loss cannot be predicted because it depends both on characteristics of individual species and the pattern of fragmentation that occurs as habitat is lost. In California, several habitats such as riparian forests and wetlands have already lost substantial acreage. Ecological theory predicts that we should anticipate the loss of species dependent upon these areas, but theory cannot tell us how rapidly these losses will occur. Many remaining small habitat areas may already be too small to support healthy populations of a number of the species present today. Because individual animals and plants live for many years, the population losses and ultimate extinctions will occur on a scale of decades rather than years. Thus the processes of loss have already begun, but the consequences are not yet evident.

Of particular concern is the fact that many of the habitats that have lost the most acreage are coincidentally also habitats that are unusually rich in species. These habitats include valley riparian forests, montane riparian forests, wet meadows, and perennial grasslands (Jensen 1988). Unfortunately these are among the habitats that have been most greatly altered and destroyed by human activities. In short, we are losing keystone habitats, those habitats that contain many more species than acres alone would predict, and we are losing these habitats first.

Maintaining biodiversity in California will require a commitment to sustaining functional examples of the habitats of the state. Because of the linkages among habitats and between habitats and species, a habitat-oriented approach rather than a species-oriented approach is preferable. The focus should be on keystone habitats that are important to many different species, as we are losing these species-rich habitats first. Although only a few of the species dependent on these habitats have been lost or are in danger of extinction, we should anticipate significant loss of species dependent upon these habitats if trends continue unabated. In some regions of California this loss is already occurring; but, as we are losing populations rather than entire species, we cannot yet see the decline. Nowhere in California is the loss of populations and genetic diversity being monitored for species that are declining but not yet endangered.

If fifty years ago one tried to predict the status of biodiversity in California today, the effort would very likely have been unsuccessful for three reasons. First, we knew far less about the many linkages within and among the genetic, species, and habitat levels of biodiversity and how those linkages influence the responses of species and habitats to human activities. Second, we could not have anticipated the types and severity of threats to biodiversity that, in fact, originated during the past half century. Third, we could not have anticipated the array of new laws and agencies and the patterns of other social and institutional changes of the past fifty years, some of which expedite and some of which impede efforts to protect biodiversity. Even had such a prediction been made, we would find it difficult to test its validity, because of the difficulties (as discussed above) in assessing the status of biodiversity today.

In some important respects, we are in a better position now to attempt a forecast. One reason is that society is more aware today than it has ever been of the present and long-range threats to the environment, of the ways ecosystems respond to those threats, and of the barriers to dealing with these threats. This is because of the dramatic increase in environmental issues which has led to new research and education. Some of this research is also improving our assessment capacity. Awareness of the present and future threats to biodiversity in California, and current perceptions of the barriers to surmounting these threats are summarized in the following two chapters, respectively. A second reason is more speculative, perhaps, but since it underlies the motivation for this book we state it boldly. The public is likely to be more proactive and less reactive to the problem of biodiversity loss in the future than it has been in the past, simply because of increased awareness of society's dependence on biodiversity. In other words, our increased knowledge of the value of biodiversity and the threats to biodiversity makes us more likely to set a course of action and then follow it. The question remains, however, as to which course California will set. In the penultimate chapter we set forth our vision of a strategic plan for overcoming barriers and coping with threats to the preservation of California's remaining biodiversity.

CHAPTER FOUR

Threats to Biodiversity in California

Public awareness of the vulnerability of California's biological diversity grew from a series of dramatic catastrophes: the multitudes of dead animals washed ashore after the Santa Barbara oil spill of 1969; the precipitous decline of the brown pelican, golden eagle, and peregrine falcon, poisoned by DDT; and the near extinction of the California condor. Most human activities, however, don't have dramatic, visible consequences. A road into the forest, a rare flower picked, or a slight warming in summer temperatures may not make headlines. Yet, if allowed to continue unchecked, the undramatic threats to California's ecosystems will eventually undermine biological diversity just as surely as will the more catastrophic threats.

The list of threats to biodiversity is long: habitat conversion; water use; commodity uses of biological resources, such as logging and grazing; pollution; and the global degradation of the atmosphere leading to climate warming and stratospheric ozone depletion. In this chapter we describe the expected trends in the magnitude of these threats, which types of habitats or species are likely to be most affected, and, briefly, the regulatory setting in California. The impacts of several large industries—agriculture, recreation, energy generation, and mining—are included within this discussion.

Population pressure, both within California and globally, is a driving force behind the loss of biodiversity. Although it is not treated separately here, the impact of the sheer numbers of Californians, and indeed of people worldwide, is reflected in every one of the threats discussed below. It is the combination of population and per capita impacts, derived from how people live and economically develop, that threatens biological diversity and wilderness in California.

Land Use and Habitat Conversion

Since the first Spanish missions were founded along the California coast in the late 1700s, California has received many waves of new settlers and industries—the livestock boom, gold rush cities, agricultural expansion—each era leaving its mark on the landscape. Consider a typical parcel of land in the Central Valley that was once oak savanna. Its history of nonindigenous use might have started in the early 1800s, with introductions of livestock, along with European grasses and fire suppression. As a result, its perennial prairie was replaced by annual grasses by the mid-1800s. Deer, elk, and other native grazers could still find forage but their numbers declined from cattle diseases, loss of streamflow due to streamside degradation, and obstruction of migratory routes by fences. In the 1940s, water projects began deliveries and rangelands were converted to irrigated fields. Native grazers and native vegetation were displaced altogether from the cropland and were isolated in the remaining grassland patches. By the mid-1950s, water draining from the fields carried nutrients from fertilizers as well as pesticides and drainage salts into streams and drainage ponds. As the area urbanized, municipal wastewater and industrial effluent added to the water pollution load. The late 1970s saw rapid conversion of the cropland surrounding these inland cities for housing and commercial development. With paving, landscaping, and channelized creeks, the developed landscape left little habitat for native species.

ENVIRONMENTAL IMPACTS OF LAND CONVERSION

As this example shows, land conversion reduces biodiversity in many ways: by the loss of the habitat that is converted, the fragmentation of remaining habitats, the assault on the environment associated with the new land use, and last, by the cumulative impact on biota of land conversion occurring across the state.

Habitat loss and fragmentation. Most land use conversions do not result in total loss of habitat for all species, but rather in conversion from one type of habitat to another. For example, when timber is harvested from mixed conifer forests, the regrowth provides a different kind of habitat. Species dependent on mature tree stands will be lost from the cutover area and new species, adapted to the young vegetation, may become established. If the logged land is reforested with a single tree species, it matures to a forest plantation quite different from the original mixed species stand.

Cultivation of undeveloped land results in nearly total habitat loss for native plant species, but many animals are still able to find nesting and feeding sites as long as critical habitat features remain. For instance, Swainson's hawks, which prefer to nest in riparian (streamside) forests and feed in open grasslands, can usually find adequate prey in hay fields and grazed pastures. But they are displaced if too much riparian vegetation is lost or if grasslands are converted to crops which do not provide adequate feeding opportunities, such as cotton, orchards, row crops, and most grain crops (CDFG 1989a). However, flooded grain fields provide valuable winter feeding grounds for waterfowl.[1]

Urban development of wildland represents total and effectively irreversible loss of habitat for most native plants and animals. Rural and suburban development is also difficult to reverse, but does not cause total displacement of native wildlife; rather its effects are mainly due to fragmentation and indirect impacts.[2] Many types of mining also result in complete loss of topsoil and habitat in the mined area.

Habitat fragmentation accompanies habitat conversion. As converted areas usually don't provide habitat for many of the original species, the landscape is fragmented into alternating patches of natural and created habitats. Habitat can also be fragmented by the erection of barriers such as roads, fences, and dams. As land use change spreads out across the landscape, the fragmentation may create isolated patches of habitat too small to support many native species, and typically these patches are subject to increased disturbance. In San Diego, urbanization has left only small islands of chaparral habitat in a sea of houses and roads. These isolated patches support lower densities of most native species than do larger natural areas (Soulé et al. 1988). Suburban and rural development, proceeding without consideration of native wildlife, continues the formation of habitat islands even though the problem could be ameliorated by leaving corridors of natural vegetation connecting habitat patches.

Indirect effects of land use. Conversion to a new land use is the start of a new collection of environmental assaults. Any type of conversion, be it from logging, agriculture, or urbanization, increases erosion due to road building and disturbance of soil and ground cover. Mines in the Sierra Nevada are among the largest sources of silt and toxic metals in the Sacramento River and San Francisco Bay-Delta (SWRCB 1990). Once established, agriculture uses large quantities of water and contributes to water pollution; urbanization brings people who need water, energy, roads, and waste disposal. The magnitude of impact, however, is dependent on how land is developed. Investment in water conservation, drainage design, and biological pest control for agriculture, and in regional planning, tertiary wastewater treatment, and recycling facilities for urban areas can greatly diminish the new impacts.

The impact of land use on aquatic habitats is demonstrated in the Tahoe Basin. By the early 1980s, Lake Tahoe had begun to lose its famous transparency, and algae populations multiplied on its surface, worrying environmentalists and developers alike. The business communities of both the California and Nevada sides of the lake were concerned about degradation of the lake's attractiveness to visitors, whereas environmentalists feared widespread changes were occurring in the lake ecosystem. A five-year monitoring program showed that construction was causing soil erosion and nutrient release into the streams feeding Lake Tahoe, leading to turbidity and algal blooms. The highest levels of sediment deposition were occurring near the areas of greatest basin development, and in fact were correlated with new construction on unstable soil types (Goldman and Byron 1986). Strict land use planning controls have now been designed by the Tahoe Regional Planning Agency to protect the water quality of the lake by controlling runoff and nutrient inputs. These efforts have received national attention both because of the beauty of Lake Tahoe and because of the establishment of a regional agency that works across the California-Nevada boundary to protect a shared resource.

The impacts of development extend well beyond the construction site for terrestrial habitats as well. For example, rural development affects an area far larger than is directly converted or paved because of the habitat fragmentation and disturbance from infrastructures such as roads, culverts, power lines, and highways, and from increased human activity—noise, trampling, shooting, introduction of exotic plants, and accidental and arson-caused wildfires.[3] Development also interferes with ecosystem processes through fire suppression, flood control, and creating unstable (landslide-prone) slopes. In general, statistics on the acres developed or utilized for commodity extraction underestimate the total impact of land conversions on biota.

Cumulative impacts of development. Finally, the long-term impact of land conversion is the cumulative impact of all the stresses on that habitat-type, throughout its range. If each county allows its vernal pools to be developed, this remarkable ecosystem, with its rare species, will be eradicated statewide. Even development of relatively common habitats creates alarming cumulative impacts; since land conversion is clustered in a few regions, development of only a few percent of California's land may completely destroy a habitat-type.

Less than 20 percent of the state's area has experienced complete loss of habitat due to agricultural, rural, or urban conversion (table 4.1). But since people like to live and work near the coast and rivers, and to farm in the floodplains and deltas, some regions have experienced severe habitat loss, and species that depend on certain habitat-types may have nowhere to go. In particular, the habitats found along the coast, riparian, wetland, and estuarine zones as well as flat grasslands of the inland valleys have been hard hit by land conversion. Species dependent on these habitats are particularly vulnerable to further development.

An additional risk of developing intensively in a particular geographic region is the potential loss of the genetic characteristics of populations found in that region. For example, selective development in the Sierra foothills reduces low-elevation populations of ponderosa pine and may be reducing the most drought-tolerant populations. In addition, the loss of these low-elevation populations due to land conversion is likely eliminating the genotypes best adapted to survive the warmer temperatures and drier soil predicted to occur with global warming.

For species with a limited range, simply building in the wrong place may cause irreversible harm, as shown by the extinction in 1986 of the Palos Verdes blue butterfly following the conversion of its last remaining habitat to a baseball field (Arnold 1986). For more common species, loss of any single isolated habitat patch may not be threatening by itself. But as conversion proceeds in a piecemeal fashion across the region, habitat is lost or isolated into islands, shrinking populations. Although each individual land use decision appears to have a negligible impact, the cumulative impact of repeated incremental losses can be local extinction.

Such was the case of the Quino checkerspot butterfly, once found

Table 4.1. *Patterns on the Land in California*

Total land area = 100 million acres; 1% = 1 million acres

Land Ownership		%
State of California		2.5
Federal Government		46.0
Dept. of Defense	2.8	
National Park Service	4.7	
Forest Service	21.0	
Bureau of Land Management	17.0	
Bureau of Indian Affairs	0.5	
Private		51.5

Land Use	%
Grazing	40
Logging	17
Agriculture	12 (10 irrigated, 2 dry)
Urban, suburban	5
Defense	3
Parks and reserves	12
Rural, roads, water districts, etc.	11
	100
Roads	180,000 miles

Vegetation Types	% Total	% Private	% Public
Conifer forest	23	8	15
Hardwood forest	10	7	3
Shrub	19	8	11
Grass	9	8	1
Desert	21	5	16
Alpine barren and rock	2	0	2

Conifers: 50% of private land is forest-industry owned.
Hardwood: 10% of private land is forest-industry owned.

SOURCE: CDF 1988.

throughout southern California. Piecemeal development of habitat across its range led to its extinction in 1988 (Murphy 1988, 1989). As is often the case with incremental loss, by the time the problem was recognized, it was too late to save the small butterfly. By the time scientists presented the conclusive data needed to petition the State Fish and Game

Commission to list the Quino checkerspot as threatened or endangered, the butterfly could no longer be found.

The ecological services that one habitat or ecosystem provides for surrounding habitats are often overlooked in assessing cumulative impact. Many habitats are closely linked; for instance, if a delta is degraded, the downstream estuary will suffer. Loss of one habitat degrades other habitats that depend on the services, such as pollen dispersal or sediment filtration, that were performed by the converted ecosystem. In addition, many species, like migratory waterfowl, deer herds, and anadromous fish, rely on more than one habitat for their survival.

TRENDS IN DEVELOPMENT AND HABITAT CONVERSION

California is poised for rapid development. Although the rate of conversion of wildland to agriculture and grazing land has slowed considerably in the last few decades (AFT 1986), California is experiencing ever-increasing rates of urban and suburban development. Population growth is the driving pressure behind urbanization and provides one of the only indicators of potential rates of land conversion.[4] For the past decade, California has had the highest growth rate in the nation in absolute numbers. This rapid growth rate is projected to continue, with the population of California growing by seven million people in the last decade of the century and doubling by 2025 (table 4.2; California Department of Finance 1989*a*, 1989*b*).

Using statistics on urbanization over the past fifteen years and projected population growth, it is estimated that between one and two million acres will be urbanized in California in the next decade to accommodate population growth (AFT 1986, CDF 1988).[5] Even the lower estimate, of one million acres converted, will add 20 percent to the existing urban land base, plus additional growth in rural areas. Most of this urbanization is occurring in the Central Valley, the Sierra foothills, and along the coast.

Although many developments take place on land that is already used for agriculture, rather than converting wildlands, often the net effect is loss of wildland habitat because the displaced farms shift to new areas. Commonly, as land is taken out of agriculture and sold for development, new lands—natural habitats—are placed under cultivation (AFT 1986). Particularly in coastal areas, both urban development and agriculture contribute to habitat conversion in this way. Although the total

Table 4.2a. *Projected Population Growth in California, 1990–2005*

County	1990	2000	2005
Alameda	1,282,400	1,420,000	1,475,500
Alpine	1,100	1,100	1,300
Amador	30,600	39,500	44,000
Butte	183,900	226,700	249,000
Calaveras	32,500	45,600	51,800
Colusa	16,400	19,600	20,700
Contra Costa	810,300	978,200	1,047,900
Del Norte	24,500	31,200	32,500
El Dorado	128,200	174,300	197,400
Fresno	673,900	855,500	942,700
Glenn	25,000	28,800	30,400
Humboldt	119,800	130,200	131,600
Imperial	110,400	142,300	154,300
Inyo	18,400	19,500	19,900
Kern	549,800	718,600	793,700
Kings	102,500	124,300	134,900
Lake	51,100	62,600	67,400
Lassen	27,800	33,400	36,000
Los Angeles	8,897,500	9,976,200	10,429,900
Madera	89,800	120,100	134,800
Marin	231,200	243,600	245,600
Mariposa	14,500	18,500	20,800
Mendocino	81,000	95,400	132,200
Merced	180,600	236,000	266,400
Modoc	9,700	10,700	11,100
Mono	10,200	13,400	14,900
Monterey	358,800	419,500	445,200
Napa	111,700	127,600	125,900
Nevada	79,600	110,400	125,000
Orange	2,424,100	2,811,900	3,047,300
Placer	175,600	238,700	267,400
Plumas	19,900	22,300	23,400
Riverside	1,195,400	1,786,500	2,027,500
Sacramento	1,051,400	1,382,200	1,533,100
San Benito	37,000	49,600	55,100
San Bernadino	1,440,700	2,098,200	2,399,500
San Diego	2,520,500	3,262,700	3,598,000
San Francisco	723,900	680,500	632,300
San Joaquin	483,800	621,700	686,300
San Luis Opispo	219,200	287,600	321,100

Table 4.2a. *(Continued)*

County	1990	2000	2005
San Mateo	652,100	712,700	726,900
Santa Barbara	371,400	434,600	462,800
Santa Clara	1,502,200	1,716,800	1,822,500
Santa Cruz	230,800	273,800	294,000
Shasta	148,800	186,500	202,400
Sierra	3,400	3,700	3,900
Siskiyou	43,800	48,400	50,300
Solano	345,800	471,900	529,200
Sonoma	392,000	494,300	542,900
Stanislaus	376,100	502,300	558,200
Sutter	65,100	78,400	84,100
Tehama	50,100	61,700	67,000
Trinity	13,100	13,800	14,300
Tulare	314,600	397,800	439,900
Tuolumne	49,000	64,300	71,600
Ventura	671,600	824,200	895,400
Yolo	142,500	174,400	187,100
Yuba	58,700	69,100	73,500
California	29,976,000	36,980,000	38,980,000

acreage of irrigated agriculture is projected to be relatively constant in the coming decade, large areas of irrigated land will be developed and large areas of relatively undisturbed habitats will be converted to agriculture.

Population growth and urbanization are not distributed evenly throughout the state. The trend of the past twenty years has been high growth rates in the coastal and desert counties, particularly in southern California, resulting in the loss of coastal wetlands, coastal bluffs and dunes, desert, vernal pools, and coastal scrub. While this trend has not slowed, new areas are also growing. Inland cities are booming, particularly the Sierra foothills near Sacramento and the San Joaquin Valley. Development in these regions threatens annual grasslands, oak woodlands, chaparral, riparian forests, and vernal pools. The Colorado River Valley and desert habitat around Palm Springs and Coachella Valley are projected to experience the fastest growth rates in the state (DWR 1987).

The extremely high growth rates evident in the foothill and desert

Table 4.2b. *Projected Population Growth in California, 1990–2005*
        Ranked by County

Rank	County	% Change	Rank	County	Absolute Change
1	Riverside	70	1	Los Angeles	1,532,400
2	San Bernadino	67	2	San Diego	1,077,500
3	Mendocino	63	3	San Bernadino	958,800
4	Calaveras	59	4	Riverside	832,100
5	Nevada	57	5	Orange	623,200
6	El Dorado	54	6	Sacramento	481,700
7	Solano	53	7	Santa Clara	320,300
8	Placer	52	8	Fresno	268,800
9	Madera	50	9	Kern	243,900
10	San Benito	49	10	Contra Costa	237,600
11	Stanislaus	48	11	Ventura	223,800
12	Merced	48	12	San Joaquin	202,500
13	San Luis Opispo	46	13	Alameda	193,100
14	Tuolumne	46	14	Solano	183,400
15	Mono	46	15	Stanislaus	182,100
16	Sacramento	46	16	Sonoma	150,900
17	Kern	44	17	Tulare	125,300
18	Amador	44	18	San Luis Opispo	101,900
19	Mariposa	43	19	Placer	91,800
20	San Diego	43	20	Santa Barbara	91,400
21	San Joaquin	42	21	Monterey	86,400
22	Fresno	40	22	Merced	85,800
23	Tulare	40	23	San Mateo	74,800
24	Imperial	40	24	El Dorado	69,200
25	Sonoma	38	25	Butte	65,100
26	Shasta	36	26	Santa Cruz	63,200
27	Butte	35	27	Shasta	53,600
28	Tehama	34	28	Mendocino	51,200
29	Ventura	33	29	Nevada	45,400
30	Del Norte	33	30	Madera	45,000
31	Lake	32	31	Yolo	44,600
32	Kings	32	32	Imperial	43,900
33	Yolo	31	33	Kings	32,400
34	Lassen	29	34	Tuolumne	22,600
35	Contra Costa	29	35	Calaveras	19,300
36	Sutter	29	36	Sutter	19,000
37	Santa Cruz	27	37	San Benito	18,100
38	Colusa	26	38	Tehama	16,900

Table 4.2b. *(Continued)*

Rank	County	% Change	Rank	County	Absolute Change
39	Orange	26	39	Lake	16,300
40	Yuba	25	40	Yuba	14,800
41	Santa Barbara	25	41	Marin	14,400
42	Monterey	24	42	Napa	14,200
43	Glenn	22	43	Amador	13,400
44	Santa Clara	21	44	Humboldt	11,800
45	Alpine	18	45	Lassen	8,200
46	Plumas	18	46	Del Norte	8,000
47	Los Angeles	17	47	Siskiyou	6,500
48	Alameda	15	48	Mariposa	6,300
49	Siskiyou	15	49	Glenn	5,400
50	Sierra	15	50	Mono	4,700
51	Modoc	14	51	Colusa	4,300
52	Napa	13	52	Plumas	3,500
53	San Mateo	11	53	Inyo	1,500
54	Humboldt	10	54	Modoc	1,400
55	Trinity	9	55	Trinity	1,200
56	Inyo	8	56	Sierra	500
57	Marin	6	57	Alpine	200
58	San Francisco	−13	58	San Francisco	(91,600)
	California	30		California	9,004,000

SOURCES: 1990 data from the U.S. 1990 Census; Projections by the California Department of Finance, 1991.

counties reflect only small absolute changes in population. For example, the 60 percent increase in population projected for Amador County by the year 2000 will only bring 13,400 new people. By contrast, Los Angeles, with a 13 percent growth rate, will add one million people (tables 4.2 and 4.3). But the nature of suburban development in the foothills, with ten-acre ranchettes and new roads, results in fragmentation of habitat that affects a disproportionate share of the landscape. The ranchette phenomenon is also prevalent in Riverside, San Bernardino, and San Diego counties. In general, the fastest rate of population growth and of land conversion is in the suburbs of existing cities.

Current land values and land ownership patterns in California facilitate rapid conversion. In particular, the continuing escalation of housing prices near urban centers is a major factor driving development.

Throughout California, suburban development is rapidly encroaching on wildlands and agricultural fields. (Photo by Charles Kennard)

Table 4.3. *California Population by Hydrologic Region, 1960–2010 (in 1000s)*

Region	1960	1985	2000	2010	Projected Increase 1985 to 2010	Projected % Increase 1985 to 2010
North Coast	315	497	611	669	172	35
San Francisco Bay	3,455	5,108	5,848	6,112	1,004	20
Central Coast	564	1,133	1,548	11,749	616	54
South Coast	8,550	14,148	17,447	19,106	4,958	35
Sacramento River	991	1,870	2,559	2,943	1,073	57
San Joaquin River	630	1,182	1,767	2,105	923	8
Tulare Lake	829	1,331	1,797	2,081	750	56
North Lahontan	26	69	86	99	30	43
South Lahontan	175	368	594	702	334	91
Colorado River	182	373	596	711	338	91
State Total	15,717	26,079	32,853	36,277	10,198	39
(% of U.S. pop.)	(11)	(12.3)	(12.8)			

SOURCE: Adapted from DWR 1987, based on U.S. Bureau of Census and Department of Finance estimates and projections.

According to Peter Detwiler, senior consultant to the California Senate Local Government Committee, "Conversion is as much an economic process as it is a physical process. When farmland prices reach $250,000 an acre, as has happened in Orange County, it is fair to say that the land has been, for all practical purposes, already converted" (AFT 1986). Land prices on the east side of Altamont Pass now reflect the development of inland cities and the region's new status as a commute suburb for the San Francisco Bay Area. The impact of rising prices and land conversion is carried over to neighboring counties when, for example, people who sold their land in Orange County bid up land prices in Ventura, and so on. Through this process, agricultural land, grazing land, and even some timberlands are threatened with suburban development.

In concert with economic pressure, the potential for subdivision and development in rural counties has grown rapidly in the past three decades as ownership of timberland and grassland shifts from industry to nonindustry interests. For example, a majority of the privately owned conifer and hardwood forests are now owned by individuals who are not part of the forest-products industry. Although privately owned land is less likely to be logged, statistics show that it is more at risk of being converted to nonresource use. Of the 180,000 acres of timberland converted for housing, grazing, and other uses between 1975 and 1985, over 90 percent was nonindustry land (CDF 1988).

Not only are nonindustry parcels more at risk from development, but in regions dominated by nonindustrial holdings, such as the Sierra Nevada, parcel sizes are much smaller than they are in the industry-dominated regions, such as northwestern California (CDF 1988). Smaller land parcels are often more difficult to manage for the protection of biodiversity since they tend to result in a landscape that is more fragmented by fences and land uses, and coordinated conservation requires the cooperation of many, potentially disparate, land owners (CDF 1988, Campbell and Wald 1989).

PREDICTIONS OF HABITATS AT RISK

Viewing the patterns of land ownership and rising land values across the state suggests that land conversion to meet future demand will be more rapid and chaotic than analysis of past trends or population growth would indicate. No matter which land is developed, accommodating current rates of growth—providing water, transportation, energy, and waste disposal for seven million new people in ten years—will change the face of California. But the impact on specific elements of biodiversity will depend on where and how development takes place. Can we predict which habitats will be converted to accommodate growth?

Population growth and economic trends can be used to estimate the rate of habitat conversion expected in the next decades, however they give only a rough indication of which particular habitats are threatened by conversion. Indicators of where conversion is occurring and which habitat-types are being converted are key to identifying threatened resources. Yet, the state has no systematic approach to keeping track of which habitats are being lost to land development. Indeed, "not even local governments keep track of land use data by habitat" (Perkins 1989). Although county General Plans indicate permissible uses for each region of the county, neither county nor state planners can describe which habitats will be the site of planned growth. In fact, it is often local environmental or historical organizations that identify conversion projects threatening highly valued natural resources—albeit on a case-by-case basis.

In one of the few systematic studies and predictions of land conversion in California, the Greenbelt Alliance (1989) found that rapid and chaotic growth threatens the continuity and natural diversity of the Bay Area's greenbelt. They project that 20 percent of the greenbelt, or 780,000 acres of undeveloped land, is at serious risk of development in the next twenty to thirty years. (The Bay Area's urbanized lands, currently 735,000 acres, will more than double if this much development occurs.) Not only will the greenbelt be considerably smaller, but also valuable habitat diversity will be lost, because, as in other regions of the state, certain types of habitats will suffer more loss than others. In particular, the Greenbelt Alliance predicts that virtually all the privately owned flatlands will be developed, leaving only steep or unstable land still green. This suggests that the Bay Area's remaining riparian, vernal pool, meadow, wetland, and floodplain habitats will be among the hardest hit.

Statewide, only limited information is available concerning which land has been or will be converted. The State Office of Real Estate collects subdivision permits for most residential subdivisions; however, no long-term trends, annual totals, or data on vegetation cover are assembled. In addition, no permits are processed for commercial, industrial, or agricultural development. Some information on agricultural land conversion, both for irrigated land and pastures, is available from the State Department of Conservation. Private rangeland is currently undergoing significant conversion to urban and agricultural uses, particularly in the San Joaquin and Sacramento valleys. Similar decreases of privately owned rangeland are expected in southern California and the central Sierra (CDF 1988). Although rangeland is not considered pristine habitat, the conversion of rangeland to urban or agricultural use represents significant and practically irreversible loss of habitat for most native species.

Estimates of historical and current habitat conversion by broad habitat categories are available from California's Department of Water Resources (DWR) and the Department of Forestry's Forest and Range Resources Assessment Program (FRRAP). Projections are harder to make. Land surveys based on aerial photography or other physical surveillance, such as those employed by DWR and FRRAP, cannot estimate the amount of land that has been legally subdivided for development but not yet physically altered. No data have been collected or analyzed on how much of each habitat-type is in different stages of development or type of land use (e.g., how much annual grassland is presubdivision, subdivided, or permitted for development). Such information, identifying habitats on the verge of rapid conversion, is needed to efficiently target species and habitats for protection.

Since the passage of the Coastal Acts of 1972 and 1976, coastal zones have been subject to some habitat-specific planning. Local Coastal Plans map and protect wetlands, bluffs, dunes, and other sensitive habitat areas. The development of coastal wetlands and estuaries is monitored or regulated by the Coastal Conservancy, California Coastal Commission, Department of Fish and Game, and regional (e.g., Bay Conservation and Development Corps) agencies. Freshwater wetlands are also the subject of recent mapping and assessment efforts. Mapping and planning has slowed the rate of conversion of these habitats, but has not stopped it.

Water Use and Water Developments

California consumes nearly one-quarter of the annual delivered water supply in the United States, in a semiarid state where 20 percent of the land receives less than 5 inches of rain per year.[6] Surface flows provide 60 percent of California's developed supply. To accomplish this, more than half of California's annual stream flow is harnessed by water projects (DWR 1987). There are over 100 major dams in California and another 1,200 large dams under State jurisdiction[7] (CDF 1988). Water is stored and transferred through the state via an elaborate system of reservoirs, pumps, and canals. Water projects are also used for flood control, hydroelectric power, and recreation. *The net result is that the amount and timing of water flow is disrupted in nearly every river, in every region of the state.*

The only major river systems of California that are still free-flowing are the Smith River and stretches of the Upper Consumnes River, Upper Kern River, and forks of the Eel River. Among smaller rivers and creeks, many have also been altered. As a result, a greater proportion of freshwater and riparian habitats have been degraded or lost than nearly any other habitat-type (Dasmann 1981, Dennis and Marcus 1983, Palmer 1986, CDF 1988, Barbour et al. 1991). Given this tremendous loss, and the keystone role of aquatic habitats, it is not surprising to learn that the majority of the threatened and endangered animals in California are those that depend on aquatic or riparian habitats.

The fate of California's water-dependent habitats rests on resolving problems arising from current water use and the operation of existing water facilities, and on the course of further water development in the future. Below we discuss the environmental impacts of water use, institutions that regulate and manage water, state projections for water demand and new water projects, and some proposed alternatives to these projects.

ECOLOGICAL IMPACTS OF DAMS AND WATER DIVERSIONS

Water projects such as dams, diversions, and stream channelization alter the natural hydrology of stream and lake systems, fundamentally changing aquatic and riparian habitats. Above a dam, stream and riparian habitats are flooded and replaced by reservoir habitat. This conversion of habitat-types is often accompanied by the introduction or invasion of reservoir-adapted fish species and the concurrent decline of native riverine species. Native populations isolated by dams, a barrier to fish migrations, are susceptible to local extinction, leading to the endangerment of whole species if many populations are threatened.

Below a dam, disruption of natural fluctuations in water flow interrupts flushing flows for hatchling fish, transport of sediment and nutrients, streambed scouring, and the periodic flooding needed for establishment of native riparian seedlings. Physical changes due to dams are exacerbated by important chemical changes in downstream flows, including warmer or cooler water temperatures and supersaturation with nitrogen. Many of the environmental impacts of diversions or dams are outlined in table 4.4. The Trinity River illustrates the combined effects of water impoundments and diversions.

The Trinity River forms high in the Trinity Alps and winds down the North Coast Ranges to the Pacific Ocean. Since the 1964 completion of the Trinity and Lewiston dams, water from the Trinity Basin has been pumped over the mountains to fill Shasta Reservoir, the largest in the state. Up to 90 percent of the Trinity's flow, about 1 million acre-feet (MAF) per year, is diverted to provide water for hydroelectric power and agricultural irrigation in the Central Valley. The construction of the two dams eliminated 109 miles of anadromous fish habitat, including 59 miles of Chinook salmon spawning and rearing grounds. Compounding the stress from the diversions, intensive timber opera-

Table 4.4. *Environmental Impacts of Water Diversions*[a] *and Dams*[b]

1. Barriers to migration of aquatic organisms
2. Barriers to migration of terrestrial organisms
3. Change in upstream hydrology
   a. raised base level causing aggradation
   b. raised groundwater table
4. Inundation effects
   a. change in habitat
   b. introduced species
5. Change in public access and public use
6. Change in downstream hydrology
   a. change in total flows
   b. change in seasonal timing of flows
   c. short-term fluctuations in flows, on a daily or weekly basis
   d. change in extreme flows
      i. smaller peak flows
      ii. change in minimum flows
   e. change in load
      i. less gravel and/or sediment brought downstream
      ii. increased scouring/erosion downstream
   f. change in riparian vegetation, which may lead to further changes in hydrology and water quality (especially temperature).
7. Change in downstream water quality: temperature, nutrients, turbidity, gases (e.g., oxygen, nitrogen)
8. Change in currents
   a. reverse flows
   b. entrainment and screening losses
   c. alteration of chemical gradients that migrating fish rely on

SOURCE: Cohen 1992.
[a] Diversions without a dam could directly result in (6) a, b, c, d, and indirectly in (7).
[b] Dams without diversions could result in any of the impacts. Change in total flows (6a) would be due to evaporation.

tions downstream have resulted in sediment loading into the Trinity River. The river's low flows, the result of the diversions, are insufficient to flush the sediment from the river, leaving gravel too silt-covered for spawning. This synergy among two threats has resulted in the loss of the Trinity anadromous fishery, with direct impact on the Hoopa Valley Indian tribe, which depends on the salmon and steelhead trout for subsistence.

The fundamental role of water flows in determining physical and chemical characteristics of aquatic ecosystems is demonstrated in the

San Francisco Bay-Delta and the Mono Lake Basin. Although each of these systems is geologically and biologically unique, there is a fundamental link between adequate flows and habitat integrity common to both.

In the Mono Basin, diversions from Mono Lake tributaries have caused significant damage to the lake's habitats and to streams, wetlands, and meadows in the Mono Basin generally. In 1941, the Los Angeles Department of Water and Power (DWP) began diverting water from tributary streams of Mono Lake. These streams were almost entirely dewatered during normal and dry water years, leading to a collapse of the fisheries. Also gone are the hundreds of acres of wetlands (fed by springs formed by subsurface creek flow) at the lake deltas, which were feeding grounds for ducks and geese of the Pacific flyway. The riparian vegetation died, and as a consequence, when water rushed through the creeks during wet years, the channels eroded and only wide boulder washes remain. Populations of several rare species have declined due to the drying of the streams, including the mountain beaver, Inyo shrew, and least bittern. Some of the butterfly species dependent on the wet meadows fed by the tributaries and springs have all but disappeared. Only a few individuals of the Mono checkerspot butterfly were seen in a 1978 survey and no apache silverspots were found (Strauss and Davis 1989).

Due to the diversions, the water level of Mono Lake has fallen 43 feet and lake salinity has increased. As the lake level has fallen, the incoming creeks have cut new and deeper channels, with the erosion and incision extending up to 2 miles upriver from the lake. Wind blowing over the exposed flatlands now causes a human health risk due to alkali dust storms that extend for up to 100 square miles around the lake. From 1978 to 1983, the falling water level exposed a land bridge to Negit Island, allowing coyotes and other predators to cross to the primary California rookery for California gulls. The land bridge to Negit Island was again exposed in the winter of 1990–1991, and the gulls abandoned the island as a rookery during the summer of 1991, moving to other islands.

A 1988 court injunction and its extension in 1991, reduced Los Angeles DWP diversions and may have saved the lake from ecological collapse by reducing diversions from tributary streams.[8] Researchers predicted that a drop of only 10 more feet in water level would have drastically reduced the productivity of brine flies and brine shrimp—the major food sources for gulls, grebes, phalaropes, and other birds. A 20-foot drop would have been accompanied by salinities that were acutely toxic for the shrimp (Botkin et al. 1988). Extinction of both species was predicted for a 30-foot drop.

Stream restoration has begun on Mono Basin streams, but physical damage to the stream channels will be difficult to undo. As a result of dewatering, followed by catastrophic floods, the channels have both widened and deepened. Restoring functioning fisheries will require making the stream channels narrower and the water level deeper, establishing native vegetation along the banks, and creating a gravel structure on the stream bottom appropriate for fish spawning. Thus far, efforts have included planting riparian vegetation and distributing gravels. Unfortunately, as water flows are increased, erosion of the steep banks threatens to undercut new vegetation, and sedimentation needed to rebuild the channels may take thousands of years.

The fisheries and wildlife of San Francisco Bay are threatened by reductions in water flows from the Sacramento-San Joaquin Delta. As freshwater flows are reduced, saltwater intrudes farther and farther up the estuary, leading to decreased viability of some estuarine and freshwater species, and increased viability of others. Changes in the quantity and timing of water flowing through the Delta can adversely affect necessary "flushing flows" for fingerlings of the spring-run Chinook salmon and other fish species. In addition, reduced flows alter circulation in the Bay, which may increase the residence time of water in the South Bay and increase chemical contamination of sediments and organisms (Nichols and Pamatmat 1988).

Drought years further exacerbate the long-term problems of inadequate flows through the estuary. The bay shrimp population, an important food source for fish, declined by 75 percent in the 1980s. By 1990, the population of the striped bass, used as an indicator species for Bay health, was lower than it had been for thirty years, with declines seen in many other fish species as well. Two historically plentiful species, the spring-run Chinook salmon and the delta smelt, are currently proposed for endangered species status, with their decline attributed to the impacts of water impoundments and diversions.[9]

As with other aquatic habitats in California, San Francisco Bay faces multiple threats. In addition to diversions and development in the watershed, the San Francisco Bay-Delta is affected by water pollution, exotic invasions (by the Asian clam and more than a hundred other species), high fish mortality in the vicinity of the Delta water pumps, and the dredging and filling of wetlands (Vogel 1991). Although the many different threats to San Francisco Bay habitats make it difficult to precisely assess the specific impact due to water diversions, scientists studying the ecosystem are nonetheless unequivocal that adequate freshwater flows are key to the Bay's biological integrity.

Ecological impacts of groundwater pumping. Although not as visible as stream diversions or dams, lowered groundwater tables have had damaging environmental effects in California. On average, 40 percent of California's developed water supply comes from groundwater, with an overdraft in the Central Valley of about 2 MAF per year. With drought, this figure rises; in 1991 the overdraft in the San Joaquin Valley alone was estimated at 11 MAF.[10]

Desert springs and wet meadows, which support many rare and endangered plants and are critical to wildlife in arid areas, depend on groundwater supplies. The Devil's Hole pupfish in Nevada, a federally listed endangered species, was nearly eliminated by groundwater pumping that lowered the water level in the only spring in which this species is found. The pupfish was saved by legal action that stopped the pumping (Cappaert v. U.S. 1976). Trees and shrubs in dry regions such as Owens Valley and the springs of Tulare Basin cannot get enough water to survive when the water table is lowered below the root zone. Spring-fed oases in Owens Valley have been dried up by groundwater drawdown. Even in less arid areas, surface and subsurface systems are often hydrologically coupled so that drawing down a water table may cause a linked stream to dry up, as is the case with the Carmel River. Surface water flows in the lower Mokelumne River have been reduced an estimated 85,000 acre-feet per year due to the continuous overdraft of groundwater around the lower reaches for the past forty years (Stork 1992).

INSTITUTIONS RESPONSIBLE FOR WATER QUALITY, WATER SUPPLY, AND WATER PROJECTS

A complete understanding of the threats to aquatic habitats would require familiarity with all of the numerous state, federal, and local institutions whose actions affect water supply and water projects in California. In addition, court decisions continue to expand the responsibilities of some of these agencies. However, for our purposes, much insight can be gained by a look at a few of the principle institutions.

Control over water flows and water projects in California rests largely with the State Water Resources Control Board (SWRCB), which has authority over appropriative water rights and water-quality regulation in the state. Under the existing system, appropriative rights are granted only for withdrawal of water for offstream use, and it is impossible to own rights for instream flows. The state water board must, however, protect instream flows by setting minimum flow standards. These standards can be set to protect fish and wildlife, to guard water quality under the Clean Water Act, and to protect public trust values. Although SWRCB is required to set minimum instream flow standards to meet environmental goals, it has done so for only a few waterways in the state. The fundamental problem is that most water rights were granted before SWRCB began a consistent program of requiring instream flows or other actions to mitigate the environmental consequences of water diversions and projects.

The public trust doctrine requires the SWRCB to consider public uses when granting private water rights. Historically, the public trust protected public rights in navigation, commerce, and fishing when private rights to shorelines and tidal lands were granted. Recent court cases have also applied the public trust doctrine to water rights decisions. In a 1983 landmark case, the California Supreme Court recognized application of the public trust doctrine to protect public recreational and ecological values impaired by existing diversions by Los Angeles DWP from the Mono Lake Basin (National Audubon Society v. Superior Court (33 Cal.3d 419)). Significantly, the court said that where SWRCB had failed to consider public trust values in past decisions it could reevaluate those past decisions to incorporate public trust values. (Biological diversity could easily be considered one of the ecological values of public trust concern.) By encouraging retrospective analysis of past water allocations, this ruling casts doubt on all water permits in the state.

The California Department of Fish and Game (CDFG) also has a role in protecting aquatic resources and regulating impacts in rivers and streams. As with SWRCB, only recently has Fish and Game begun to take a strong stance to protect fish and wildlife in debates over water supply. For example, CDFG played a critical role in stopping diversions from the Rush Creek tributary of Mono Lake. In the Rush Creek decision, the Los Angeles DWP was required to release enough water to keep downstream fisheries healthy and productive through enforcement of Section 5937 of the Fish and Game Code. Interestingly, the

Mono Lake case was the first time the Department of Fish and Game had ever enforced this section. Some CDFG staff members fear that if Section 5937 were fully and consistently enforced, the legislature would overturn it. The Rush Creek decision should affirm the legal authority of CDFG to enforce this section of its code.

California's water projects are built and managed by numerous state and federal agencies as well as by local utilities. The lead state agency in project management is the Department of Water Resources (DWR), which oversees the State Water Project and plans for the state's water supply. DWR also oversees new development and operation of many of the state's existing reservoirs and aqueducts, which are owned by twenty-three local, private, and state agencies, and two federal agencies (Bureau of Reclamation—BuRec, and Army Corps of Engineers—ACE). The federal Central Valley Project, directed by BuRec, and the State Water Project together manage 25 percent of California's developed water supply. Historically, DWR has given emphasis to planning new water projects at the expense of alternative supply technologies and demand management that could protect riverine and lake habitats.

The licensing authority over construction and operation of all non-federal hydroelectric projects is held by the Federal Energy Regulatory Commission. The state's ability to control the operation of dams, and thus the fate of downstream reaches, is under attack in a series of legal battles over the rights of FERC to preempt the minimum flow standards or other protective powers of SWRCB (see chapter 5). In addition to FERC, federal agencies with authority over water projects and water flows in California include the Army Corps of Engineers and the U.S. Environmental Protection Agency. With formal recommendations from the U.S. Fish and Wildlife Service, these agencies are involved in issuing permits for disposal of dredging materials and filling that might affect any navigable waterways, including wetlands, under Section 404 of the Clean Water Act.

WATER DEMAND AND STATE PROJECTIONS

Competition for water resources is often touted as a contest between northern and southern parts of the state. In fact, the major competition over water is between the agricultural sector and other users. Most of the water in California is used in the Central Valley and Imperial Valley for agriculture. Agriculture accounts for approximately 83 percent of offstream water use in the state (table 4.5; DWR 1988).

Urban (municipal and industrial) demand accounts for most of the remaining offstream use (table 4.6).

The state Department of Water Resources projects large increases in water demand from 1985 to 2010, with total (applied) annual use increasing by over 2.8 MAF by the year 2010, a 6 percent increase resulting in the withdrawal of 43.2 MAF in developed supply (table 4.5).[11] According to DWR, agricultural water use will decrease by less than 1 percent over the next twenty years. Irrigation, which peaked in 1980, is now declining slowly due to crop switching, small reductions in irrigated area, and improved efficiency, including lining conveyance channels to reduce seepage losses. Overall, DWR projects only small gains in efficiency through conservation in the agricultural sector.

Industrial water use is projected by DWR to remain stable, as recycling and reuse keep pace with growth in this sector. Clean Water Act provisions on effluent water *quality* have had a beneficial impact on the *quantity* of water used by industries, as industries have found recycling water cheaper than treating and discharging water to meet CWA standards (DWR 1987).

According to DWR projections, urban growth is driving the demand for additional offstream water use in California. This is because the state's population is growing much faster than are savings through home water-use efficiency. Statewide urban consumption of water is projected to increase about 30 percent in the next twenty-five years (table 4.6). The projected increase of 2.1 MAF in urban use will far offset the small projected savings in irrigation and conveyance, a decrease of only 0.27 MAF by 2010.

These DWR demand projections are based on a limited set of assumptions about economic growth in California and the potential for conservation and are likely to be considerable overestimates. In general, water supply agencies have a history of exaggerating future water demand (DWR 1983, Cohen 1989a). Nevertheless, these projections give insight into DWR's approach to water planning and water development. They suggest that DWR is not concentrating on managing water demand to free up water for instream uses or to minimize the need for new projects. Such status quo thinking among the lead state and federal agencies inevitably leads to plans for many new projects.[12]

Proposed new water development. California's wetlands, lakes, estuaries, rivers, and riparian forests are slowly drying up under existing water allocations. In addition, many proposed new water developments

Table 4.5. *Water Use and Water Supplies in California, 1980–2010*
(1,000 acre-feet per year).

Sector	1985	2010	Projected Change 1985 to 2010	Projected % Change 1985 to 2010
Total Consumption[a]				
Irrigation	32,911	33,494	583	2
Urban	6,573	8,709	2,136	32
Wildlife and recreation	927	964	37	4
Energy production[b]	39	57	18	46
Total	40,450	43,224	2,774	7
Net Water Use				
Irrigation	26,941	26,736	−205	−1
Urban	5,576	7,188	1,612	29
Wildlife and recreation	818	864	46	6
Energy production	84	128	44	52
Conveyance losses	764	703	−61	−8
Total	34,183	35,619	1,436	4
Water Supplies				
Local surface water development[c]	9,257	9,182	−75	−1
Imports by local water agencies	1,034	1,066	32	3
Colorado River[d]	4,985	4,200	−785	−16
Groundwater	5,955	6,060	105	2
Central Valley Project	6,955	7,800	845	12
Other federal water development	1,273	1,272	−1	0
State Water Project[e]	2,425	3,209	784	32
Waste water reclamation	252	521	269	107
Total	32,136	33,310	1,175	4
Groundwater overdraft	2,028	1,835	−193	−10
Shortage[f]	19	474	455	2,395
Reserve supply	931	1,175	244	26

Source: DWR 1988.

[a]DWR refers to total consumption (total delivered supply or total withdrawals) as applied water use. Net water use is calculated by adding individual water uses and "evapotranspiration, losses from a water distribution system that cannot be recovered, and outflow leaving an area [and returning to surface water or groundwater]" (DWR 1987).

[b]Water used for power plant cooling and enhanced oil recovery. Does not include evaporative losses from reservoirs for hydroelectric power generation.

[c]Reflects reduced diversions from San Joaquin River.

[d]1985 includes surplus deliveries; 2010 assumes no surplus flow is available.

[e]1985 includes surplus deliveries; 2010 includes Los Banos Grandes Reservoir, Kern Water Bank, enlarged Harvey O. Banks Delta Pumping Plant, purchase of CVP interim supplies, and North and South Delta water facilities.

[f]Shortage is "the difference between projected net water use and the sum of dependable supply and groundwater overdraft."

Table 4.6. *Total Urban Water Use by Hydrologic Regions, 1980–2010 (in thousands of acre-feet).*

Region	1985	2010	Projected Increase 1985 to 2010	Projected % Increase 1985 to 2010
North Coast	160	181	21	13
San Francisco Bay	1,088	1,222	134	12
Central Coast	269	379	110	41
South Coast	3,118	4,021	903	29
Sacramento River	625	835	210	34
San Joaquin River	436	670	234	54
Tulare Lake	481	729	248	51
North Lahontan	27	40	13	48
South Lahontan	120	223	103	86
Colorado River	249	409	160	69
Total	6,573	8,709	2,136	32

SOURCE: DWR 1988.

for water supply, power, flood control, and recreation further threaten our waterways. In Coastal and Central California, DWR plans expanded reservoirs (such as Los Banos Grandes) and aqueducts or canals (such as the South Coastal Aqueduct to Santa Barbara County) to boost the water supply to urban and agricultural users.

Water conveyance projects, to move water from the northern part of the Sacramento Valley to the southern half of the state are an important component of plans by DWR and local water districts to supply more water to California's urban and agricultural consumers. One of the most publicized of these, the Peripheral Canal, was rejected by voters through a state initiative in 1986. Nevertheless, DWR is still proposing to transport water through the Delta for the same purpose with a project now called the Delta Facility. The Delta Facility would form part of DWR's larger development plan for the Sacramento Delta, known as the North and South Delta Projects. This project is described as allowing the closure of some Delta pumps and thus reducing fish mortality at those sites. Unfortunately, these canals will increase diversions of water and some of the planned reservoirs will require installation of new pumps. In addition, several other planned water projects depend on expanding the current pumping system.

Some accounts give the impression that the era of building big dams and other projects has passed. The Conservation Foundation (1987) found that "due to diminishing economic returns from new construction and environmental objections to reservoir siting, the rate at which reservoir capacity is being added in the United States has fallen off dramatically." Similarly, according to DWR (1987) planning documents, "California will meet its future water needs primarily through a wide variety of management actions." Yet the same DWR planning documents report that to meet their projected demand, and to offset reductions in diversions from the Colorado River, DWR is planning to increase surface water diversions within California. Specifically, DWR proposes large increases in supplies from the federal Central Valley Project and expansion of the State Water Project by bringing new and existing facilities fully on-line, including the Delta Pumping Plant, the Los Banos Grandes Reservoir, the Kern Water Bank, and the North and South Delta water facilities.

Thus, for some, the era of big-dam construction is not at all over. There are more than thirty active and deferred proposals for large dams on rivers in California (table 4.7). Two dams over 400 feet tall are currently in licensing (Middle Bar on the Mokelumne and Clavey) and another 400-foot dam has its preliminary permit (Devil's Nose on the Mokelumne). Both the Clavey Dam and the Devil's Nose Dam would flood miles of upstream river (three and nine miles respectively). Even worse, each would drastically diminish flows for twenty miles downstream by directing the river's flow through power tunnels. Numerous small dams and reservoirs are also proposed by private and public entities. For example, thousands of permits have already been issued by FERC for small hydroelectric projects.

Three large proposed water-storage projects, Los Vaqueros, Buckhorn Canyon, and Los Banos Grandes reservoirs, are for offstream water storage. For offstream reservoirs, water would be diverted from rivers and used to flood canyons or small stream valleys, destroying oak woodland and riparian habitats. The Los Banos Grandes Reservoir would be the sixth largest in the state (after Shasta, Trinity, Oroville, New Don Pedro, and San Luis) and would flood one of the last native riparian sycamore forests in California. Moreover, plans for filling the Los Banos Reservoir each year call for additional pumps and running existing pumps at full capacity to divert what DWR calls "excess" water flowing through the Delta to the San Francisco Bay during the winter (DWR 1987). Scientists estimate that in 1992 as many as one out of four winter-run Chinook salmon juveniles trying to migrate out past the existing pumps was killed (DWR 1992). The huge Auburn Dam (a

Table 4.7. *Major Dams Proposed on California Rivers*

River	Project	Sponsor	Purpose	Status	Notes
American	Auburn Dam	BR	irrig, multi	const halted* Congress funds water-need study	Major storage reservoir would flood 48 miles of canyon
American	Auburn Dam	ACE	fl con,	ACE study recommends Dam	Periodic flooding of 20 miles of North and Middle fork
American South Fork**	Upper SOFAR Projects	El Dorado Irrig. Dist. SMUD	power ws	Licensed by FERC, planning in progress	Popular whitewater rafting river
Clavey	Clavey	Turlock ID	power	In FERC licensing proceedings	State Wild Trout Stream. Dam 400' high, flood 3 miles upstream. Power tunnel 20 miles long
Consumnes	Nashville Dam	Local Counties	power, multi	inactive	Only undammed Sierra Nevada river reaching the Central Valley
Fall River	6 small dams	local gov't & private dev.	power	FERC prelim permit issued (inactive)	3d highest waterfall outside Alaska, and national river tributary
Hardscrabble Creek	3 small dams	Cal Nickel Co.	water supply for mining	Inactive	1st dams in Smith River basin

River	Dam/Project	Sponsor	Purpose	Status	Comments
Kern	Hobo Dam	private dev	power	FERC preliminary permit	Southern Calif.'s principal rafting river
Kings River	Rodgers Crossing Dam	Kings River Cons. Dist.	power, multi fl con	deferred	Outstanding whitewater run. Protected by federal law in 1987
Kings River	Raising Pine Flat Dam	Kings River Cons. Dist. and ACE	power, fl con	ACE study compl. (inactive)	Will innundate lower whitewater run. River not protected
McCloud	McCloud River Dam	City of Santa Clara	power	deferred	Trout fishery. Construction prohibited by state law
Mad River	Butler Valley Dam	ACE	ws, fl con	deferred	Voted down in local referendum
Merced River	Bagby Dam	Merced Irrig. Dist.	power, multi	inactive pending	W&S river legislation
Mokelumne	Middle Bar Dam	San Joaquin Co.	reservoir	FERC prelim. permit	Dam over 400'. Popular canoeing and kayaking run. Would close portion of river to public
Mokelumne	Devil's Nose Dam	Amador Co.	power	FERC license applied for	Dam 400' high. Would flood 9 miles upstream. Power tunnel 20 miles long
San Joaquin, NF	Granite project	irrig. districts	power	inactive	Diversion planned from Ansel Adams Wilderness
Santa Margarita	multiple dams	BR, local districts	water supply	proposed	Many projects. Flood 20 miles of stream in San Diego Co.
Stanislaus, North Fork	Ramsey-French Meadow	CCWD, NCPA	power	inactive	Would disrupt commercial whitewater rafting

Table 4.7. (*Continued*)

River	Project	Sponsor	Purpose	Status	Notes
Yuba	Marysville Dam	ACE, YCWA	multi	study in progress	Major storage reservoir. Yuba projects threaten proposed State Park
Yuba: North, South, and Middle Forks	4 dams***	YCWA	power, multi	in planning	Funded by water sales
Yuba, South Fork	Excelsior Ditch Project	private dev.	power	license issued	State Park threatened

SOURCES: Palmer 1986; Stork 1989, 1992.
NOTE: Many large offstream storage reservoirs are not listed in the table.
* Reauthorization required.
** In addition to South Fork: Silver Fork, Alder Creek, and Webber Creek
*** Wanbo, Indian Valley, Edwards Crossing, Humbug, and Washington Dams

ABBREVIATIONS:
ACE   American Corps of Engineers
BR   Bureau of Reclamation
CCWD   Calaveras County Water District
EBMUD   East Bay Municipal Utility District
FERC   Federal Energy Regulatory Commission
NCPA   Northern California Power Agency
SF   San Francisco
SMUD   Sacramento Municipal Utility District

YCWA   Yuba County Water Association
dev   developer
fl con   flood control
irrig   irrigation
multi   multiple purposes
prelim   preliminary
ws   water supply

$2.5 billion project that could flood up to forty-three miles of canyon) would double the reservoir capacity of the existing 1.7 MAF Auburn dam system, but might only result in an additional 200,000 acre-feet of water actually stored for consumption.

ALTERNATIVE APPROACHES TO DEMAND AND SUPPLY MANAGEMENT

These proposed new water projects are not necessarily required in order to meet future demand. There are many policy and technical options for managing water demand and supply that have the potential to reduce the threat to biological diversity implied by DWR's projections of demand and supply. Just as energy conservation allowed America's economic productivity to grow while oil use was cut in the 1970s, water conservation can reduce the demand for water in California without reducing economic activity or closing the state to new residents. In another parallel to energy, where controlling late afternoon electricity demand can offset the need for new power plants, management of water demand may reduce the need for additional supplies by controlling when and where water is used as much as by lowering overall consumption.

Unfortunately, despite the potential for agricultural water conservation in California to offset the large increase in residential demand that DWR projects, DWR places little emphasis on managing water demand through conservation. For example, a 20 percent savings by large agricultural users would more than double the water supply available for urban, recreation, and wildlife uses. According to some analysts, a savings of only 10 percent would make enough water available to alleviate the need for the large water projects now proposed (e.g., Horner et al. 1984). The success of conservation programs in all sectors—residential, industrial, and agricultural—during the drought years of 1976 to 1977 and 1987 to 1991 showed that conservation could greatly reduce water demand throughout California. The amount of water saved in the future through conservation depends in large part on the economics of water use, as determined by water pricing and the extent to which agricultural water subsidies are restricted (see chapter 5).

As with conservation, establishing alternative supplies of water (supply management) can meet consumer needs without more diversions. Alternative supply strategies range from purification technologies to water reuse to conjunctive use to reallocation of water rights. Desalinization, currently providing water for Santa Barbara, is an energy-intensive but potentially valuable source of new supply. Grey water, water from clean municipal uses such as laundry, is more and more frequently reused on golf courses and other water-intensive sites that do not require potable water. Conjunctive use of ground and surface water, such as recharging groundwater during exceptionally wet years and withdrawing that groundwater during dry periods, may offset the need for wildlife-threatening diversions during droughts as well as off-setting the need for new supply projects. Reallocation of water rights with compensation through water marketing and transferable water rights is another increasingly discussed option. With the exception of desalinization, these supply options—although economically and technically feasible—are dramatically underutilized because the legal and institutional frameworks necessary for their development do not yet exist in California.

Water marketing: Potential and peril? Some environmental advocates see water marketing as a way of easing the political and economic pressure to develop new water projects. Water rights that can be transferred give water-users the option of selling their water rights to another entity if, for example, such a sale would result in a higher profit than using the water directly. This arrangement facilitates economically efficient use of water, but it is unclear whether this kind of efficiency alone results in environmental benefits such as increased flows. However, under marketable rights, conservationists or state agencies might be able to purchase outright the flows required to protect aquatic habitats.

Water transfers could involve water made available in three ways: through conservation (i.e., more efficient use), though stopping or altering use (e.g., fallowing land or crop switching), and through more groundwater pumping or increased surface-water diversions. From an environmental perspective, transfers based on the latter source are much less likely to be beneficial than are those based on conservation.

The positive potential of water transfers is demonstrated by the Los Angeles Municipal Water District (MWD), which has junior rights to water in the Coachella and Imperial Irrigation districts. MWD has been freeing up 100,000 acre-feet per year for its use by lining irrigation district canals and paying for water conservation efficiency in Imperial Valley farmland. Lining the canals does have a small environmental cost, as it reduces the water seeping into the opportunistic riparian vegetation along the canal banks. River flows are not changed, however, and the need for new developments or diversions is offset.

In contrast, the Yuba County Water Association (YCWA), which has been selling water during the recent drought years, transfers water by releasing water from the New Bullards Dam and Englebright Dam. The flows attract anadromous fish who spawn on the natural gravel bars. When the transfer is completed, the water is cut off and the river level falls, exposing and killing the eggs. The river is treated as a conveyance canal, rather than as a living river. The water sales, and therefore the flows of water being conveyed for sale, are timed following market demands (heavy demand in summer and fall and light in spring) not natural flows (which are heavy in spring and light in summer and fall).

In some water districts, water marketing appears to be backfiring from a conservationist perspective. Problems arise when sales fuel new development in water districts that reinvest proceeds in more water development. For example, YCWA is committed to reinvesting proceeds of water sales in water district projects. Although some of this investment will be used to strengthen delta levees, they have also commissioned feasibility studies for several new projects on the Yuba River.

SUMMARY

Current water projects and diversions are causing severe degradation of many of California's aquatic habitats. When we look to the future of aquatic biodiversity in California, it is clear that only sufficient instream flows can stop the slide toward extinction of numerous species of fish, plants, and waterfowl. Maintaining adequate instream flows for aquatic habitats is not simply a matter of preventing more projects and diversions in the future, because current water diversions are already causing the degradation of rivers and estuaries. California is now in a difficult situation; currently allocated rights to water resources are causing irreversible harm to the state's resources. Thus, even to maintain habitat quality at current levels, many tough issues must be addressed.

Yet protection of aquatic habitats is particularly difficult under the state's existing institutional arrangements in which many different state, federal, and local agencies all have the power to affect instream flows. Despite the importance of water supplies for many of California's habitats and wildlife, no agency with control over water management has a clear mandate to protect biological diversity.

Water conservation is necessary to free up sufficient flows, and luckily, the potential for water conservation in California is sizable, particularly in the agricultural and new-development sectors. Yet, although water conservation and efficient supply may minimize the need for new diversions and water projects, they will not necessarily result in higher instream flows. Demand for offstream water use may be so strong that the water freed up by conservation will simply go to additional consumption rather than to increasing stream flows. For example, municipal conservation may simply be used as a way to allow further development without having to expand water supplies.

Moreover, changing laws to allow the purchase of water rights for instream flows might result in pressure for the state to buy instream flows instead of setting minimum flow standards. This would result in tremendous expenditures to pay for what is now attainable through the enforcement of existing statutes on protection of fisheries, water quality, and public trust values. However, as advocates of water marketing point out, given that setting new minimum flow standards may involve long legal battles, the purchase of instream water rights could be a more rapid way of getting water flowing through aquatic habitats.

The pressure to sacrifice biological diversity for water use is bound to increase as demand for water grows because of California's increasing population, industrial expansion, and irrigation needs. In addition, trends in urbanization, population distribution, and energy policy affect the pressure for channelization, riparian conversion, flood control, hydroelectric development, and other projects. By all indications, the demand for California's already scarce water resources is growing. The only way to protect California's aquatic habitats, and the many species that depend on them, is simultaneously to have large-scale conservation and to guarantee instream flows. This will require a fundamental change in the way that California manages water demand and operates water projects, giving highest priority to maintaining what is left of our aquatic habitats.

Commodity Use of Natural Resources

The natural resource commodities, such as fish, forage, and lumber, that we extract from ecosystems play a crucial role in the state's economy and in forming the material basis of our life. California's commercial forests supply 10 percent of the nation's lumber, with a commodity value of $1.3 billion annually.[13] The state's livestock industry ranks eighth in the nation, second among all agricultural commodities in the State.[14] To support these industries, over 55 percent of the state is used for grazing or logging (table 4.1) and much of the coast supports highly productive fisheries. In addition, fishing and hunting provide popular recreational opportunities. On a regional basis, natural commodity industries play an even more dominant economic role. For example, 85 percent of all the land in the five-county North Interior region (Lassen, Modoc, Shasta, Siskiyou, and Trinity counties) is used for forestry or grazing. Wood and wood product industries are critical to the regional economies of the North Coast (Del Norte, Humboldt, and Mendocino counties) and North Interior. Overall, the value of processed lumber produced in California averaged 1.3 billion dollars per year between 1978 and 1985. The timber industry accounted for over 90 percent of basic (manufacturing) employment in three counties and over 50 percent in ten counties, in 1984. Statewide employment in these industries has averaged about 58,000 people in the past decade (CDF 1988).

California's bountiful harvest of natural resources depends on the health and integrity of the ecosystems that produce it. The continued production of wood, forage, and fisheries depends on the functions of a healthy ecosystem such as nutrient cycling, water flow regulation, and seed dispersal. Yet our harvest of these goods fundamentally affects vital ecosystem services by disturbing vegetation regeneration, soil fertility, and river flow. Some alteration of the environment is inevitable. However, because so much of the state's territory is used for commodity extraction, harvest and management practices that lead to environmental degradation pose a major threat to habitats and species throughout California. Poor management practices are also a threat to the long-term economic sustainability of commodity industries. Management decisions are not just local or state, as over one-half of California's commercial forest and rangeland is under the jurisdiction of the U.S. Forest Service (USFS) or U.S. Bureau of Land Management (BLM; figures 4.1 and 4.2).

With population growth and per capita consumption increasing, consumption of natural resources is accelerating. Never before has our grasp on "renewable resources" been so tenuous; anadromous fish and riparian forests are not being managed as renewable resources but are instead being depleted rapidly. For example, only 10 percent of Cali-

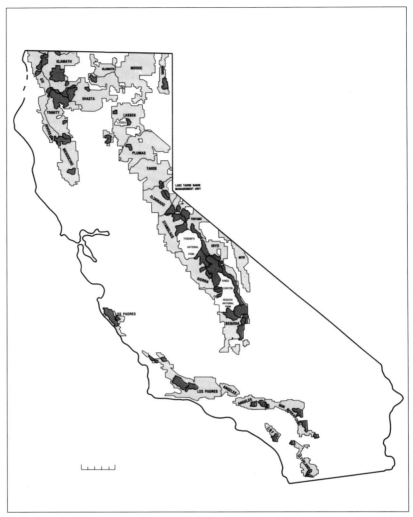

4.1. U.S. Forest Service land in California: National Forests (light grey) and Wilderness Areas (dark grey).

fornia's old-growth forests remain—nearly all of it on public lands, and fishery indices for many salmon runs and the striped bass of the San Francisco Bay-Delta declined steadily throughout the 1980s. In 1992, the size of some salmon populations had fallen so low that the commercial fishing season was severely restricted. By ignoring the fact that an ecosystem's production of natural commodities depends on its overall health, extraction practices without regard to natural limits have led

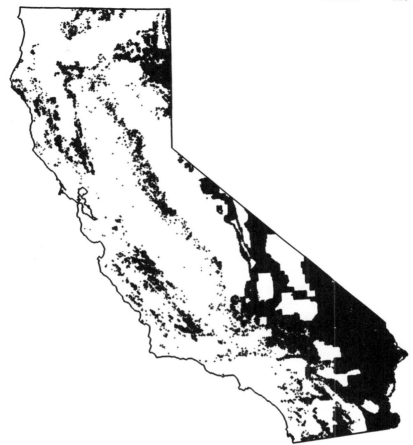

4.2. U.S. Bureau of Land Management land in California.

to two mutually interactive problems: the declining productivity of natural commodities, and the loss of habitats and species. These problems are not inevitable with commodity use. Rather, they reflect a lack of balance between preservation and harvest and a lack of commitment to the land use and resource management practices necessary to maintain this balance.

FORESTRY

Of the eighteen million acres of productive conifer land in California, two million are in parks or preserves and much of these are at high elevations. On commercial conifer lands, the typical practice of harvesting more rapidly than reforested areas can reach maturity is leading to the net loss of mature forests. For example, on privately owned industry lands, harvest each year exceeds growth by 22 percent, thus rapidly reducing standing inventory (CDF 1988). Although California's forests are highly productive, at current rates, harvestable timber on private industry lands will decrease 35 percent in only fifteen years, from 46 billion board feet to only 30 billion board feet, according to FRRAP computer simulations (CDF 1988).[15] Overall, California's commercial forests are logged three times faster than the national average (in board-feet extracted per acre per year). As private forests are logged, there is increasing pressure to accelerate logging of public forests, which have a multiple-use mandate.

Environmental impacts of logging. The most serious terrestrial impacts of logging are loss of old-growth habitat, fragmentation of remaining habitat, extirpation of species dependent on mature forests, alteration of tree stand composition (particularly from reforestation practices) and the long-term loss of soil fertility from erosion, removal of biomass, and disturbing beneficial microbial activity in the soil. In many logging operations, road building and the roads and skid trails left behind are the most damaging activities. Use of herbicides to control undergrowth removes shrub species and pollutes streams.

The impacts on riparian and aquatic habitats are primarily due to removal of riparian vegetation and erosion from logging and road building. Removal of riparian vegetation leads to erosion of the banks, more intermittent stream flow, loss of shade causing warmer water, and less filtering of sedimentation carried by runoff. Sediment clouds the water column and can bury the gravel beds needed for fish spawning and insect habitat. The excess nutrients in sediments can change the stream's algae composition, with ripple effects throughout the food chain.

Old-growth forests (forests in late seral stages of succession) provide habitat for a high diversity and abundance of wildlife species (CDFG 1989*b*). Recent controversies over logging center on the cutting of old-growth forests, particularly low-elevation Douglas-fir and redwood forests. Over the last hundred years, nearly all privately owned old-growth redwoods were logged and only 1 percent of the historic old-growth ponderosa pine forests remain. Current rates of timber harvesting, if unchecked, could destroy what is left of the state's remaining old-growth Douglas-fir, ponderosa pine, and mixed conifer forests, particularly on private lands. Logging is proceeding although scientists and forest managers do not know how much old growth remains or how much can be cut while still maintaining viable populations of species that require old-growth habitat. Nor do they fully understand the effects of fragmentation of large, continuous forests into smaller patches.

Management of timber harvests. Particularly for forests in early stages of succession (new growth), the threat to biological diversity posed by logging depends on whether or not good management practices are followed. Forest management is the key to limiting environmental degradation from timber harvesting and to protecting future timber resources. Four aspects of management have particular environmental importance: harvest rate, reforestation, erosion control, and stream protection. Reforestation makes a tremendous difference in the habitat value of cutover land for many years after the cut (Maser et al. 1988). Roads, slash burning, and lack of reforestation are major sources of erosion; hence, sound practices can minimize erosion.

Although nearly all logging results in some forest degradation, good timber harvest practices, including streamside protection zones and road restoration, can greatly ameliorate the damage by leaving riparian vegetation intact, reducing the length of water flow paths on hillsides, and minimizing the clearing of ground cover vegetation. There are proven techniques for protecting riparian and stream habitats, many of which require leaving a swath of trees uncut. Unfortunately, there is a limit to the effectiveness of any erosion control practices on steep or unstable slopes.

Although forest managers have the technical ability to protect habitats, current forest practices commonly replace natural forest ecosystems with a monocultural plantation. To the extent that good management practices are well known, the threat from logging remains because of bureaucratic and economic barriers to the implementation of these practices, some of which are discussed in the next chapter.

Better management of privately owned timber land will require both improved timber harvest rules and enforcement to ensure that approved timber harvest plans do comply with these rules. Some improvement of enforcement has been occurring, after years of inertia on the part of the California Board of Forestry. The Board of Forestry has primary responsibility for timber harvest rules, although it required an act of the California Legislature, the Z'berg-Nejedly Act of 1973, to finally make reforestation practices mandatory. The Board's inaction is partially a result of the resource-extraction orientation of its mandate and the in-

An ancient redwood grove, Humboldt County. (Photo by David Swanlund courtesy of Save-the-Redwoods League)

terests of Board members, who share this orientation. The enabling legislation of the Board of Forestry gives priority to enhancement and management of forest commodity resources and requires only that the Board "consider" the effects of forestry practices on the multiple values of the ecosystem. Under common interpretations of this mandate, enhancement of the timber-products industry and short-term economic goals are often favored over conservation. Improvement of Board of Forestry and CDF policies may require outside influence to reinterpret or rewrite the Board's mandate as the protection of the long-term productivity of forest land, and thus protection of biological diversity, and to allow coordination with other agencies concerned with protecting biological diversity.

Stumps from old growth and regrowth redwood on private land in Humboldt County.
(Photo by Charles Kennard)

Management of federal timberland. Federal regulations are considered to be much more stringent than those of the state, and they give clear statutory protection to biological diversity as part of the multiple-use mandate of the Forest Service and Bureau of Land Management. In practice, however, the goals and standards for conservation are not always achieved on federal land.

On public lands, several promising efforts are being made to provide protection for old growth and riparian ecosystems. Specifically, the Tahoe National Forest staff recommended revisions, in 1991, to the existing Long Range Management Plan that incorporate the most current information from landscape ecology, conservation biology, and habitat suitability models for old-growth-associated species. The Forest Service staff recommended protection of large blocks of old-growth habitat connected by riparian corridors. These blocks and corridors are to be distributed evenly across the landscape to provide habitat and dispersal and migration capability for the full array of species that require old-growth forests. These recommendations specifically avoided the single-species emphasis that typifies many early conservation plans.

Similarly, in the Pacific Northwest, the congressionally commissioned Portland Panel (also known as the Gang of Four) report is the first National Forest planning effort to comprehensively address multiple species management, including fisheries stocks, rather than single-species protection in late-successional forests (Johnson et al. 1991). Their conclusions were similar to those recommended for the Tahoe National Forest, namely that in order to protect the myriad of old-growth-associated species (such as the California spotted owl, fisher, flying squirrel, and several salmon populations), large blocks of habitat and riparian corridors must be maintained intact and well distributed throughout the landscape.

Market forces. Although the National Forest Plan recommendations and the state forestry accords are slowly moving through political review—processes that may take several years—market pressure for lumber continues unabated. Population growth may increase demand for board lumber, since over 70 percent of the logs cut in California are used in the state (CDF 1988). In addition, tree species that were traditionally undesirable for harvest are now being cut due to changes in markets for lumber, paper, and other wood products. Tan-oak harvesting has increased dramatically, not only for wood chips, but because it is particularly good material for making facsimile paper. One of the most dramatic turnarounds in tree demand concerns the yew tree of the Pacific Northwest forests. Once burned as a weedy species, the tree is now prized as a possible source of cancer-fighting chemicals. In 1990, medical scientists announced that an extract made from yew bark, called taxol, is one of the most effective treatments of ovarian cancer known. With the bark from an entire mature tree required to make enough taxol for one treatment, the value of the yew tree has skyrocketed and medical associations have joined environmentalists in decrying the traditional management of forests as mines of lumber.

Overseas markets such as those in Japan and Mexico have become large consumers of raw logs shipped from the West Coast despite the fact that sales of raw materials give far less benefit to the local economy per acre of harvest than do locally processed forest products. The on-going shift to raw-log markets increases the size of harvest needed to support local workers. Although California is approaching international markets much more cautiously than are Oregon and Washington, the Board of Forestry is interested in developing these raw materials markets (CDF 1988). Even if California lumber is not shipped to Japan, the overall demand for lumber will increase as a result of the expanding international market.

Private land sales and corporate takeovers are emerging as a threat to sustainable management, as exemplified by the 1985 takeover by Maxxam Group of the family-owned Pacific Lumber Company. Pacific Lumber's sustainable yield practices and impressive reserves of virgin forest left them vulnerable to corporate takeovers. Maxxam immediately began liquidating the inventory of old-growth forest to pay back the debt incurred in the takeover. As demonstrated by the Pacific Lumber case, sustainable management results in an undervaluation of timber holdings at high discount rates when compared with rapid extraction and sale of the trees, as discussed in chapter 5. Thus, businesses tending toward sustainable management are ripe for takeover by companies intending to extract resources quickly.

Preservation of old-growth forests. Even with the best management practices, logging alters forests. To preserve at least a mosaic of the mature habitats that support native species, some stands must be left uncut. Furthermore, some forest habitats are too rare or important to log now or to leave vulnerable to market pressure in the future. Recognizing this situation, the Save-the-Redwoods League and others have worked for more than fifty years to get old-growth redwood forests protected in parks. Due in part to their efforts, there are approximately 76,000 acres of old-growth coastal redwood and giant sequoia forests in California parks, and a total of 200,000 acres of redwood forests in all stages of succession. Nevertheless, only two-thirds of the land needed to protect major redwood watersheds is safe from logging (Save-the-Redwoods League 1979). Because unprotected stands have been cut, less than 20,000 acres of old-growth redwoods were left on private land in 1988. Most of these were owned by Pacific Lumber-Maxxam Corporation and were threatened by immediate plans for logging.

Unlike the redwood tree, famed for its majesty and unparalleled size, the Douglas-fir, red fir, and ponderosa pine were historically overlooked by preservationists. Yet these trees form remarkably rich and varied habitats, vital to the biological diversity of the state. The extensive stands of Douglas fir throughout the Pacific Northwest, once viewed as inexhaustible, have now been cut so extensively that the spotted owl and possibly other species may have been pushed to the brink of extinction. Low-elevation forests, of Douglas-fir in the North Coast and of ponderosa pine and mixed conifer in the Sierra Nevada, are under-represented in our parks and wilderness areas, leaving most of California's old growth vulnerable to logging. Because some animal and plant species require undisturbed habitat, logging old growth, even with improved regulation and management, may result in extinctions. Moreover, if logging of mature forests continues, small parks may not offer sufficient protection for wide-ranging species such as the wolverine, fisher, martin, and Sierra Nevada red fox.

Management and protection of hardwood communities. Hardwoods, mainly oak woodlands, cover 9.5 million acres of California, of which virtually none is in preserves or otherwise protected from logging or conversion. The logging of hardwoods is not regulated by state government, despite the fact that three-quarter million acres of oaks and other hardwoods have been logged for firewood in the last fifty years and that development of oak woodlands continues to proceed rapidly (CDF 1988). Regulation of oak removal is the jurisdiction of local governments and varies greatly from county to county.

Traditional regulatory approaches to protecting lumber species, such as requiring permits for cutting, will not in themselves protect the oak woodlands since not only the oak tree but the whole habitat is threatened. In fact, the threat from logging per se is diminishing. The inventory of black oak, used for lumber, is currently increasing (Bolsinger 1988). Cutting of valley oak and live oak for firewood was a major cause of loss in the 1980s, but cutting has slowed since 1986. Now the major threats to oak habitats are from grazing and conversion for ranchettes, urbanization, and agriculture. Even if oaks are not cut, a housing tract set in the woodland leaves only a suburb with trees in it. Scientists do not know how large a contiguous expanse is needed to preserve the habitat value of the oak woodland.

The Integrated Hardwood Range Management Program (IHRMP), started by CDF and the University of California in 1986, has begun studies of oak regeneration, the multiple assaults facing the oak woodlands, and oak protection (Huntsinger et al. 1988). Nevertheless, loss of hardwood habitats is of increasing concern. Most hardwood habitat is in the hands of private, nonindustrial owners, and cutting of hardwoods has not been regulated in most counties. With IHRMP, however, the Department of Forestry is becoming involved in research and education about hardwoods, which may be a stepping stone to conservation of the state's oak habitats.

LIVESTOCK GRAZING

Cattle and sheep grazing is the most pervasive use of wildlands in California. It occurs on nearly every habitat-type and in all counties but Imperial and San Francisco. Over 41 million of the state's 85 million undeveloped acres are grazed. Of these, more than half are federally owned, with the remainder in private hands (table 4.8, figure 4.1). Cattle populations are declining slowly in California although beef remains one of the state's biggest agricultural commodities. Use of public rangeland is projected to remain constant over the next few decades, whereas private rangeland is giving way to development. California's Department of Food and Agriculture and Department of Forestry have programs concerned with ranching interests but the state has no agency specifically regulating grazing or rangeland resources, in contrast to the state's active regulation of timber harvest and forest resources by the Board of Forestry and CDF.

Environmental impacts of grazing: native animals, plants, and soils. Grazing threatens many native plant and animal species as well as aquatic habitats. Because they carry transmittable diseases, the presence of domestic livestock poses a direct threat to bighorn sheep, pronghorn antelope, elk, and other native grazers. For example, the entire Warner Mountain herd of sixty-five bighorn sheep was killed in 1988 by a virus believed to have been transmitted by contact with a single domestic sheep (CDFG 1989*a*). Grazing livestock were a major cause of the decimation, around the turn of the century, of the bighorn sheep and pronghorn antelope in California (Dasmann 1981).

Although the condition of California rangeland has improved in this century, due mainly to reduced numbers of livestock (USGAO 1988*a*), grazing remains the principal threat to many plant species. According to the California Native Plant Society, more than seventy species of rare or endemic plants statewide are threatened by grazing. Seventy-five percent of the counties (forty-four) in California have at least one such plant species (Smith and Berg 1988). Few of these plants, however, have been studied in detail.

Special habitat concerns. The impact of grazing on oak habitats is of particular concern because grazing affects most of the state's vast stretches of oak woodlands and savanna—in 1985, over 77 percent of all oak woodland owners used their land for grazing (CDF

Table 4.8. *Livestock Grazing in California*

Table 4.8a. *Acres Grazed and Forage Used by Ownership, 1985*

Ownership	Acres Grazed (1,000's)	AUMs* Consumed (1,000's)	Percent of Forage Consumed in California Provided by Land Type
Private	17,853	12,793	91
Public			
Forest Service	12,800	568	4
BLM	9,336	387	3
Defense	263	84	1
Other federal	64	47	1
State and local	567	160	1
Total public	23,029	1,246	9
Total	40,882	14,038	100

Table 4.8b. *Forage Production by Cover Type, 1985*

	Percent AUMs Consumed	AUM/Acre	Acres Grazed**
Annual grassland	50	0.7–3	6,184
Perennial grass	1	0.1	1,404
Meadow & riparian	4	0.5	1,123
Hardwoods	28	0.01–3	20,305
Conifer	7	0.2	4,913
Shrublands	4	0–2	280
Desert	1	0.03–0.06	3,510
Total	95		37,720

Table 4.8c. *Ownership of Grazed Land by Cover Type*

Cover Type	Owned By
Annual grassland	All
Perennial grass	All
Meadow & riparian	U.S. Forest Service
Hardwood lands	Bureau of Land Management, private
Conifer	Private
Shrublands	Bureau of Land Management, U.S. Forest Service
Desert	Bureau of Land Management, U.S. Forest Service

SOURCES: CDF 1988; US GAO 1988a.
*AUMs = forage equivalent to one cow's monthly consumption
**Acres estimated as (% AUMs) × (total AUMS) / (average AUMs/acre). Note that these acreage estimates do not correspond with other estimates of cover type in California, such as figure 3.1.

1988)—and because grazing is one of the factors linked to the widely observed reproductive failure of valley oaks and other oak species. In addition to trampling vegetation, livestock selectively graze on certain species—favoring young and riparian vegetation—and they may eat plants so close to where they emerge from the ground that the plant cannot grow back.

Although range conditions statewide show improvement, riparian areas remain severely degraded, particularly on federal rangeland (USGAO 1988*b*). In fact, the most acute and serious threat to biological diversity from grazing may be the continued degradation of riparian and aquatic habitats on both private and federal land (USDA 1984, USGAO 1988*b*). Rivers degraded by livestock have only intermittent flows, provide less forage and water, and support, at best, reduced populations of native fish. Riparian zones are important for terrestrial vertebrates in rangeland habitats, as these habitats tend to be relatively arid and have less tree cover than, for example, the coniferous north coast. The loss of riparian vegetation caused by grazing or erosion has a marked effect on plant and animal populations (CDF 1988).

Management of rangelands. Rangeland erosion is widespread in California, threatening soil fertility and plants of rangeland, riverine, and lake habitats. Livestock grazing accelerates erosion by disturbing soil and river banks and by removing protective plant cover and roots. Except on very sensitive soils, erosion is largely a problem of inadequate management practices such as overstocking, too little fallow time, or grazing at the wrong times. In heavily degraded range, plants are killed, leaving expanding patches of bare soil, particularly where livestock congregate (Heady 1975).

Practically all of California's nineteen million acres of private rangeland have erosion problems. According to U.S. Soil Conservation Service (SCS) surveys, more than 75 percent of the state's rangeland could be greatly improved by better management, but on nearly one-quarter of the acreage, erosion problems are so severe that treatment is not practical (USDA 1984). In addition, there are over 9,000 miles of streambanks with erosion problems (USDA 1984). Systematic soil surveys are available only for private land, but there is no indication that public land is in significantly better condition.

The problems of poor rangeland management may be particularly severe on federal lands, although data are insufficient to fully assess the condition of federal rangeland. Since nearly one-quarter of the state is grazing land overseen by the federal government, lack of information in this sector alone creates significant gaps in assessing and managing the condition of California's wildlands.

Surveys by the U.S. General Accounting Office suggest that *most* of the riverine areas on federal land are degraded, as is a significant fraction of the upland range. Pressure by environmental groups and others concerned with the long-term management of western rangeland has resulted in some improvement in stewardship by BLM and USFS. For example, a successful lawsuit by the Natural Resources Defense Council in 1974 led to the requirement that an environmental impact statement be filed by BLM or USFS before grazing rights are allotted. Other groups, such as the Sierra Club, are challenging the subsidy given to ranchers using federal rangeland, because the subsidy is linked to environmental damage resulting from overstocking (see chapter 5). Unfortunately, although slow changes may be occurring in agency procedures, the actual condition of riparian habitats and rangeland does not show steady improvement (USGAO 1988*a*, 1988*b*).

Much of federal rangeland is of low forage productivity, with the result that on average thirteen times more federal land than private land must be grazed to support a given herd of livestock (CDF 1988). Although more than half the rangeland in California is federal, federal land provides less than 10 percent of the range forage consumed statewide. In part, this disparity is due to the fact that most private rangelands are used year-round, whereas many federal range allotments are used only seasonally. For the most part, however, the disparity is due to the great quality difference between private and federal land. In conclusion, most federal land provides very little forage while subjecting very large natural areas to disease, trampling, erosion, and riparian degradation.

Trends in riparian protection and restoration are unsatisfactory, with neither private ranchers, BLM, or USFS demonstrating a serious commitment to protection. It appears that on both private and public land, erosion will continue to be a serious problem on rangeland unless management practices are improved and degraded range and riparian areas are restored. On privately owned land, the SCS can advise ranchers on erosion control but has no legal authority over ranching practices. On federal land, there are formal policies requiring improvement of rangeland with erosion problems, but implementation of policies generally only occurs as a result of pressure from outside the management agency, such as from a Regional Water Quality Control Board or a lawsuit filed by an environmental organization, as discussed in chapter 5. Despite the availability of technical solutions, it appears that grazing will continue to cause erosion of rangeland soils and the degradation of riparian and aquatic habitats.

AGRICULTURE

Many of the threats to biological diversity from agricultural activity have already been discussed in this chapter. The development of agriculture results in conversion of the most fertile land and the flattest land, thus selectively taking floodplains, deltas, and wetlands. Most of the best agricultural land has been converted, and the consequent loss of many ecosystems has already occurred. Conversion for new agricultural land has slowed.

As agriculture thrives as one of California's biggest industries, the numerous negative impacts show no sign of abating. Perhaps the most widely felt ramification of agricultural practice is the redistribution of water throughout California, due to agricultural consumption of 85 percent of California's developed water supply. At the physical nexus of this demand for water, the Sacramento-San Joaquin Delta, there are now fisheries associations, environmental organizations, water utilities, state and federal agencies, and developers struggling for control over water flows and diversions. Mandatory water conservation during the drought years affected urban communities throughout the southern two-thirds of California, and many aquatic habitats received water only on a low priority basis. Although the vast majority of the state's freshwater wetland habitats have already been lost to conversion, the enduring wetlands play a key role in the natural landscape. Yet these habitat remnants are still at risk from conversion to cultivation, with many wetlands protection laws specifically exempting land zoned for agriculture. In addition, irrigation water that flows back into rivers or drainage canals carries salts, metals, nutrients, and pesticides. The impact of these pollutants on the species of wetlands, estuaries, and other receiving waters are discussed in the next section.

Agricultural businesses are regulated very differently than are other natural resource industries. The Department of Food and Agriculture (CDFA) is not part of the Resources Agency, and many environmental and natural resource laws either pass over or explicitly exempt agriculture. Nevertheless, agricultural production remains dependent on ecosystem functions, such as soil structure development, genetic variation, moderation of the climate, and water availability. Conversely, agricultural practices exert a strong influence over the state's species and habitats.

Although the influence of agricultural practices in California have been negative—historically through conversion of habitats and destruction of riparian forests, and now through heavy water use and pollution of drainage water—not all modes of agriculture are intrinsically in conflict with maintenance of biodiversity. Organic farming, without pesticides or fertilizers, avoids most of the water and air pollution associated with chemical-based agriculture.

HUNTING AND FISHING

Although hunting and fishing are sustainable at appropriate levels, overhunting and overfishing affect biological diversity directly by decreasing the numbers of the target species. Sometimes populations of nontarget species, such as dolphins caught in tuna nets, also decline. There are also ecological ripple effects from the reduction of these populations, due to disruptions of predator-prey, competitive, and other species interactions.

Fishing and hunting also affect biological diversity through the practices used to manage fish and game. Management of habitats to increase numbers of game species may be deleterious to nongame species. For example, a natural wetland displays a mosaic of elevations, soil types, and plants, which provide an array of sites favoring different species. Management of Central Valley wetlands, which is focused on enhancing waterfowl habitat, results in the restoration and maintenance of only a fraction of the natural wetland formations at the expense of native plants and birds (Jensen 1983).

Control of hunting and fishing, mainly through licenses, is administered by the Department of Fish and Game and the Fish and Game Commission. The Commission sets policies for CDFG, which manages game species and certain habitats. The Fish and Game Commission often appears biased in favor of game animals over other habitat values, with adverse consequences for biological diversity. For instance, feral pigs eat native plant bulbs and root up large areas. Particularly in Marin and Sonoma Counties, where feral pigs are reproducing rapidly, the pigs' feeding behavior is threatening rare and endangered plants. Rather than attempting to eradicate the feral pigs, or at least allow unlimited hunting, the Fish and Game Commission restricts the hunting of feral pigs.

In CDFG, where the source of most income is hunting and fishing, the Department's funds for protection are spent heavily on game species, such as deer, trout, salmon, and migratory waterfowl. For instance, CDFG maintains a staff of fifty for studying deer in California, whereas a single staff member in the Inland Fisheries Division is responsible for fifty different species of nongame fish. This allocation of resources, inappropriate from the point of view of preserving biodiversity, arises from the interests of the funding sources as well as from institutional bias (see also chapter 5). CDFG now has a number of divisions and programs devoted to protecting nongame species and habitats (e.g., Environmental Services Division, Natural Heritage Division, and the Non-game Program in the Wildlife Division), but weak financial support for these programs hampers their effectiveness.

Pollution

Most pollutants are released into the environment as by-products of industrial or other processes, either routinely, as with carbon dioxide (CO_2) emissions from power plants, or through malfunction, as with hydrocarbons released from incomplete combustion or oil spills. A few pollutants, such as pesticides, are actually intended as toxins in the environment. Other compounds, such as phosphate and selenium, are essential nutrients in trace quantities and are harmful only when present in excess.

Assessing the risk to any species or habitat in California from a particular pollutant is extremely difficult since there are huge data gaps at each phase of such an assessment. Estimates of the amount of pollutants, such as pesticides, in runoff and other dispersed sources of water pollution are very crude, with slightly better data available for air pollution emission rates and point-source water discharge. Compared to release data, there is little understanding of the environmental fate of pollutants, due to complicated transport and chemical reactions. Finally, scientists know shockingly little about the effects on most species of any given exposure to the pollutants we release. In this section we concentrate on release trends for the major types of pollution and describe the harmful impacts of a few well-studied pollutants.

Calero Reservoir, Santa Clara County, is two miles from the settlement of New Almaden, the center of a mercury mining district, which closed down in the 1970s. The reservoir supplies drinking water to neighboring municipal utilities. (Photo by Charles Kennard)

Despite great advances made under the Federal Water Pollution Control Act and subsequent Clean Water Act amendments, water pollution still threatens wildlife in many of California's aquatic and wetland habitats. A 1990 study found that almost three hundred waterways in California pose a threat to aquatic life as a result of toxic contaminants, excessive nutrients, or erosion (SWRCB 1990). Many current problems result from dispersed, non-point sources of pollution, such as agricultural fields, urban runoff, and construction sites. These dispersed sources of water pollution pose the greatest threat to aquatic ecosystems, although harmful pollutants are still being discharged from industrial and municipal pipes as well (tables 4.9, 4.10, and 4.11).

Water quality in California is the responsibility of the State Water Resources Control Board, which has authority for enforcing the

Table 4.9. *Sources of Pollutants in San Francisco Bay*

Pollutant	Sewage Treatment Plants	Industrial Effluent	Urban Runoff	Non-Urban Runoff & Riverine
Metals:				
Cr	X	X	X	X
Pb		X	X	X
Ca		X		
Hg		X	X	**
Se		X		X
Cu	X	X		X
Ag	X			
Zn	X	X	X	
Ni		X		
Tin				X
Organics:				
PCB		X	X	
Pesticides				X
tAH	X	X	X	

SOURCES: TSMP 1984, NOAA 1987, Gunther et al. 1987.
** = in some pesticides and in mining residues in Delta outflow
PCB = total Polychlorinated Biphenyls
tAH = total Aromatic Hydrocarbons

Cr = Chromium	Se = Selenium
Cu = Copper	Ca = Calcium
Pb = Lead	Zn = Zinc
Ag = Silver	Ni = Nickel
Hg = Mercury	

Clean Water Act in California. To achieve local implementation of the Clean Water Act, SWRCB has ten Regional Water Quality Control Boards (RWQCB) that write basin plans, conduct research, and enforce regulations. The Regional Boards regulate both non-point and point source pollution in both freshwater and coastal waters. Because water quality is affected by water flow as well as pollutant loading, SWRCB, which has responsibility for water flows, must consider water quality in setting standards for minimum flow and timing of flows. Many different agencies oversee activities that influence coastal water quality, including SWRCB, the State Lands Commission, the Department of Fish and Game, and the Coastal Commission.

Point source water pollution. Point sources of water pollution from industrial pipes, wastewater treatment plants, and other

Table 4.10. *Concentration of Trace Elements in Sediments in Estuaries*

| | Heavy Metals (ppm dry wt) | | | | | | Organics (ppb dry wt) | | |
	Cr	Cu	Pb	Ag	Cd	Hg	tAH	DDT	PCB
California Estuaries:									
Bodega Bay	240	**	**	170	10	5	**	**	4
San Diego Harbor	150	220	40	60	100	100	5,000	8.4	422
San Francisco:									
average	365	25	10.5	18	5	8	1,500	2.25	30.5
Hunter's Point	355	20	50	**	5	**	2,900	2.7	40
Oakland	190	65	353	2	5	30	170	5.4	61
Richmond	260	5	2	60	5	**	1,200	0.3	12
San Pablo Bay	650	10	**	10	5	2	100	0.5	9
U.S. Estuaries:									
Appalachicola	70	20	40	2	2	2	200	1.4	NA
Boston Harbor	200	150	100	250	150	100	26,440	210	17,100
								31	
Hudson-Raritan	180	180	180	200	270	230	4,500		444
Lower Chesapeake	50	10	15	2	30	**	100	2.1	33
Mississippi Delta	70	20	30	5	40	2	600	7	33.7

SOURCE: NOAA 1987.

NA = not available.
** = below detection

tAH = total Aromatic Hydrocarbons
DDT = total DDT residues
PCB = total Polychlorinated Biphenyls

Cr = Chromium   Ag = Silver
Cu = Copper   Cd = Cadmium
Pb = Lead   Hg = Mercury

Table 4.11. *Waterways in California Polluted Primarily by Point Sources*

Location	Contaminant	Responsible Facilities
South San Francisco Bay	Heavy metals	City sewage treatment plants and outflow from storm drains
Spring Creek	Metals	Iron Mountain Mine
South Fork of West Squaw Creek	Metals	Balaklala Mine
Little Backbone Creek	Metals	Mammoth Mine
Little Grizzly Creek	Metals	Walker Mine
Sacramento River	Dioxin	Simpson Paper Co, Anderson
Pacific Ocean	Dioxin	Simpson Paper Co, Fairhaven
Pacific Ocean	Dioxin	Louisiana-Pacific Corp.
San Joaquin River	Metals	Gaylord Container Corp.
Suisun Bay	Metals	Exxon, Tosco, and Mountain View Sewage Plant
Carquinez Strait	Metals	Shell
Carquinez Strait	Metals	Stauffer
Mokelumne River	Metals	New Penn Mine
Kanaka Creek	Metals	16 to 1 Mine
Leviathan Creek	Metals	Leviathan Mine
Las Tables Creek	Metals	Buena Vista Mine

SOURCE: SWRCB 1990.
Total: 30 sewage treatment plants and industrial facilities.

identifiable sites of origin have been the traditional focus of water quality control. Although problems still persist in many areas, the once widespread pollution from point sources has been relatively well-controlled through regulation since the Clean Water Act (CWA) was passed in 1972.

Nearly all types of aquatic habitats in California, including lakes, streams, estuaries, bays, and open ocean waters, receive municipal wastewater. The most common pollutants in municipal wastewater, excess nutrients and heavy metals, cause adverse impacts in many of these receiving waters. Nutrients from inadequately treated waste cause eutrophication, characterized by blooms of algae, decreased water transparency, depleted oxygen, and in extreme cases, asphyxiation of fish.[16] In addition to trace metals, discharge often carries oil and solvents discharged by system users and chlorine from the treatment plant.

The threat to aquatic habitats from sewage in the future will depend not only on the number of system users, but also on the mass of contaminants that users discharge and on the technology employed for treatment. Even with improvements in treatment technology and increasingly stringent standards for discharge quality, the dramatic increases expected in the number of sewage-system users may make controlling pollution from discharge difficult and extremely costly.[17] In addition, if current trends in population growth for rural California continue—as seems likely—there will be fewer and fewer lakes and streams in California free from pollution by wastewater. Seepage from septic tanks also increases the total nutrient loading as the number of dischargers increases.

Sewage discharge is becoming an important source of trace metals, solvents, and other toxic contaminants in aquatic habitats. Effective control of toxic household products in discharge could be achieved by banning certain products (for example, the ban of phosphates in laundry soaps resulted in a significant decline in lake eutrophication) and by providing convenient disposal alternatives. Educational programs to reduce household toxics in wastewater are being developed in a few areas under RWQCB encouragement.

In a few municipalities and districts in California, population growth has been slowed by Clean Water Act limits on effluent loading from sewage treatment plants or septic tanks. For example, proposed developments have been stalled or denied the necessary permits under the Clean Water Act (CWA) because the capacity of the existing sewage treatment system could not meet effluent standards if the system load was increased. Local areas have limited growth by voting down referenda to expand sewage treatment capacity or by electing directors of their local wastewater utility who choose not to expand facilities.

The wide variety of chemicals[18] discharged at point sources by industrial facilities into aquatic habitats threaten not only aquatic species, such as fish, but also the waterfowl, birds of prey, and mammals that eat contaminated fish. Bioaccumulation of selenium in fish is thought to contribute to the decline of the striped bass and also to the high levels of selenium in diving ducks of San Francisco Bay, where contamination is as severe as that found in dabbling ducks of Kesterson National Wildlife Refuge and other polluted agricultural drainage ponds (Pease and Taylor 1992). Statewide, pollution from industrial discharge of chemicals regulated under CWA is less serious than it was twenty or even ten years ago. However, many harmful chemicals are not yet regulated under CWA. In addition to placing more chemicals under regulation, further control of discharge will require more stringent enforcement combined with new approaches to regulation of pollutant mixtures.

The historic emphasis of the Clean Water Act on controlling the concentration of individual pollutants in discharge, with the use of best available technologies, is now inadequate to achieve CWA goals. Compliance with standards for each individual pollutant can still result in toxic mixtures of chemicals. Industrial processes discharge a wide variety of chemicals, the combined effect of which is usually unknown. In addition, the accumulation of pollutants released over time may result in toxic levels of pollutants.

Regulations to control the total loading of pollutants and to protect water quality have been promulgated by RWQCBs but these regulations have proven technically difficult to enforce. Most research has been conducted on a single species and a single toxic substance. Current scientific knowledge is generally inadequate to allow prediction of the effect of mixtures of chemicals or to measure the impact of specific chemicals once discharge has occurred. Thus, it is difficult to set standards for discharge permits that explicitly limit the impact of discharge on receiving waters, compared to the relative ease of setting standards for concentrations of individual pollutants in the discharge. Except where harm to animals has already been documented, knowledge of effects at ambient levels (i.e., in the habitat) is limited even for a single pollutant and a single species. To bypass the need for predictive data, USEPA and water quality control boards are developing new tests. These tests evaluate the toxicity of the receiving waters (and the specific mixtures of chemicals in each sample) by determining the reproductive impacts from exposure, for a variety of test organisms. Such methods are beginning to be used to regulate water quality in the aquatic habitat, as opposed to that in the discharge pipe. At least forty-seven states are now using this kind of ambient toxicity test to determine compliance with discharge permits (Taylor 1992).

Non-point source water pollution. Non-point source pollution does not come from a single, identifiable point of discharge like an industrial outflow pipe, but rather comes from many diffuse sources, like street runoff or dairies. The importance of non-point source pollution in California is demonstrated by the 1990 assessment of water quality by the State Water Resources Control Board (SWRCB 1990). In this statewide study of water quality and pollutant inflows for nearly two thousand water bodies, more than 90 percent of the pollution problems were attributed to non-point sources. Historically, non-point source pollution has received little attention from regulatory agencies, but in many regions of California it is now a more serious concern than is point source pollution. In fact, sediment loading to streams and lakes from erosion of agricultural fields, currently regulated as a non-point source, is thought to be the single most important water pollution problem in the nation.

In California, the major non-point sources of pollution are runoff from agricultural lands, construction sites, mining operations, timber harvesting, and city streets. Different regions of California are subject to different non-point sources: sedimentation from timber harvesting threatens salmon and trout habitats in the northwest and the Sierra; mining threatens Delta and foothill waterways; construction is an important source where building occurs on erosive soils such as those in the Sierra foothills, Lake Tahoe Basin, and coastal bluffs; grazing-induced erosion and nutrient loading threatens aquatic habitats particularly in eastern and northern California; urban runoff is important in the San Francisco Bay and South Coast regions; and agricultural drainage threatens waterways and wetlands in the Central Valley and Delta regions. Not surprisingly, the ecological impacts of pollution also differ from place to place, depending on the type of pollution and the type of habitats receiving it.

Runoff from cities carries pollutants such as oil, solvents, and sediment through sewer pipes to ocean, bay, or river discharge sites. Originally treated as non-point sources due to the dispersed layout of sewer and storm drains, large cities will now be held responsible for the discharge from their drainage systems. Under a 1989 modification of the Clean Water Act, municipalities of over 100,000 people are treated as point source polluters and regulated with point source standards and liabilities by RWQCBs. If the new law is implemented strictly and achieves its stated goals, some urban areas will keep runoff pollution below today's level even with projected population growth. Several cities in California have proposed implementation plans but programs have yet to be carried out.

Kesterson: A case study in agricultural drainage problems. In California, water pollution from agriculture is proving to be both the most serious water quality threat to wildlife and the most difficult to regulate. California's most critical problems arise from soluble metals and salts in drainage water from agricultural fields (USEPA 1984). This drainage water is directed to evaporation ponds that have become de facto wetlands for millions of waterfowl and shorebirds. The acute toxicity of these contaminants to waterfowl, fish, and other wetlands residents is vividly demonstrated by considering the impact of selenium accumulation in the Kesterson National Wildlife Refuge. We can also see the elusiveness of policy and technical solutions to such problems.

As early as 1960, the risk of selenium contamination in drainage waters was recognized by the State Department of Water Resources. They concluded that the combination of poor natural drainage, high rates of evaporation, and leachable metals in the irrigated soils of the San Joaquin Valley would result in concentration of metals and salts in the drainage water, thereby rendering it unfit for "beneficial uses." In 1962 the USFWS concurred in a letter to the Bureau of Reclamation, predicting that selenium would bioaccumulate in wildlife and fish inhabiting wetlands fed by drainage water (Schultz 1985). Nevertheless, the continued irrigation of fields in the San Joaquin Valley increased the need for evaporation ponds, and dwindling water supplies for wetlands made drainage water seem a logical source of water for Valley wetlands.

Numerous early studies, such as those by DWR in 1966 and by US FWS in 1977, rejected the use of drainage water in Kesterson wetlands because they estimated that Kesterson would become too contaminated for wildlife after only three years of receiving such drainage water (Schultz 1985). Nevertheless, in 1978 drainage water began flowing into Kesterson National Wildlife Refuge. By 1981 high selenium levels were found in the migratory waterfowl feeding there. When the public learned, in 1983, of thousands of deaths and deformities among the ducks and wading birds of Kesterson National Wildlife Refuge, national attention finally focused on the problem of selenium in agricultural drainage waters.

Wildlife researchers have described the potential for more Kesterson-like problems in the San Joaquin Valley as "explosive," with potentially widespread and catastrophic consequences for waterfowl and other wetland species (Moore 1989b, Skorupa 1989). Unfortunately, the contamination problem is now evident outside Kesterson. Levels of selenium greater than or equal to those found at Kesterson are now found in birds and fish in the San Francisco Bay-Delta and the Tulare Basin at the southern end of the San Joaquin Valley (White et al. 1987, Pease and Taylor 1992). In 1989, one in four ducks was born deformed in some Tulare Basin ponds, whereas at Kesterson the average was about one in twenty (Skorupa 1989). Some agricultural drainage is released into rivers and channels that eventually flow into the San Francisco Bay or Salton Sea, bringing selenium into these ecosystems. Selenium is also released into the San Francisco Bay in discharge from oil refineries along the Bay margin. As a result, double-crested cormorants in Humboldt Bay, Suisun Bay, San Pablo Bay, central and south San Francisco Bay, and the Salton Sea have liver selenium at concentrations found to impair reproduction. The double-crested cormorant has attracted special concern because of its decline in California and much of North America (Remsen 1978).

The serious implications of contaminated evaporation ponds are due not only to pond toxicity, but also to the large acreage of evaporation ponds with respect to total wetland and aquatic habitat in the San Joaquin Valley. In the Tulare Basin, where 98 percent of the San Joaquin Valley evaporation ponds are located, total pond area is estimated at about 7,000 acres and wetlands at 5,000 to 9,000 acres (virtually all of which are managed for waterfowl). Large areas of evaporation ponds and scarcity of wetland and aquatic habitats make the ponds attractive not only for local birds, but also for international populations of waterfowl and shorebirds. Up to 60 percent of the migratory birds of the Pacific flyway depend on the wetlands of the Central Valley for wintering grounds (USFWS 1978). In fact, Central Valley habitat may already represent a limiting factor for these populations, because although breeding grounds in Alaska and Canada remain relatively intact, wetland wintering grounds in the Central Valley have dwindled to only 4 or 5 percent of their historic extent due to development and water diversion (Sacramento Valley Waterfowl Habitat Management Committee 1983). To make matters worse, by 1987 the Central Valley Regional Water Quality Control Board had applied for more than 10,000 acres of new evaporation ponds in the San Joaquin Valley (San Joaquin Valley Drainage Program 1987).

Natural wetlands are also at direct risk of selenium accumulation, since competition for scarce water resources results in agricultural drainage water being used to maintain wetlands. For example, wetlands in the Grasslands District of western San Joaquin Valley received half or more of their water supply from agricultural drainage until 1985, when this practice was discontinued because of findings of potentially harmful levels of selenium, boron, and other trace elements (San Joaquin Valley Drainage Program 1987).

Despite decades of warning, state and federal agencies were unprepared when confronted, in 1983, with massive dieoffs of waterfowl. They had no preventative program, interim safety measures, or cleanup plan. Although fish and wildlife continued to die, the refuge itself was not closed until 1986. The state now has an extensive mapping and monitoring program. Selenium contamination and toxicity in the San Joaquin Valley is one of the best studied environmental problems in California; however, there are no solutions in sight for the thousands of acres of habitat still receiving selenium-contaminated water.

Another lesson from Kesterson is that the agencies with the jurisdiction to protect wildlife, such as the U.S. Fish and Wildlife Service and the California Department of Fish and Game, generally have only an advisory role with respect to the industries and activities that affect wildlife. In contrast, the agencies with the power to set and enforce policies regulating activities that lead to selenium contamination, such as the California Department of Food and Agriculture and the State Water Resources Control Board, typically do not place a high priority on protection of biodiversity.

Offshore oil development. Offshore oil development poses a major hazard to the marine habitats of California's coast. Experience shows that oil spills threaten whole populations of marine mammals, birds, tidal organisms, and fishes with rapid extirpation and that the long-term effects on marine food chains extend the damage for many seasons. Routine operations alone harm sensitive species; new development creates additional levels of disturbance while increasing the probability of catastrophe. The most pressing problems are the oil rigs currently in operation and the heavy tanker flow through the state's major harbors.

California's coastal shelf, which has ongoing oil extraction activities and may be opened for further exploration, provides critical habitat for over twenty species of whales, porpoises, and dolphins, including seven endangered species of whales. The state's offshore habitats are the main breeding grounds (south of Alaska) for many of these marine mammals and are home to the world's populations of the grey whale (seasonally) and the California sea otter. The California sea otter is extremely vulnerable to oil spills, and a U.S. Mining and Mineral Services study concluded that otters could not be kept out of a spill once one had occurred. Perhaps equally important, the U.S. Fish and Wildlife Service found that disturbance by *existing tanker traffic alone* is already threatening the otter population in the northern portion of its range. Even barring an oil spill, offshore construction activities may impede or obstruct grey whale migration from feeding grounds in Alaska to calving grounds off Baja California (Wald and Notthoff 1989).

The California Coastal Commission can restrict oil development through its powers to restrict the development of auxiliary facilities onshore and offshore within three miles of the shoreline. The Regional Air and Water Quality Control Boards protect the shoreline from chronic and accidental oil contamination by regulating technologies and practices for oil transfers, refining, and transport. The state has limited control over development of oil resources in federal waters, as only federal regulations apply beyond the three-mile limit.

Many special habitats would be at risk if the federal government leases offshore tracts for oil exploration and extraction, as has been proposed for California's central coast. These habitats include Bodega Bay, Cordell Bank Marine Sanctuary, Gulf of the Farallones Islands Marine Sanctuary, Tomales Bay, San Francisco Bay, Año Nuevo, Monterey Bay, Big Sur, and the many estuaries, wetlands, and prime fishing and fishery grounds of the central coast.

The 1980s saw repeated federal proposals for leasing tracts of California's outer continental shelf to oil companies for exploration and development. A respite came in 1991, when the federal energy strategy omitted offshore development along California's coast, but the longer-term future of the coast is undecided. Although the state legislature has passed bills and resolutions limiting or opposing offshore oil leasing, these actions are not binding to the federal government. Similarly, the state can appeal for federal consistency with state policy, but it is not able to unilaterally prevent federal leasing of tracts more than three miles from shore, since these decisions are made by the Department of Commerce. Thus, except for congressional intervention over specific locations, the fate of the outer continental lease program rests with the executive branch of the federal government.

Plastic pollution of marine habitats. According to a report published by the State Lands Commission, "plastic pollution poses special hazards for marine life because plastic products neither sink nor decay. Tens of thousands of sea birds, seals, sea otters, whales, dolphins, porpoises and sea turtles are killed or maimed each year after eating floating trash or being snared in plastic debris" (California State Lands Commission 1989). The whales and seals found beached after swallowing indigestible garbage provide unfortunate examples of the threat that plastic pollution poses, not only to seagulls and other familiar denizens of the beach, but also to rare and endangered animals. The large numbers of animals killed worldwide by trash are testimony to the global impact of a single human activity—dumping trash—when it is multiplied by large numbers of people doing it.

Although California cannot eliminate plastic pollution from out-of-state sources, much of the problem originates from products sold in California. The simple technology change from pull-tops to "push-in" drink cans completely eliminated a source of pollution. Other items, such as the plastic rings for six-packs, still pose serious threats to wildlife, due to ensnarement.

AIR POLLUTION

Air pollution emissions in California result from the combustion and refining of fossil fuels, industrial processes, feedlots, woodstoves, and myriad small enterprises such as bakeries and dry cleaners. Pollutants directly emitted from these sources (called primary pollutants) include oxides of nitrogen and sulfur, hydrocarbons, carbon monoxide and carbon dioxide, ammonia, and particulate matter. Chemical transformations in the atmosphere can convert these primary pollutants into different harmful substances (called secondary pollutants), which are often more damaging to ecosystems. Our focus here is on two of these secondary pollutants, nitric acid and tropospheric ozone, currently the two air pollutants of greatest ecological concern in California.[19]

Tropospheric ozone. Ozone is formed in the troposphere (the lower atmosphere, where we live and breathe) when hydrocarbons and oxides of nitrogen combine in the presence of sunlight. In many of California's urban areas, particularly the Greater Los Angeles air basin, ozone is widely recognized as a threat to human health. It is a powerful oxidant, irritating lungs, degrading rubber and building materials, and injuring plant tissue.

Downwind from Los Angeles, high ozone concentrations have resulted in obvious damage to the foliage and reduced growth of trees and chaparral. For example, in the San Bernadino National Forest, sixty miles east of Los Angeles, over a million ponderosa and Jeffrey pine trees were already showing ozone damage in 1977 owing to emissions

in the Los Angeles Basin (Westman 1977). Ozone has also been implicated as the cause of degradation of coastal sage scrub communities of
southern California (Westman 1979).

Moreover, the damage is not limited to vegetation in the hills and
mountains immediately surrounding southern California cities. Ozone-
damaged Jeffrey and ponderosa pines have been observed in Sequoia,
Kings Canyon, and Yosemite National Parks (Hinrichsen 1988), and
ozone in Lassen National Park is approaching a level that can cause
damage. Trees species known to be harmed by ozone include ponderosa pine, Jeffrey pine, white fir, limber pine, incense cedar, and California black oak (Woodman and Cowling 1987). Although there is no
documented ozone damage to mature giant sequoias, their seedlings
have shown measurable reduction in root growth under increased ozone
levels during controlled experiments, which raises questions about the
long-term implications of ozone exposure to these magnificent trees
(Hinrichsen 1988). Urban growth in the Sacramento and San Joaquin
valleys, the regions exporting ozone to the Sierra Nevada, suggests an
increasing threat to giant sequoias and other species unless air pollution
is controlled.

The ecological impact of ozone in combination with other commonly occurring air pollutants appears to be synergistic, with greater
damage than the pollutants would cause if each acted alone. Ozone
damage to leaves makes plants more susceptible to diseases and insect
infestations and more vulnerable to low-level exposure to other pollutants. Thus, it is difficult to quantify the total ecological damage wrought
by elevated ozone concentrations.

To comply with the Clean Air Act, most cities in California have
active programs to reduce emissions of those chemicals that cause ozone
formation. Reducing urban concentrations to meet health standards is
proving extremely difficult, however, since so many activities contribute
to the problem. The Los Angeles area has one of the worst ozone problems in the nation, with many heavy industries and 10 million people
living and driving in the air basin. In response, the Air Resources Board
and California's South Coast Air Quality Management District
(SCAQMD) have a far-reaching comprehensive program to reduce
ozone. Many measures to control ozone precursors have been implemented, including gasoline standards, automobile modifications, and
protocols for loading and unloading of oil tankers. The more innovative actions, including the use of much cleaner fuels and electric cars are
still considered too expensive to be widely implemented. Furthermore,

it may be that controlling population growth will eventually be necessary to check air pollution problems. In Los Angeles, San Francisco, and other cities, population densities are already so high that even residential barbecues, bakeries, and dry cleaning release enough hydrocarbons to be a serious problem. Similarly, in rural areas, smoke from woodstoves poses a recognized health threat.

In many respects, California's Air Resources Board and the Regional Air Quality Control Districts are leaders in the nation in setting stringent air quality standards. These offices have not always willingly exercised their full legal power in addressing transportation and growth control issues. Environmental groups have been an important factor in pushing for stringent emissions controls, through research, negotiations, and lawsuits. Protection of air quality has slowed growth or development in various parts of California. Permits required under the Clean Air Act for new traffic corridors or modifications of old ones, for proposed developments that would increase traffic, and for industrial expansion that would release pollutants, have been denied in airsheds that already violate federal or state air quality standards.

Acid deposition. Commonly termed acid rain, acid deposition consists of sulfuric and nitric acid dissolved in rain, snow, fog, or dew, or in dry particles falling from the atmosphere. The acids are formed when nitrogen oxides or sulfur dioxide in the atmosphere combine with oxygen and water. When these acids fall to earth they have the potential to acidify soils and waters and thereby render the habitat unsuitable for many species. Due to acid deposition, numerous lakes in the northeastern United States, Ontario, and Scandinavia have become sufficiently acidic to cause the decline of fish, amphibian, and plankton populations. In many areas of Europe and the eastern United States, where air pollution (especially ozone) and acid deposition levels are high, forest damage has been severe. Like ozone, acid deposition does not generally act alone: the observed forest damage may result from the combined effects of ozone, acid deposition, and possibly other pollutants.

Rain and snow in California are only about one-fourth as acidic as in the northeastern United States or Europe, but several California ecosystems are so sensitive to acid deposition that California Air Resources Board (CARB) scientists are concerned (CARB 1988). In particular, alpine lakes in the Sierra Nevada are particularly vulnerable to episodes of acidification during snowmelt and rainstorms. At Emerald Lake, in the central Sierras, ARB researchers have found that acid levels in lakes and streams rise for brief periods during snowmelt and some summer storms (Melack et al. 1989). In Colorado and eastern United States lakes, these acid pulses are linked to impaired reproduction in salamanders and other species (Harte and Hoffman 1989). As yet, no one has demonstrated biological damage in California lakes from acid deposition. Similarly, there is presently no evidence that acid deposition is damaging forests or other vegetation in California. Deposition of nitrogen has been implicated in the loss of frost hardiness of tree species in Europe and the northeastern United States, but no studies have been done yet in California. Research to determine whether continuing acid deposition here could cause forest mortality is being undertaken as part of the ARB's Atmospheric Acidity Protection Program.

The severity of acid deposition in California depends primarily on the severity of pollution from automobiles, since the single most important cause of acidic rain and snow in California, nitrogen oxides, are emitted primarily by automobiles. If vigorous regulatory action is not taken, we expect more people will be driving more miles, and hence, acid deposition will become an increasingly serious threat in the future. If this happens, more severe acidic episodes are likely in the lakes and streams of the Sierra Nevada; this could result in losses of populations of fish, amphibia, and aquatic insects. Similarly, ozone pollution in California will increase if hydrocarbons and nitrogen oxide emissions from vehicles are not controlled, although industrial releases of hydrocarbons are also important contributors to ozone formation in many places.

PESTICIDES

Pesticides are unique among pollutants in that they are purposefully designed and released to kill plants and animals. The "miracle cure" image surrounding early pesticide use was shattered when it was learned that the side effects of their use included the near extinctions of the brown pelican and the peregrine falcon due to the bioaccumulation of DDT. It was not the toxicity of pesticides that was a surprise, but rather their mobility and persistence in natural ecosystems. Although some pesticides have been banned or controlled, pesticide use remains widespread, and the residues of past and current pesticide applications pose a threat to fish, wildlife, and vegetation.

Historically, pesticides have been used more heavily in California than almost anywhere else in the world (Risebrough 1969). The first widely used pesticides, organochlorines (e.g., DDT), were persistent in the environment. They bioaccumulated in food chains, thereby becoming more concentrated at higher trophic levels. Today, more than a decade after DDT was banned, residues remain high in terrestrial and aquatic organisms as well as in sediments and soils. For example, peregrine falcons reintroduced into California's central coast are suffering nearly complete reproductive failure due to DDT-induced eggshell-thinning. This population survives only because all eggs are collected and artificially incubated. In the San Francisco Bay, DDT concentrations in sediments have not decreased since DDT use was limited in the 1970s (R. Brown 1987). Although many organochlorine pesticides have been banned, some, such as Dicofol (used against cotton mites), are still widely used in California. In laboratory tests, Dicofol has caused reproductive impairment like that from DDT, but it is not known how much or how fast it bioaccumulates in nature.

Organochlorines have been largely replaced with less persistent chemicals like organophosphates. These pesticides, however, are usually more acutely toxic than their predecessors and are highly soluble in water. Their use has been linked to population declines in a number of species. The widespread spraying of Malathion in 1980 resulted in losses of steelhead trout, carp, striped bass, starry flounder, and mosquito fish. Unfortunately, we will never know the full magnitude of the damage because monitoring was terminated shortly after spraying stopped (Dreistadt and Dahlsten 1986).

The threat to endangered species from pesticides was acknowledged in the USEPA (1988) report, stating that "certain pesticides may pose a threat to the survival of America's endangered species if used in their remaining habitat. For example, pesticides may directly kill endangered plants or animals, or pesticide drift, runoff, or leachate may contaminate water, soil, or vegetation used by endangered species." California, with a large number of endangered species and unique habitats combined with heavy pesticide use, is particularly vulnerable to the toxic effects of pesticides.[20]

Pesticide release in California. Agriculture is by far the largest source of pesticides in the environment. Pesticides are also applied throughout California on rangeland, timberland, parks, school grounds, highway borders, and residential gardens. Current trends in pesticide use in California are both positive and negative. On the positive side, the number of pounds of *registered* pesticides applied annually has decreased from 141 million pounds in 1970 to 85 million pounds in 1986 (CDFA 1971, 1987).

It is difficult, however, to translate the reduced usage of registered pesticides to a change in environmental toxicity. No records are kept on the use of the many unrestricted pesticides (although these are not necessarily less toxic than registered pesticides; they may simply be lacking in sufficient testing data). Even if total mass were known, these figures do not give pounds of active ingredients, but rather of the pesticide when mixed with sand or water, as applied. Each new generation of pesticides has new formulations, giving rise to new concentrations, toxicities, and mobilities.

Understanding the environmental burden of pesticides, even if the formulation and mass of all pesticide applications were known, is beyond current scientific knowledge. First, USEPA and California Department of Food and Agriculture (CDFA) have complete data on toxicity and environmental fate for only a small number of the compounds in use. Second, the ability to monitor for pesticides in the environment is very limited because some pesticides are toxic to aquatic organisms at concentrations well below our ability to detect them. Third, and finally, there are no ready translations of the concentration of pesticides in sediments or animal tissue into a measure of harm to individuals or populations. There is a growing literature on concentrations of pesticides in organisms, water, and soil in California. Unfortunately, the actual toxicity of pesticides in the environment—from acute or chronic exposure or through ecosystem-level impacts—is the least well-known part of the impacts equation.

Regulation of pesticides. Both state and federal agencies have fallen far short of their legislative mandate to regulate chemical pesticides, beginning with the failure to fill the basic data gaps described above. After nearly twenty years of regulating pesticides, the USEPA has not acquired the legally required data on the toxicity and environmental fate of the majority of registered pesticides. Moreover, the integrity of much of the existing data is questionable (AOR 1985, Shabecoff 1987). The State of California has historically based its regulation of pesticide use on USEPA data on human health effects and environmental impacts of each pesticide. Over the years there has been ever-tougher state legislation pressing CDFA and the USEPA to fill these data gaps on pesticides. Yet even this modest goal, only the first step in actually regulating pesticides, has been unsuccessful. CDFA was slow to respond to legislative mandates to collect data on pesticides and has undermined other regulations with selective implementation.[21] One result is that after twenty years of regulation, the effects of many pesticides remain unknown and regulation of these uninvestigated pesticides is minimal. In 1991, the Wilson administration moved pesticide regulation from the CDFA into a dedicated pesticide unit in the newly created California Environmental Protection Agency.

In conclusion, considering the lack of data on the environmental effects of most pesticides, the poor record of environmental agencies in collecting that information, and the high costs of testing all marketed chemicals, it is doubtful that the threat from pesticide use can be ameliorated by regulation, unless regulation results in drastic reductions in pesticide use. Proposals for restrictions in pesticides have been met with fierce opposition by many representatives of agricultural interests. They claim that the economic viability and biological productivity of agriculture cannot be maintained without relatively unrestricted development and use of pesticides. Yet, the most modern trends in agriculture belie this dependence. For example, the California Cooperative for Organic Farming is overseeing a growing and successful industry of organic farms throughout the state. Evidence comes from a much less likely source as well. A 1989 report by the National Academy of Sciences found that large reductions in pesticide use are possible without adverse impact on food production, and that pesticide-free farming is in many cases more productive and cost-effective than is its chemical-based counterpart (Schneider 1989).

Global Atmospheric Change

Through myriad actions repeated across the globe—some as small as using an aerosol spray can or replacing the coolant in an automobile's air conditioner, and some as large as operating 1,000-megawatt coal-fired power plants—humans have set in motion the worldwide degradation of the thin shell of atmosphere that makes life on earth possible. Chief among these global atmospheric changes are greenhouse warming (climatic change) and depletion of the ozone layer in the upper atmosphere.

Action taken by California to limit emissions of greenhouse gases and ozone depletors will help to slow the rate of atmospheric degradation, especially since California emits a disproportionately large share of these chemicals. Nevertheless, the sources of the emissions are global and California cannot unilaterally prevent further ozone degradation or climate warming. Furthermore, emissions to date have already resulted in discernible depletion of the protective ozone layer and have probably already altered our climate. By the time strong emission control policies are implemented, the atmosphere—as a shield from harmful radiation and a temperature regulator—will behave quite differently than it did at the turn of the century or any previous time in human history. Consequently, no matter what steps California adopts to protect the atmosphere, the state faces the prospect of significant environmental change.

Unlike the threats discussed thus far, which occur in a specific location or involve a specific species, the degradation of the atmosphere will affect every natural community, everywhere. The effect on biological diversity will be the sum of the impact of atmospheric degradation coupled with location-specific stresses on the environment.

STRATOSPHERIC OZONE DEPLETION

Ozone, a molecule made up of three oxygen atoms, is the only gas in the atmosphere that significantly limits the amount of harmful solar ultraviolet radiation (UV) reaching the earth. Thus, the scientific discovery that a class of widely used chemicals is rapidly destroying this protective ozone layer has generated public concern.

As the ozone layer is depleted, more UV reaches the earth's surface. Scientists have observed a significant decrease in stratospheric ozone, not just above the Antarctic where the most dramatic depletion has occurred, but around the globe (Bowman 1988). Between 1969 and 1986, North American latitudes experienced a decrease in ozone of 4.7 percent in the winter and 3 percent year-round (Shea 1988).

The emissions of certain ozone-depleting chemicals, the CFCs, are being reduced under the conditions of the international protocol adopted in Montreal in 1987. Although the United States has a general ban on CFC use in aerosol cans, many other consumer products, such as refrigerators and air conditioners, are not yet controlled. Furthermore, other ozone-destroying chemicals, such as the halons, are also uncontrolled. The major point source emissions in California are the electronics, aerospace, metal product, and chemical industries, many of which are defense contractors. At 1987 emissions rates, it has been estimated that the ozone layer would have been reduced by up to 16 percent in the next fifty years. Unfortunately, ozone depletors are so long-lived in the atmosphere that even with complete cessation of emissions, the ozone layer is not expected to return to 1970s levels until the middle to late twenty-first century.

Ozone depletion has potentially serious consequences for both aquatic and terrestrial communities, primarily because UV strongly inhibits photosynthesis and plant growth. In addition, UV harms developing larvae and is active in biologically important chemical reactions in water and in the atmosphere. While UV is known to cause cataracts in humans, its impact on the eyes of other animals is largely unexplored. With more research, the impacts of ozone depletion on animals may emerge as being equally serious as impacts on plants.

The impacts of elevated UV on plants. Plants are extremely sensitive to enhanced UV, with even small increases in exposure to UV inhibiting photosynthesis and productivity in most species.[22,23] As would be expected, plant species differ in sensitivity to UV. Plants found where UV is naturally higher, such as high altitudes or tropical latitudes, can tolerate higher levels of UV than can low-altitude temperate plants (Barnes et al. 1987).

Some low-altitude plants, however, have successfully invaded subalpine and alpine habitats. Understanding how some plants have invaded high-UV environments and others have not is important in understanding the capacity of plants to survive still greater intensities of UV than they experience now. The dynamics of plant invasions in response to increased UV are also crucial to understanding how plant communities will change in response to a changing atmosphere. Unfortunately, nothing is known about the role of UV in preventing the successful establishment of most low-altitude species in high-flux environments (i.e., how many introduced species *did not* become successfully established because they could not adapt to the high-UV flux) (Caldwell 1981).

The ability of plants to develop protective mechanisms against UV is very limited. For example, leaves oriented away from the sun don't reduce exposure very much because UV is reflected toward the leaf from all directions. Leaves with high reflectance decrease UV absorption but also decrease absorption of light needed for photosynthesis (Caldwell et al. 1983).

The persistence of particular species in the face of increasing levels of UV may depend on whether the acquisition of increased tolerance requires hereditary (genotypic) or developmental (phenotypic) change. Phenotypic response is rapid, whereas genotypic change probably could not keep up with the rate of ozone depletion projected to occur over the next thirty years (Caldwell et al. 1983). It should be stressed, however, that no experimental research has been published on the ability of plants to adapt genetically to high levels of UV (Roy 1989).

The impacts of elevated UV on vegetation communities and habitats. Although experiments with many varieties of agricultural plants show that increased UV inhibits plant growth, the consequences of ozone depletion for undomesticated plant species and especially for natural communities are very difficult to predict. The direct impact of increased UV on terrestrial plants will be to decrease primary productivity and to lower plant resistance to other stresses. The result of these two factors will be to increase vulnerability of plants to diseases and pests and to change the species composition of some plant communities. New plant community compositions may result from changes in the competitive balance of species as well as from reductions in primary productivity per se. Altered competitive ability has been seen in wheat, wild oats, and rye plants exposed to enhanced UV in field experiments by Barnes et al. (1987). Between wheat and wild oats, the oat leaves shriveled and the wheat thrived. Rye, however, did poorly while the wild oats flourished. The modification of plant communities and plant productivity will have profound ecosystem impacts, affecting herbivores, carnivores, decomposers, and soil formation.

Aquatic ecosystems may be even more severely impacted than are terrestial ecosystems. Algae, the base of most aquatic food chains, are particularly sensitive to UV. Penetration of UV into water, which depends on how calm and clear the water is, generally reaches deep enough (1–5 meters) to affect most of the surface layer where algal photosynthesis takes place. Alpine lake habitats appear to be the most at risk from increased UV, as algal productivity is often UV-limited, even under current conditions (Shea 1988). In addition to decreasing productivity, elevated UV affects the species composition of algae communities, favoring large plankton over smaller diatoms and nanoplankton (El-Sayed 1988).

We know very little about the effect of increased solar UV radiation on freshwater animals, although we can draw inferences from the handful of studies performed on marine organisms. Aquatic animals, in addition to suffering a decreased food supply because of reduced primary productivity, will have direct responses to UV. Laboratory tests on marine animals revealed deleterious effects on the activity, developmental rates, and survival rates of larvae of various species of crustacea and fish (El-Sayed 1988, Shea 1988).

Ozone depletion and other environmental changes. There are many possible synergies between stratospheric ozone depletion and other threats—such as global warming, acid deposition, and smog—to biodiversity. Increased UV could enhance global warming since a decrease in the rate of photosynthesis without an accompanying decrease in the rate of decomposition would decrease the amount of carbon sequestered by natural ecosystems (in living plants and soil carbon). This could result in a net release of carbon dioxide into the atmosphere thus fueling global warming. The direct effect of decreasing concentrations of ozone (another effective greenhouse gas) is not expected to lead to a cooling because it would be counteracted by the direct effect of more UV penetrating the atmosphere. Increased UV may enhance the formation of acid rain by increasing concentrations of hydrogen peroxide, a catalyst to acid formation, in clouds. In the lower atmosphere, an increase in ultraviolet radiation will accelerate the photochemical reactions leading to smog and tropospheric ozone.

In addition to making environmental stresses more severe, for example by catalyzing the formation of atmospheric acidity, stratospheric ozone may also make ecosystems more vulnerable to various threats through its impact on plant productivity and animal reproduction. Alpine lake species appear particularly threatened because they are vulnerable to acid deposition. Algae in alpine lakes is UV-inhibited even at current UV levels, and climatic change will likely alter the chemistry of alpine lake water.

GLOBAL WARMING

Climatic change is caused by increases in certain gases in the atmosphere—called greenhouse gases—that trap heat, thus raising the temperature of the lower atmosphere. The most important of these is carbon dioxide (CO_2), which is emitted by fossil fuel combustion and by deforestation.[24] Other greenhouse gases include methane and chlorofluorocarbons (CFCs). The most important anthropogenically controlled sources of methane are rice paddies, livestock, landfills, biomass burning, and the extraction, transportation, and combustion of fossil fuels.

CFCs are problematic not only because of their effect as ozone depletors, but they are also extremely potent and long-lived greenhouse gases.

Because of increasing atmospheric concentrations of greenhouse gases, the earth may be warmer in the next century than it has been in human history. Accompanying the warming will be changes in all aspects of climate, including frequency of droughts in the Sierra Nevada mountains and of Santa Ana winds in southern California. The effect on biological diversity of this warming is likely to be much more severe than past, natural climatic changes due to the rapid rate of change and the existence of other anthropogenic stresses.

The rate of warming expected—a 3 to 8 degrees Fahrenheit increase in global average temperature in the next seventy years (figure 4.3)—is ten to forty times faster than any climatic warming the earth has experienced since the last Ice Age. At this rate, plants will have to move north by about 5 miles per year (or uphill at 3 feet every 45 days) just to stay in their current temperature zone. This is much faster than the seeds of most bushes and trees can disperse, and certainly soil development will not keep pace. Genetic adaptation to this rate of change is extremely unlikely.

Sea level rise and aquatic habitats. As temperatures rise, ice and snow in the polar regions will melt, causing sea level to rise, and the warmer temperatures will induce thermal expansion of the ocean that will also raise sea level. The result of these two processes is predicted to be a 1- to 2-foot rise in sea level off California within the next seventy-five years. Coastal wetlands and other tidal habitats will be drowned by the rising sea. In one of the only studies of its kind, Moffatt and Nichol (1987) found that a substantial portion of the San Francisco Bay-Delta mudflats and tidal marshes would be submerged by a 2-foot rise in sea level, significantly impacting endangered species such as the salt marsh harvest mouse and the clapper rail. Wetlands may form again in time, if enough open land is available and if sediment loading occurs at just the right rate (Moffatt and Nichol 1987, Williams 1985). The historic loss of wetlands contributes to their vulnerability to future rises in sea level, in that we have destroyed and continue to destroy natural habitats at the drier, uphill end of existing wetlands.

Managed coastal wetlands, such as Suisun Marsh, will suffer from

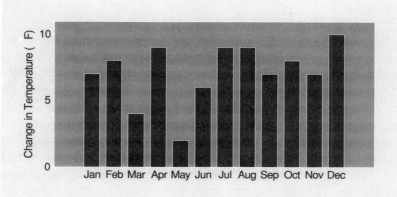

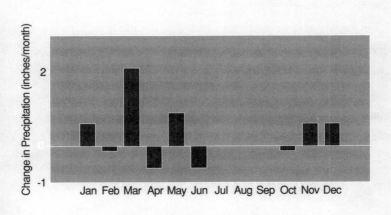

4.3. *The predicted difference in monthly temperature and precipitation in central California due to global warming. The difference between today's climate and the climate with doubled concentrations of greenhouse gases, about seventy-five years in the future, is based on results of General Circulation Model simulations. Data supplied by the Goddard Institute of Space Studies.*

changes in water quality as their supply-water becomes increasingly saline due to saltwater intrusion. According to Moffatt and Nichol (1987), water control structures currently being built are not equipped to deal with predicted changes in sea level and will not be able to provide a safe water supply to the wetlands in the face of the likely increase in saltwater intrusion.

Water availability will be affected not only by increased evaporation (from higher temperatures), but also because of altered patterns of rain and snowfall. It is likely that some regions of California will be drier and others wetter, but current predictions are too rough to pinpoint such changes. In addition, scientists predict that warmer temperatures will make snow melt earlier (Gleick 1988). Changes in the amount of rain, snow, and runoff will affect soil moisture and plant growth. The threat from existing water diversions shows the importance of water flows for estuaries and rivers: for example, the importance in the timing and quantity of flushing flows timed with anadromous fish spawning.

There will likely be unfortunate synergies between the ways in which climatic change alters water flows and the many ways in which aquatic habitats are already threatened by human activities. Sea level rise will cause more saltwater to flow up the San Francisco Bay-Delta, compounding saltwater intrusion problems caused by water diversions. In addition, if climate warming induces an earlier spring runoff, late-season runoff may be much reduced, thus reducing summer flows that are already diminished by water diversions. The effects of acid deposition may also be exacerbated by climatic change. If snowmelt in the Sierra is more rapid, then the spring snowmelt—which already is responsible for the annual acid pulse into Sierra lakes—may become more severe.

Species distribution and community composition. As the climate changes, some species in a community will find themselves in an area in which they can no longer survive or successfully reproduce. At the same time, these areas will become hospitable to new species. To the extent that plants and animals can shift ranges in response to these changes, familiar plant and animal communities will be replaced by new community assemblages.

The ability of any single species to shift its range depends first on its ability to travel. Animals that migrate or have wide ranges, and plants with light or easily dispersed seeds may be able to keep up with the rapid rate of climate change. Plants and animals that are poor at dispersal or migration, or that require specialized interactions with other organisms (such as soil microbes or pollinators), may not be able to shift their range and will instead decline in numbers. But even the most mobile species will face natural obstacles to migration, such as oceans and mountains, as well as manmade obstacles like freeways, cities, and agricultural fields. Although less daunting than oceans and mountains, human developments cause such ubiquitous fragmentation that they must be seen as a principal obstacle to species movement. In addition, cities and other converted habitats destroy potential sites of new settlement.

Ecological processes.   Climate shapes ecosystems not only through the direct influence of temperature and rainfall on organisms, but also through its control of important processes such as disturbance, weathering, and nutrient cycling. Climate warming will affect biological diversity through changes in biological and physical ecosystem processes (Harte et al. 1992). Wildfires, coastal upwelling, and springtime snowmelt are only a few specific examples of the physical ecological processes that shape habitats in California. Many unique habitats in California have evolved with the historical patterns of these processes. For example, both fire frequency and the extent of the Gabroic serpentine formation limit the range of the Gabroic chaparral habitat to El Dorado County. Much of the Gabroic formation is undergoing suburban development, reducing the potential habitat area. If, as a result of climate warming, fire frequencies increase beyond the ability of the Gabroic chaparral species to regenerate, there will be nowhere suitable for this habitat-type (Harte et al. 1992). A computer simulation of climate change and wildfire in El Dorado County showed grass and brush fires becoming much more frequent as a result of climate warming, with smaller but significant changes in timber and oak woodland fires (Fried and Torn 1990, Torn and Fried 1992). Such predictions can lead to wiser policies regarding how much Gabroic formation to preserve and how much to allow to be subdivided for housing, as well as aid management decisions for the many other habitats in this area. Research is needed, however, to translate the impact of change in wildfire to impacts on plant regeneration, animal behavior, and rates of erosion.

Species at risk.   Species that are now at the margin of their climatic tolerance, such as some desert species, may have no suitable habitat under a warmer climate. Geographically isolated communities and populations, such as the Santa Cruz Island fox, will be unable to keep up with changes in the location of suitable habitat. Species or habitats with very small ranges may find themselves without an established colony in a suitable climate even if currently protected in a park or reserve (Peters 1988). Climatic change will exacerbate the stress on plant and animal species that are already rare and endangered in California, most of which are found in isolated populations or have small ranges.

It is highly likely that most species will experience a degradation of habitat and decline in numbers as a result of rapid climatic change, as the repercussions of climate warming ripple through species interactions and physical processes. We may be able to design parks and preserves to aid the survival of individual species, but there are no ready solutions for the ecosystems threatened by climatic change (Peters and Darling 1985). It is ironic that the alpine habitats, which have the greatest proportion of land in preserves of any major habitat-type in California, may be forever lost as the climate warms, since a more moderate climate may allow lower-elevation species to invade high mountain ecosystems. For all of these reasons, parks may be even less effective than they are today. Furthermore, in the face of constantly changing environmental conditions, we will know even less than we do today about how to design parks and much less about the species for which we should design any particular park.

Finally, human responses to climate change may cause some of the most certain impacts, and possibly the most severe. If, as has been suggested, we build more and bigger dams to prepare for the changes that global warming may cause in the hydrocycle (dams are proposed to prevent flooding caused by a less predictable snowmelt and to enlarge storage capacity in case stream flow is concentrated into fewer months of the year), we may sacrifice the state's last free-flowing rivers.

Much is known about the causes of stratospheric ozone depletion and the greenhouse effect, and we understand at least qualitatively what the major physical consequences of these two phenomena will be (for example, ozone depletion will lead to increased ultraviolet radiation, which inhibits photosynthesis and damages skin tissue, and climatic change will lead to exacerbated heat waves, sea level rise, and changes in soil moisture). Moreover, from experience with other climatic anomalies, such as El Niño events, floods, droughts, and heat waves, we know that global warming will exert severe stresses on the biosphere. Some major uncertainties do remain, however. In particular, we are not able to predict the local climatic consequences of the greenhouse effect with the confidence with which we can predict the average global effects. The expected responses of plants and animals to both increased ultraviolet radiation and to a changing climate are only beginning to be understood in detail.

Despite these gaps in knowledge, we can be virtually certain that serious ecosystem disruptions will occur, both in California and globally, to the extent that the atmosphere is altered over the coming decades. Because these threats are synergistic with the more familiar threats such as water pollution or land conversion, global change must be taken into account even in conventional environmental impact assessments.

Conclusion

Projecting the trends of this complex and dynamic picture, in which most elements of biological diversity are threatened by many different environmental perturbations, is increasingly difficult. We expect new problems to emerge as California's population grows, technologies change, and the scale of human activities increases. For the first time, we are threatened by changes in the global biosphere that originate, in part, outside the control of California or the United States. It is clear that we can no longer use past trends of loss or degradation to predict the future.

No simple ranking of the threats to biological diversity from the most important to the least is possible. Different threats target different habitats or species, and some are primary threats whereas others work in concert. Nevertheless, threats can be evaluated by combining information on what is threatening critically rare or endangered habitats and species and on trends in threats that will lead to more habitats or species becoming critically endangered.

Recognizing that for most habitats and species the peril comes from multiple threats acting in combination, it is still useful to evaluate the significance of individual threats. A few threats are unlikely to be the primary agent of a significant loss of biological diversity—they generally cause low-level degradation. These include air pollution, toxic wastes and groundwater contamination, and many threats associated with recreation—collecting and hunting. Although these activities degrade habitats or stress certain species, we doubt that they will result in the widespread endangerment of species or habitat-types. Mining and off-road vehicles (ORVs) continue to cause significant damage to desert biomes in the state. Of greater concern are pesticide use, stratospheric ozone depletion, and invasions of introduced species, because of their potentially far-reaching ripple effects in ecosystems and because our ability to predict actual impacts is limited. The biggest risk is posed by those threats that are already causing significant damage throughout California or in critically rare habitats. Not coincidentally, for most of these, we have no ready solution. Currently in this category are land development, water diversions, logging of old-growth forests, grazing in deserts and riparian habitats, and water pollution (including offshore oil development). Also in this high danger category is global climatic change, for which our scientific understanding is sufficient to assure us that consequences in the next seventy-five years may overshadow many of the current threats to biological diversity.

Some of the controversy over the significance of individual threats to biodiversity arises because multiple threats and unchecked incremental loss are now the norm. Multiple threats give rise to the harmful synergies that make environmental degradation more severe and less predictable than it would be otherwise. In the future, these problems will also be joined by the importance of the global scale of disturbance, leaving no place unaffected as well as by the growing uncertainty over the causes of problems and the impacts of specific actions. Each time habitat is lost, the options for future conservation are diminished. Pollution, conversion, degradation, introductions, and most clearly, extinctions, all change forever the landscape we call home. Perhaps California's greatest challenge is to control the threats to biodiversity enough to preserve options for the future that we can live with.

Some ecosystem services are being taxed to their limit. Specifically, the ability of nature to provide clean air and clean water cannot keep up with pollutant loading in many regions. The protection of these essential environmental elements is already requiring regulation of growth and land use. In attempting to control ever-expanding vehicle traffic, Air Quality Management Districts, are, by proxy, taking on new growth control in many urban areas of the state. In a few areas, water utilities are capping growth by restricting the availability of new water permits. Where voters have rejected construction of development infrastructure, such as new water supply systems, or have voted in environmentalist utility administrators, citizens are linking growth and land use with these fundamental ecosystem services. Although in most counties local control over land use is weak, the finite limits of the natural environment are creating strict barriers to growth.

Every one of the threats discussed here has a common ingredient—people. The greater our numbers, the more severe the threat. Population size is, however, not the whole story. If we can maintain or improve our level of prosperity by engaging technologies, resource management practices, and lifestyles that reduce damage to the environment, then the impact of our numbers is reduced. But if the population of California doubles over the next thirty-five years, as present trends suggest, then in thirty-five years there will be roughly twice as many people in the state building homes, discharging wastes, requiring transportation and consumer goods, and doing all the other things that threaten our natural ecosystems. These effects could easily undo the progress that we hope will occur over the coming decades in adopting less destructive practices. Hence, for conservation measures to succeed, California must both come to grips with population growth and begin a transition toward less destructive lifestyles, technologies, resource management practices, and economic systems.

CHAPTER FIVE

Barriers to Biodiversity Conservation in California

Despite increasing scientific and public awareness of the causes and consequences of loss of biodiversity in California, many habitats are being degraded and species are being lost at accelerating rates. In this chapter we explore the substantial barriers to the conservation of biodiversity in California. Understanding these institutional and sociopolitical obstacles is a critical step in designing a strategy to conserve biological diversity. Simply evaluating the technical aspects of biodiversity and threats presented in chapters 3 and 4 will not suffice. We emphasize barriers to effective state action here, while recognizing that federal and local governments, as well as private organizations, play crucial roles in protecting California's biodiversity.

Numerous parks and nature reserves have been established to protect ecosystems and provide recreation, but the parks and reserved areas of California do not contain complete representation of the state's biotic riches. Moreover, parks cannot protect biodiversity from all threats. Laws and regulations have been written to supplement the protection afforded by parks by providing a safety net to prevent extinction and by regulating some of the activities that degrade habitats. Unfortunately, some laws fail to achieve their goals because of problems with enforcement and inadequate implementation. In addition, few laws are designed with the explicit purpose of preventing the decline of biodiversity. For example, the California Environmental Quality Act (CEQA) assures that data are available in decision making, but does not require that land use planning include biological diversity. In many cases, waiting to take action until a species is endangered means waiting until it is too late, yet our laws encourage this pattern.

The absence of a governmental mandate to sustain and protect California's biodiversity contributes to its loss. Agencies' actions are often uncoordinated with respect to addressing threats to habitats. Conflicts are also common between state government and the management of federal land, which makes up 46 percent of California. But the state does not take a consistent stand to encourage the federal government to protect the biological resources within its jurisdiction. Certain threats—those that accumulate over time or space and those that result from a multitude of stresses—are particularly hard to address. Competing economic interests combined with the absence of a statewide overview of these threats and of basic knowledge of their mechanisms often results in controversial battles between land use development and conservation interests. Contemporary views of the economic value of development which neglect the value of functional ecosystems and the benefits of natural areas contribute to these conflicts, as do the significant gaps in our knowledge of the status of biodiversity and our lack of understanding of many basic ecological processes. We conclude that the existing system of laws and institutions is ill suited to balancing short-term economic gains that result in loss of biodiversity against the long-term costs of these actions.

Limits to the Protection Parks Can Provide

Parks and reserves are the core of California's conservation efforts, providing an essential sanctuary of undisturbed habitat. Many species cannot thrive on lands that are also used for commodity extraction or agricultural purposes, and zoos cannot reproduce ecosystem functions or natural evolution. Reserves provide both. Geneticists recommend parks as the best means of maintaining adaptive genetic variation. Parks are a much more permanent designation of land for secure long-term habitat and species protection than are zoning, moratoriums on harvest, or plans for federal multiple-use lands.

However, parks and reserves cannot be the sole means of protecting biological diversity, for there are significant limitations to the amount of protection that we can depend on our park system to provide. Too often, after parks have been designated, it is assumed that the species and ecosystems found within them are protected. Yet parks are not adequate protection for all species or habitats, nor against all threats, and there are practical limits on the amount of parkland that can be designated in California. In short, important elements of biological diversity simply slip through the holes of the park safety net.

PARKS ARE AN IMPERFECT REFUGE

At best, parks and reserves are an imperfect refuge because they are not, and cannot, be walled-off from the outside world. Park boundaries are lines on maps across which people, pollution, and wildlife regularly pass (Schonewald-Cox 1988)—as demonstrated by park management problems such as selenium pollution at Kesterson National Wildlife Refuge, or human disturbance of harbor seal nesting areas. In addition to causing pollution, land and resource management outside park boundaries can have serious impacts on the habitat quality of a park or preserve. Park habitats may be invaded by introduced species—such as landscaping plants or agricultural pests—from adjacent, nonpark lands. Hunting may still threaten a species, even though a portion of its habitat is protected as a refuge, if animals cross outside of the parks' boundaries regularly.

Parks provide inadequate protection for migratory species, for animals with large home ranges such as the wolverine, black bear, and eagle, and for species particularly sensitive to pollutants (such as ponderosa pine and ozone pollution, condors and lead poisoning). Migratory waterfowl require a string of sites to use for feeding, resting, and breeding as they move from their wintering areas to their summer breeding areas. Assuring the integrity of both their summer range in Canada and Alaska, and their overwintering wetlands in the Central Valley, plus safe stopover sites is a large challenge. No one park, or even one state or nation, can accomplish this task alone.

Many parks are not large enough to encompass the territories of large animal species, thus these animals are at risk from pollution, hunting, and habitat loss outside the park sanctuary. As a result many people advocate establishing corridors of relatively undisturbed habitat to connect parks and protected areas. Where feasible, establishing a network of corridors and protected areas would help expand the effective size of parks. But in many areas designing such a network will be difficult. Moreover, for certain types of habitats such as rivers and lakes, park status is inadequate if the park does not encompass the entire wa-

Snow geese flying over the Sacramento National Wildlife Refuge, one of many stops along the Pacific flyway. (Photo by Charles Kennard)

tershed. Many reserves do not have dedicated water rights, increasing their vulnerability.

These examples of species and habitats that cannot be easily protected within parks raise concerns about the adequacy of parks for protecting *all* components of biological diversity. If reliance is placed only on parks, then adequate attention may not be given to securing minimum instream flows, controlling pollution, managing resources, land use planning (e.g., to leave migration corridors between parks), and other actions needed to complement parks.

Climate change is expected to put severe stresses on the species and habitats of California, creating a stronger need for all avenues of protection. Larger and diversified parks are certainly called for in response (Peters and Lovejoy 1992), but certain impacts of climate change will make parks less effective and make park design much more difficult. Some plants and animals are likely to shift their ranges, each species at its own rate, in response to a warming climate; similarly the tree line may shift upslope in the mountains. Scientists cannot yet predict which species will be protected by existing parks over the next century or how best to design and locate new parks. Estuaries and wetlands, two of the most important habitats to protect because of their rarity and keystone role in maintaining the state's biological diversity, exemplify the complications introduced by climate change: to what elevation should our estuary and wetlands preserves be extended to make them secure from the threat of sea level rise?

The perception that parks alone are sufficient leaves many species unprotected and, in fact, diminishes the value of the parks themselves. If parks are perceived as self-sufficient refuges, the regions surrounding parks may not be managed to protect biological diversity, and our parks may soon become habitat islands, surrounded by development and degraded by pollution. The central role of parks in a conservation strategy varies, depending on the compatibility of the land uses adjacent to parks. To maximize the benefits that parks can provide, we must also recognize their limitations and treat parks as an integral part of a many-faceted conservation program that addresses cross-boundary problems, resource management, and water and land use planning.

THERE ARE LIMITED OPPORTUNITIES FOR BUILDING THE PARK SYSTEM

The study of conservation biology is adding immeasurably to our ability to design and manage preserves. Even with better design concepts, however, practical obstacles to creating an effective park system remain. Opportunities for building a park system are always limited; there are limits to how much land the state can purchase, and many desirable sites have been developed, are slated for development, or are under the control of the federal government.

California cannot afford to purchase all its wildland for parks, nor is it desirable to do so since many counties are supported by resource industries, and as a society we depend on their products. Furthermore, such an approach severely restricts local and state flexibility in development. Instead, we need better management practices that allow commodity production and conservation to coexist.

Even without economic constraints, much of California's land is not available to be purchased for parks. Private owners may be unwilling to sell their land or they may have already partially developed it. In addition, about half of the undeveloped land in California is managed by the federal government, which dedicates some land to parks, but the majority of federal land is currently dedicated to logging, grazing, recreation, and military uses. Although the state cannot add these lands to its park system, aggressive review of federal land management programs and aggressive use of other avenues including the California Endangered Species Act, Wild and Scenic Rivers Act, CEQA, pollution control laws, and federal consistency doctrines can increase the value of federal land for biodiversity (see *Conflicts between Federal and State Interests*).

For many sensitive areas, protection as a park is the best conservation strategy; delaying park establishment only allows further loss. With development and habitat conversion occurring piecemeal across the state, it is increasingly difficult to find contiguous stretches of natural habitat without areas that have been logged, damaged by off-road vehicles, filled, dredged, plowed, or developed. Critically rare habitats are rapidly disappearing; there are few large stands of old-growth redwoods left, few pristine wetlands remain, and there are few undisturbed aquatic habitats left. Although many are looking to restoration ecology to save us from the damage we have already caused, ecologists in this new field are only beginning to understand how to "repair" ecosystems. The possibility of partial rehabilitation of damaged ecosystems is not substantial insurance against their loss.

In summary, the problem presented here is a dual one. Parks alone are not adequate and the amount of parkland that California can acquire is limited. As a result, we cannot rely solely on parks, the conceptually simple solution, and must instead develop a bigger "tool box" of conservation techniques.

Cumulative Effects of Incremental Losses and Multiple Threats

If habitat degradation and declines in plant and animal populations always stemmed from readily identifiable and isolated human activities, the task of protecting biodiversity would be far easier than it is. In the real world, many instances of habitat or population loss are due to the cumulative effect of several threats acting at the same time and from the slow accumulation of individually insignificant losses over time. After describing incremental losses and multiple threats, we discuss how they confound the ability of existing institutions to protect biodiversity.

The case of the California condor illustrates the cumulative effect of both incremental losses and multiple threats. What pushed the California condor to the brink of extinction? In one important sense it was blindness—inability on the part of society to perceive the consequences of the progressive shrinkage and degradation of this magnificent bird's habitat. As acre after acre of its habitat were degraded by grazing, or oil drilling, or lost outright to urbanization, and as birds were killed by hunters, pesticides, and poisoned coyote-bait, the condor was pushed out of the wild. The stress on the condor population from any one subdivision or any one expansion of oil drilling activity into its range, or any one shooting incident was undetectable and, indeed, negligible. But these losses accumulated to the point where the bird was doomed.

The multiplicity of the threats, as well as the nearly unproveable effect of individual actions, contributed to the bird's demise. Had there been only one threat to the bird, such as shooting by hunters, it would have been easier to take actions to protect the bird. With a single, clearly identified causal agent, public opinion and agency attention could have focused on that single threat, and action to protect the bird would have been more likely (though, by no means, a certainty). In reality, there was no single cause and perhaps all the major threats to the condor needed to be addressed simultaneously for the bird to be protected in the wild.

INCREMENTAL LOSS

Incremental loss is, unfortunately, an all too common occurrence in California. The selenium disaster at the Kesterson National

Wildlife Refuge, the loss of old-growth forest along the north coast, the filling of San Francisco Bay, and the loss of coastal shrub habitat in San Diego and of vernal pools in the Central Valley are all the consequence of accumulation of individually small, incremental losses. The human mind is better at perceiving sudden calamities than slow accumulation of danger. Thus a major oil spill or an accident at a nuclear power plant grabs headlines and leads to discussion of future preventive action. But when losses accumulate gradually, leading to possibly greater harm than that from the calamitous events, society rarely notices.

As we look to the future, many of the new threats to biodiversity will also act incrementally. Emerging threats to ecosystems, such as global warming or increased ultraviolet radiation due to stratospheric ozone depletion, are likely to heighten our need to acknowledge and effectively address incremental losses. If preventive action against global warming is not taken, the rate of warming in California is expected to be almost a degree (Fahrenheit) per decade during the next century. Although that rate of warming is unprecedented in human history, it still is sufficiently slow that perceptible damage to ecosystems will most likely set in over time periods of several decades, not years. Detecting such damage is far more difficult than detecting damage from, say, a new dam on a river or a malfunctioning sewage treatment plant discharging wastes into a bay or the cutting of an extensive area of old-growth forest.

Monitoring incremental losses is difficult because a long baseline of data is required to detect change. Rarely are research projects funded for long enough time periods so that the needed baseline data can be acquired. Often it is not even clear where and when to begin a monitoring effort to detect incremental loss in its early stages because awareness of the problem is lacking.

MULTIPLE THREATS

Multiple threats, as well, occur frequently in California. The brown pelican is a symbol of the threat from bioconcentration of DDT in food chains. Less well known is that the pelican is still threatened, not only by DDT, but also by oil pollution, human disturbance of breeding colonies, loss of food fishes because of overharvesting by people, loss of nesting sites, fishing gear entanglement, and bacterial infection resulting from overcrowding in harbors (CDFG 1989a). Numerous species in California face a similar multiplicity of threats. Nearly every threat discussed in chapter 4 impacts the California freshwater shrimp *(Syncaris pacifica)*, whose survival, in its three-county range, is jeopardized by water diversion, watershed erosion, stream sedimentation, removal of riparian vegetation, agricultural development and urbanization, and potentially, climate change.

The San Francisco Bay-Delta exemplifies the way in which an entire ecosystem can be subjected to multiple threats. The combination of water inflow, point source and non-point source water pollution, landfill, dredging, reduced food supply due to destruction of wetlands, overfishing, and introduced species are all degrading the estuary and leading to the decline of its aquatic life. The variety of assaults on the ecosystem makes it extremely difficult to pinpoint the effects from any single type of threat. This fuels an ongoing debate about what threats should be allowed to continue, and what activities should be modified to protect the ecosystem. Each industry or interest can blame the actions of others for the problem.

Historically, threats to ecosystems tended to be fairly localized in space. Last century, a low rate of land conversion resulted in ecological stresses that were largely confined to the converted land. (Hydraulic mining, a notable exception, had wide-ranging impacts, rearranging hillsides and rivers and affecting the entire Delta.) Now, with fragmentation, loss of corridors, and destruction of keystone habitats, the influence of land conversion leads to the cumulative loss of certain habitats throughout the state, and perhaps more importantly, affects nearly every habitat in the state.

With impending climate change, stratospheric ozone depletion, acid deposition, and other global or regional pollutants that respect no political boundaries, stresses will increasingly overlap and nearly all ecosystems will be subjected to multiple threats. Thus, the already significant overlap of threats will likely be more widespread in the future. For example, California's forests may be increasingly subjected to climate warming, tropospheric ozone, acid deposition, and ultraviolet radiation from ozone depletion, as well as logging and other threats from direct land use.

The complexity of interactions among different stresses makes it difficult to obtain a scientific understanding of their impacts on populations and habitats. When a single stress is suspected, scientists may use well-established (but often expensive) laboratory or field procedures to determine the impact of that stress. This is particularly true for water pollutants. Further insights into situations where a single cause–effect relationship is suspected are also often obtained by using correlation analysis. But when many stresses are suspect, experimental testing and correlation analysis are difficult. More time and funding are necessary to carry out the multiplicity of tests needed to sort out the dominant combination of stresses and more data are needed to carry out the correlation analyses.

The total effect on a population of a combination of threats is often much greater than the sum of the effects due to each threat acting separately. The reason for this synergistic behavior is that one threat can render a population more vulnerable to another threat. For example, air pollution has been shown to increase the susceptibility of ponderosa pine to infestation by bark beetles. Thus, if the bark beetle population were growing because urbanization had reduced the habitat of one of its major natural predators, the combined impact on ponderosa pine of air pollution and urbanization would be greater than the sum of the individual effects. In another example, fish that are subjected to elevated water temperatures are often more vulnerable to chemical pollutants. In this way, cooling water discharge may interact synergistically with water pollution.

CHALLENGES POSED BY INCREMENTAL LOSSES AND MULTIPLE THREATS

Incremental losses and multiple threats strain the capacity of existing institutions and laws, most of which are ill adapted to protect biodiversity from these cumulative effects. Several reasons for this were discussed earlier: the scientific uncertainty associated with understanding the complex interactions that occur when multiple threats are at work, the difficulty in even perceiving a problem is coming in early stages of incremental loss, and the tendency for people to shift the blame on a threat caused by another party. Here we focus on government institutions and laws themselves.

Consider, first, the California Environmental Quality Act (CEQA) and National Environmental Policy Act (NEPA) processes for evaluating the hazards of different projects. When a project involves significant environmental change, CEQA and NEPA require that the project's impact be characterized as fully as possible. If that same ecosystem is also threatened by another project, the impact report is required to characterize the potential impact due to the "cumulative impacts"[1] resulting from both proposed projects. Under California law, the environmental impact statement must discuss past, present, and reasonably anticipated projects regardless of whether or not they are under the jurisdiction of the same lead agency. These provisions are expressly designed to address the problem of piecemeal development and the resulting incremental impacts. However, there is no standardized method for evaluating cumulative effects. Although impacts such as the cumulative effects of a housing project on traffic flow or on a water system's capacity to meet human demand are routinely examined in environmental impact documents, cumulative impacts on biodiversity are typically overlooked. Both the accumulation of each increment of damage and the multiple stresses that arise from different types of projects are usually omitted, as are synergistic effects. A major reason for this is that cause and effect relationships and even the very concept of "system capacity" is much better defined and understood for traffic flow or water supply than it is for habitat integrity and wild populations.

Some stresses, like that of climate warming, threaten virtually all habitats and natural populations, yet there is no requirement under CEQA or NEPA to include in an impact statement a description of the combined effect of the stress of climate change with those of the proposed project. Thus, the environmental impact documents describe the effects of projects that are, effectively, situated in a world that is different from what the real world will look like during the lifetime of the project. Under such a situation, it is unlikely that an accurate characterization of the threats to biological diversity can be gleaned from the environmental impact documents. Because of the cumulative and synergistic interactions among threats, it is quite likely that the impacts of proposed projects will be underestimated as a result.

Agencies that deal with natural resources or the environment are further challenged by the ways in which multiple threats do not fall neatly within the traditional boundaries among these agencies. Protection of our forests from air pollution is the responsibility of the California Air Resources Board, whereas logging is regulated by the California Department of Forestry or the U.S. Forest Service. To the extent that there are cumulative or synergistic interactions between these two threats, neither agency has a mandate to provide protection. Currently California has no means of coordinating the regulation of these combined stresses. The problem here is not simply one of authority but one of understanding as well. No single existing agency today is responsible for understanding all the combined threats to a particular habitat. This structure for regulatory activity already neglects the current level of multiple threats. As multiple threats intensify in the future, it will only become increasingly inadequate.

Without a strong conservation plan, the permitting process undercuts the ability of agencies to protect biodiversity against multiple threats and to prevent incremental losses. Permitting is intrinsically a case-by-case process; it treats projects in isolation and it is usually carried out under legal, political, and economic pressures so great that long-term impacts from incremental loss are unlikely to be considered. Although CEQA requires assessment of the cumulative impacts, the environmental impact report need not provide as complete a discussion of the combined impacts as it does for those attributable to the project itself (Duggan et al. 1988). This enhances the tendency of local governments and agencies to look only project by project.

Where a planning process plays a greater role in the formulation of public policy, some of the damaging consequences of sequential decision making on a case-by-case basis are minimized. Long-range planning can provide the needed time horizon, but state agencies and local governments, lacking a mandate to protect biodiversity, currently do not devote time or resources to designing plans to assure that cumulative effects on biological diversity are minimized. With the excuse of scientific uncertainty about cause–effect relationships in hand, it is all too easy for agencies to simply follow the path of expediency and ignore the cumulative effects of incremental losses and multiple threats entirely.

Currently, a demonstrated and clear cause–effect relation is necessary for regulatory action to be taken to protect biodiversity. The environment is considered to be safe unless proven at risk. The "burden of proof" issue (the question of whether a proposal should be considered desirable unless proven undesirable or undesirable unless proven desirable) arises often in matters of public policy. It is particularly relevant to policy decisions regarding the protection of natural habitats (and the associated goods and services they provide the public), for in such decisions both public welfare and private freedom are abundantly championed by both industry and environmentalists. Our system of government provides no a priori right answer for where the burden of proof should lie in such cases, but by precedent it has fallen on the defenders of natural environments. In situations where incremental losses or multiple threats occur, demonstration of a convincing cause–effect relation is often difficult to obtain for reasons discussed above. The existing assumption about where the burden of proof lies thus tips the balance against protection.

Gaps in Mandate

There are many reasons why agencies do not take responsibility for all the tasks that fall within their jurisdiction. Lack of funding or changes in political climate may cause them to be lax in their implementation of laws, or even actively seek to dismantle particular programs. Leadership is also a significant ingredient in the functioning of an agency or institution. Institutions, moreover, have histories that influence both their goals and actions. This institutional history can create blind spots, making it hard for institutions to see new issues as part of their responsibility. Biological diversity is falling through the cracks between the traditional resource management agencies, which do not see protection of biodiversity as their responsibility or mandate, and the newer environmental agencies, most of which have authority over pollution control but not over resource protection.

State government agencies that regulate activities affecting biodiversity can be divided into two contrasting types—organizations responsible for providing resources for human use or consumption, and organizations responsible for protecting human health from a host of environmental threats. None of the existing offices, boards, or departments in California's state government has as its primary responsibility the conservation of biological diversity. (Table 5.1 lists some of the state natural resource and environmental departments.) Most of the departments and boards that deal primarily with pollutants and pesticides are now part of the recently formed California Environmental Protection Agency, a new effort to coordinate these related regulatory functions. In contrast, the many departments responsible for the use and stewardship of natural resources do not belong to a single larger government entity. For example, the Department of Water Resources and the Department of Forestry and Fire Protection are both within the Resources Agency, but the Department of Food and Agriculture is not.

Recognition of the threat posed by air, water, and soil pollution has led, over the past twenty years, to the passage of many laws to regulate pollution. Many of the state and federal laws regulating pollutants and toxics, such as the Clean Water Act, the Clean Air Act, the Federal Insecticide, Fungicide and Rodenticide Act, the Resource Conservation and Recovery Act, and the Hazardous Substance Control Act, require that standards be established and enforced which will protect hu-

Table 5.1. *Major California Government Departments that Regulate Use of Resources or Pollution, Organized by Historic Mandate.*

Natural Resource (use mandate)	Environmental (protect mandate)
Dept. Fish and Game	Air Resources Board
Dept. Food and Agriculture	Dept. Health Services
Dept. Forestry and Fire Protection	Regional Water Quality
Dept. Transportation	Control Board
Dept. Water Resources	Waste Management Board
State Water Resources Control Board	

man health and environmental quality. In practice, with the notable exception of the Clean Water Act, nearly all the standards that have been established are based on studies of human health impacts. Until quite recently, little work has been done to determine the impacts of pollutants on plant and animal species or on ecosystems. Nevertheless, when regulations successfully decrease pollution, they usually improve the environment for biological diversity. Thus, the protection mandate of the environmental departments has unplanned benefits for biological diversity.

In contrast, the activities overseen by departments responsible for providing resources for human use—water, timber, agriculture, transportation, or catchable wildlife—are activities that can and do threaten biological diversity. In pursuit of their resource use mandate, these agencies may promote actions that adversely affect biological diversity. Actions designed to protect biodiversity such as restricting harvest or diminishing water diversions, or decreasing pesticide use may be seen by staff members as being in conflict with the primary mission of the agency. Many other activities such as protecting endangered species, monitoring contaminants, inventorying resources, or reviewing environmental documents have been considered peripheral to the main goals of the organization.

LEGISLATIVE MANDATE IS ONLY ONE COMPONENT

Several ingredients influence an agency's realized mandate—the responsibilities and authorities written into the laws of the state, the expectations and beliefs of the constituents, and the staff's perceptions of the agency's highest priorities. The enabling legislation established each agency's responsibilities and sphere of influence and was written to address then-contemporary concerns, not unforeseen future concerns. All of the natural resource departments were established long before the concept of biodiversity was articulated and before the threats to biodiversity were so plainly visible. The enabling legislation may include broad language encouraging conservation but could not possibly include language directing the agencies to take specific actions to protect biodiversity. Although there are also some new legislative directives, many of the older directives are still in effect. In addition, the legislature, through the selective funding in the budget process, encourages some tasks within the agency's mandate and impedes others.

Long-time constituents also influence an agencies' activities. Constituent groups that became involved with the agency when it was first established are most likely to have their goals and needs met. These long-time constituents, who are receiving benefits from the activities of a resource agency, will support the agency, work toward getting additional funds or programs from the legislature, and try to protect the agency from legislative or regulatory attacks. Other constituents, whose needs have not been successfully met by the agency, may go to another agency to achieve their goals, or may turn to the legislature or the courts to try to force the agency to be more responsive. Thus the constituents who have been involved for a long time and who receive tangible benefits from the agencies tend to reinforce the traditional mandate of the agency and not encourage new mandates that may conflict with their interests.

The Department of Food and Agriculture (CDFA) has responsibility for matters affecting plant and animal industries in California; pest control and monitoring, marketing services, measures and standards, and food inspection services are all part of the department's programs. CDFA's historical mandate is to facilitate agricultural production in California, and its primary constituents are the many businesses of the agricultural and range industries.

CDFA is not typically concerned with biological diversity nor human health issues, even though until 1991 it also had responsibility for pesticide regulation. Pesticide regulation is now part of the California Environmental Protection Agency, a shift that occurred in part due to criticism of the CDFA for its performance in protecting human health from risks due to pesticide use. This criticism first led to legislative reforms to strengthen pesticide regulation in mid-1980s particularly through the Birth Defects Prevention Act and the Pesticide Contamination Act. These laws focused on improving the data on the adverse effects of pesticides on human health. Both forbid reregistering any chemical for which the health effects data are incomplete. CDFA has been criticized for its implementation of these laws, particularly the Pesticide Contamination Act, which is designed to prevent the contamination of drinking-water aquifers. These laws were designed to address human health effects of pesticides, not the effects on the state's ecological health, yet if implemented there would be some benefit to biodiversity. Because CDFA's primary mandate is agricultural production, and its largest constituencies are the agricultural and range industries, the agency faced substantial internal conflicts between pesticide use and control in its role as pollution regulator. Regulating pesticide use to minimize adverse effects on biological diversity is even further from its central goal.

The Department of Forestry and Fire Protection (CDF) and the Board of Forestry provide an example of traditional natural resource agency's views concerning biological diversity. The department oversees timber harvest on private land and provides fire protection; the board sets policy. In recent years there has been growing public concern over the loss of fish and wildlife, the erosion of streams, degradation of water quality, the loss of riparian vegetation, and the loss of old-growth forests due to timber harvesting. Until quite recently, the Department and the Board of Forestry have not been supportive of positions that would protect biological diversity or old growth. CDF personnel and Board of Forestry members can effectively resist changing CDF's mandate by perpetuating resource consumptive attitudes and by failing to implement resource protection. Several battles have been fought over the approval of controversial timber harvest plans in the past few years. These court fights haven't changed the views of at least some staff members. As one CDF forester said, regarding efforts to stop permits to cut old-growth redwoods so that they could be bought for preservation, "We know that the old growth is going to be cut. We know the last redwood tree will be cut. Our directive is not for preservation" (Kay 1989). Despite new programs in CDF oriented toward sustainable resource management, such as the Integrated Hardwood Range Management Program, change in the agency may be slowed down by staff who resist a broader mandate. CDF has many new programs and may be vulnerable to the problems facing agencies in transition, which are discussed in the following section on the Department of Fish and Game.

THE DEPARTMENT OF FISH AND GAME: AN AGENCY IN TRANSITION

The state agency whose responsibility comes the closest to protecting biodiversity is the Department of Fish and Game (CDFG). The mandate of CDFG has been changing, exemplifying how laws, constituents, and staff all influence the role CDFG plays in protecting biodiversity. Historically, the department has been responsible for the management of huntable and fishable species and a majority of the staff work on related issues. In addition, the oldest constituents of the CDFG are the sportsmen's groups. Many people and environmental groups believe that hunting and fishing are still the highest priorities in the department. This historic emphasis on game species is reinforced by the financial constraints of the department. Hunting and fishing license fees are the CDFG's primary source of revenue. These revenues have been falling in recent years, leaving CDFG in financial trouble. Without a stable source of funding adequate to support CDFG's nongame programs, threatened and endangered species programs, and environmental review activities, the agency's orientation cannot easily change, even if the public, constituents, and staff desire change. The legislature has hampered CDFG's ability to carry out its expanding mandate by refusing to fund these programs although these are arguably the programs that provide services to the general public.

The responsibilities and authorities of CDFG have changed dramatically over the past twenty years. There is an entire unit, the Environmental Services Division, responsible for review of environmental assessment documents and for water quality issues. Although CEQA and NEPA were passed over twenty years ago, this branch is relatively small and poorly staffed in comparison with their work load (see also the next section, Gaps in Enforcement and Implementation). This is in part a function of politics outside the department; during the eight-year tenure of the Deukmejian administration, positions were systematically cut from this division, weakening the environmental protection component of CDFG.

The department also has a newly established Natural Heritage Division. This division includes some of the endangered species staff, the Natural Diversity Data Base (an inventory and monitoring program), the Lands and Natural Areas Program, and the Wildlands Program. This division is in its infancy and suffers from a lack of staff and funds. It has no constituency with private economic interests and has not yet developed an active powerful constituency among environmental groups. Funding is a substantial problem, hindering its success; licenses are an inappropriate source of revenue for a nongame unit, and the legislature has appropriated only meager General Fund dollars for this division. As a result the department has started fundraising from private sources to support these programs.

CDFG is caught between its old and new mandates. It has new legislative responsibilities, but no new funding sources and limited staffing. Staff members working on issues primarily under the old mandate are often at odds with staff working on the newer issues. They compete for funds and priority within the department. Leadership, many of whom have been in CDFG for more than twenty-five years, is often torn between their belief in the old mandate and the growing public pressure for new responsibilities. The constituents of the agency are now very diverse and often diametrically opposed to each other, leading to explosive, highly politicized battles. When these battles concern local land use issues, decisions made by local department personnel may reflect a staff member's personal views of the responsibilities and mandate of the department more than statewide policy. As a result, there is a perception that rules and regulations are inconsistently applied.

CDFG is in drastic need of a new image and structure. Internally, the department recognizes its changing responsibilities and in the early 1990s began a process of internal review to create a vision for the department in the next century. However, even though changes have already begun internally, without legislative support for more staff and new funding sources, it is unlikely CDFG will be able to accomplish its many responsibilities.

Summary. Departments responsible for resource use and management have not fully incorporated protection of biodiversity in their responsibilities nor do they have well-developed relationships with their new constituents who wish to see more comprehensive protection. Departments responsible for regulating environmental pollutants don't see biodiversity protection as their responsibility and therefore may not regulate pollution or toxics to meet such a goal. If the only threats to biodiversity were from pollution, the existing institutional structure would probably work. All that would be needed is to create a biodiversity protection unit within each environmental agency. However, because many of the threats to biodiversity are from the activities associated with the use of resources—timber, grazing, water diversion, land use—protection of biodiversity must be part of the mandate of the natural resource agencies. Finally, some stresses result from the interaction of threats from pollution and from resource use. To address these threats, coordination is required between natural resources departments and environmental regulatory departments.

Gaps in Enforcement and Implementation

California has some of the strictest pollution control regulations and most forward-looking natural resource policies in the nation. Despite the good intentions of these laws and policies, failures in enforcement and implementation of state and federal law mean the goals of these policies are not always achieved. Waterways remain polluted nearly twenty years after a "zero discharge" standard was declared. Populations of endangered plants are legally eliminated despite the California Endangered Species Act. The acreage of high-quality wetlands is decreasing despite a "no net loss" policy.

What are the barriers to realizing the benefits of California's existing conservation and protection policies? Enforcement and implementation require an agency with the political support, the legislative authority, the commitment, and the resources to enforce laws and policies. The resources for enforcement include staffing, funding, and technical knowhow. The absence of any one of these factors can reduce enforcement of even the strongest laws.

INADEQUATE RESOURCES

Many state employees watch with great frustration and disappointment as habitat degradation occurs. They are powerless, not because there are no laws or policies at their disposal, but rather because they do not have the resources to enforce or implement them. At a minimum, enforcement requires monitoring, staffing and funding; throughout California there are cases of habitats degraded and wildlife lost because of inadequate resources hampering protection efforts.

For example, the Department of Fish and Game has at most a single wildlife biologist who is responsible for all wildlife management functions plus environmental review of all environmental impact statements for each county. County staff plus a few regional staff members in each of five regions and fewer than twenty staff members in Sacramento were responsible for reviewing more than 13,000 environmental documents in 1989 (K. Smith 1989). Because CDFG participation in environmental review processes required under CEQA and NEPA suffers from understaffing, "projects that may potentially affect rare, threatened or endangered species and important natural communities do not receive sufficient attention to assure that the existing legal protections are being implemented" (Jones and Stokes 1987).

An overloaded review process also plagues CDF efforts to protect biodiversity on timberland. Timber Harvest Plans (THP) are filed with CDF before logging permits are granted, which should allow CDF staff to ensure that the logging plan will protect riparian areas and other special concerns. Because of inadequate staffing, however, most THP receive only a half-hour's review by CDF (Goddard 1988). Despite the importance of checking descriptions in the field, staff almost never have time to visit the timber harvest site to verify or evaluate the THP.

Inadequate staffing to implement regulations has been exacerbated by budget cuts. Some of these cuts are targeted specifically to diminish the effectiveness of the organization. For example, the Deukmejian administration cut the budget of the Coastal Commission to achieve a stated goal of lessening the ability of the Coastal Commission to regulate coastal development. Coastal Commission staff reductions of 44 percent by 1984 crippled the enforcement division. One result was that, in 1984, over a thousand documented violations awaited resolution but the statute of limitations ran its course before even 15 percent of the cases could be resolved (Rosener and Gregersen 1987).

Inadequate resources also affect the health of California's parks. Frequently, there is money available to acquire lands or to develop campgrounds and recreational areas within parks, but little is available for ecological management of the lands, and even less for resource inventories. Capital projects like acquisition can be funded through bond acts, but management and data collection must be funded out of the annual budget. No consistent revenue source has yet been identified to ensure the protection of these valuable lands once they are acquired. As acquisitions continue, there is an increasing budget short-fall of funds to manage these lands and to inventory the biological diversity found on the preserves to allow informed decisions about what to protect next.

Outside the departments traditionally concerned with natural resources, staffing for protection of biodiversity may be even thinner. For example, in the California Department of Transportation, only two staff members were added to one environmental review section during a period in which over a hundred engineers were hired (C. Brown 1989).

FLAWED STATUTES

Laws may be crafted or amended in such a way that they are extremely difficult to enforce. Some laws are written so as to give a great deal of discretion to the regulatory agency, running the risk of a wide range of interpretation and impacts. Either can result in a marked difference between the spirit of law and its actual impact. For example, the California Endangered Species Act does not prohibit the destruction of listed plants because it differs from the Native Plant Protection Act, which permits losses. As a result the CESA "does not preclude the direct taking of state-listed threatened or endangered species by a private landowner. As a result, listed plant species and habitats of both plants and animals on private lands are being legally eliminated" (Jones and Stokes 1987). In this case, as in many others, enforcement is in part hindered by ambiguities in the law that leave CDFG staff without sufficient guidance and authority for action. In Santa Rosa, when state-listed plants were being moved by a developer who had not yet received approval for developing, CDFG staff were uncertain whether or not they had the authority to stop the removal of the endangered plants. Public outcry and media attention, rather than resolution of the policy, stopped the destructive transfer.

Legal loopholes for specific purposes can undermine programs resulting in unexpected and serious consequences for biodiversity. Once a loophole exists, it is difficult to ensure that only the targeted group takes advantage of it. Because on paper the programs remain intact, the public may not realize that they are not getting the benefit of existing legislation. For example, agricultural activities such as plowing do not require permits and are therefore not subject to review under CEQA. Developers with land zoned for agricultural use have taken advantage of this by plowing and discing wetlands in order to legally remove endangered plants from the land before applying for a development permit (see *Land Use Conflicts*).

AUTHORITY AND ABILITY

Even when laws do not directly allow evasion (i.e., have loopholes), their success may be limited if agencies do not have both the authority and tools with which to enforce them. Despite a clear policy stated by the Clean Water Act to protect water quality, control of sediment pollution (from erosion) is nearly impossible under current institutional arrangements. The U.S. Soil Conservation Service (SCS) has responsibility for managing soil resources. Responsibility for controlling erosion from agricultural fields is the responsibility of the Regional Water Quality Control Boards. The Regional Boards have the authority and technical ability to address water pollution, but do not have the experience, staff, and facilities to enforce water pollution regulations governing agricultural erosion. SCS has the funding and technical ability to address soil and erosion problems, but not the regulatory responsibility.

Under CEQA, project approval may require that projects be modified or mitigation measures taken to avoid or mitigate negative environmental impacts of the project. These mitigation measures are often not enforced, however. For example, in one central coast development, "trees in a monarch butterfly habitat were slated for protection from development. Accordingly, only 32 percent of the trees were to be removed. Instead, actual development destroyed 80 percent of the trees" (Cervantes et al. 1989).

Much too often, the mitigation of wetlands loss required as a condition for development permits for San Francisco Bay wetlands has simply not been carried out and too rarely have the regulatory agencies enforced this permit requirement (Eliot 1985). In the face of large profits to be made from development, currently allowable agency actions amount to only a slap on the wrist of the noncomplying developer. Agencies cannot levy heavy penalties or deny future permitting requests in response to noncompliance. In late 1988, a State Assembly bill was passed to establish a monitoring program to "ensure the implementation of measures that public agencies impose to mitigate or avoid the significant adverse impacts identified in an environmental document" (AB 3180; Cervantes et al. 1989). This bill, designed to ensure implementation, has led to the inclusion of mitigation monitoring plans in all EIRs.

In a related problem, existing laws, even when enforced, are inadequate to meet California's "no net loss" policy of protecting wetland habitat. Under current state and federal laws, wetlands development is rarely stopped if mitigation, in the form of marsh restoration or creation, is promised. Yet, restoration technology and monitoring are infant sciences. Restored or created wetlands may never achieve the habitat quality of natural wetlands, or achieve replicate ecosystem processes such as carbon storage. At best, created wetlands may take several years to approximate even the structure of natural wetlands (Zedler 1989, D'Avanzo 1990). If these restored areas don't achieve parity with less disturbed wetland habitat, then the wetland losses are never actually mitigated. In addition, no habitat exists for the wetlands species in the years between displacement from their original habitat and the maturation of the restored wetland.

POLITICS

Political pressure may erode support from appointed upper management for strict interpretation, enforcement, and implementation of existing statutes. Support for protecting biodiversity suffers where upper management is less willing than staff to take a strict conservation position. The political nature of appointed positions puts a premium on compromise. Long-term influence requires not alienating major actors and not losing one's job or losing program funding. The tenure and future of political appointees relies in part on their implementation of the political agendas of those responsible for their appointment.

Even with a strong legislative mandate, political appointees and the political process of establishing departmental funding levels can greatly influence the capabilities of an organization to enforce the law. The California Coastal Commission exemplifies this experience in California. The Coastal Commission was established in 1972 by voter initiative to regulate coastal development. Regional commissions were established and commissioners appointed. Local land use plans were written. Over time the organization changed, but most analysts agree that the Coastal Commission significantly affected the pattern and pace of development in the coastal zone. The early commissioners had a strong proregulatory bias and took stances that favored environmental protection over development. Under the Deukmejian administration, new commissioners were appointed who did not favor a strong regulatory approach. In addition, the Deukmejian administration drastically cut staff and program funding of the Coastal Commission. The combination of new appointments in the commission and decreased funding resulted in an increase in permit waivers to development applications and a decline in the permit denial rate (Rosener and Gregersen 1987).

Ideological conflicts with biodiversity protection are evident in California's politically appointed boards and commissions, particularly where there are no composition requirements to ensure a balance of interests. The Board of Forestry and the Fish and Game Commission have no requirement for a member who represents biodiversity conservation interests, yet have often had members who are part of the interest groups regulated by the community.

Influence from outside the agency can also impede enforcement through threats such as lawsuits (e.g., Nollan v. Coastal Commission), lack of future cooperation, or lobbying against future funding or expansion requests. Without high-level state support or substantial public outcry, the Regional Water Quality Control Boards may find themselves too weak to take on agricultural interests in the Central Valley, and Fish and Game too weak to take on urban developers. Strong regional interests caused the State Water Resources Control Board to withdraw the Draft Water Quality Plan for the San Francisco Bay-Delta rather than to follow their own proposed protocol of accepting comments and revising the draft (SWRCB 1988).

Enforcement is also a significant problem on federally managed land, not only because of insufficient funds and staff, but also because of the lack of upper management support. Riparian zones provide an important example in that they are one of most critically rare and degraded habitats in the state. Because BLM and USFS manage 40 percent of the state's land, their actions regarding riparian areas are integral to California's success or failure in preserving and restoring riparian habitats. Both agencies have formal policies giving priority to riparian restoration and protection. For example, the USFS manual prescribes preferential treatment of riparian-dependent resources (e.g., riparian species) when conflicts arise among land use activities (USGAO 1988*b*). Agency field staff, however, are often discouraged from pursuing riparian protection goals. Field staff at BLM report that they are not supposed to push riparian restoration if the permittee does not want it, and that BLM upper management not only refuses to support any action in opposition to permittee wishes, but actively discourages field staff in such endeavors (USGAO 1988*b*).

Conflicts Between State and Federal Interests

Because the federal government manages a substantial portion of California's land and water resources and regulates certain pollutants, both coordination between federal and state actions and effective state control over resources are critical to protection of California's biodiversity. In some cases, such as wetlands protection under the Clean Water Act, federal agencies have been more aggressive in enforcing environmental regulations than have state agencies. However, federal control over natural resources has not always led to improved environmental quality, and at times the state's interest in environmental protection conflicts with federal interests. Because of the complexity of state and federal policies no simple solution for resolving conflicts between state and federal control and regulation of resources will suffice. However, as the examples presented below indicate, the existing conflicts diminish environmental protection.

Species protection often falls through the cracks created by unclear divisions of state and federal responsibility. One telling example of the perceived lack of state responsibility for biodiversity on federal lands was given at the October 5, 1989 meeting of the California Fish and Game Commission (FGC). At this meeting, the FGC decided not to list as threatened or endangered an alpine plant, the Ramshaw meadows abronia, *Abronia alpina,* because although the species meets the scientific qualifications for listing, it is found only on federal land and thus "is not the state's problem."

HABITAT PROTECTION AND RESOURCE MANAGEMENT

The problems arising from federal control of natural resources go far beyond the protection of any individual species. Three federal departments, Agriculture, Defense, and the Interior, manage over 40 percent of California's land area (table 4.1), which amounts to nearly half the state's undeveloped land. The uses of this land that impact biological diversity, over which the state has only limited control, include logging, grazing, oil extraction, mining, and bomb/munitions testing and military maneuvers.

In terms of acreage, the single largest land use in California is grazing, and most of the state's rangeland is managed by two federal agencies, the Bureau of Land Management (BLM) and the Forest Service (USFS). Grazing on public rangeland demonstrates many of the problems resulting from federal management of natural resources, in that the state has little information about the condition of habitats on federal rangelands and little control over management of those lands or the grazing fees levied for their use.

Inventories of species and natural resources on rangeland and assessments of range condition are simply not available for most federal lands. Neither BLM nor USFS have up-to-date assessments of their land (only one-half the western federal allotments have been surveyed in the past ten years), which impedes both state and federal conservation activities. Federal decisions about grazing levels and allocation of range improvement funds are ostensibly based on inventories or monitoring of vegetation and range condition (USGAO 1988a). This lack of current information directly impedes federal success at reducing grazing on overstocked allotments.[2] In addition, to protect wildlife the state needs habitat assessment and population trend data for federal grazing land, particularly since it comprises over 25 percent of the state's wildlands.

Management of rangeland or timberland involves conflicts between immediate resource extraction and long-term preservation of habitats. In the face of these conflicts, BLM and USFS have a record of favoring immediate extraction over protection of biodiversity, both in terms of management policies and allocation of restoration resources. The result of current spending patterns by these agencies is that little improvement is being made in range condition, monitoring, or riparian and aquatic restoration. Since pressure from the livestock industry supports current agency priorities, the threat from inadequate range management will likely continue unless environmental organizations or the state successfully intervene.

Nevertheless, in contrast to private owners of rangeland, federal agencies have formal policies to which the state can attempt to hold them accountable (table 5.2). Among the most powerful of these are doctrines requiring BLM and USFS actions to be consistent with state resource policies.[3] The success of a recent attempt by CDFG to have USFS change the grazing policy of a National Forest Management Plan so that it would be more consistent with state policy suggests that these federal consistency doctrines could be increasingly used by the state in protecting habitats on federal rangeland (CDFG 1988b).

Table 5.2. *Laws and Regulations Pertaining to Federal Grazing Land*

Livestock Grazing on Federal Land

* U.S. Forest Service grazing permit system first introduced in 1906.
* Taylor Grazing Act of 1934:
  Established grazing permit system to prevent further overgrazing and deterioration. Created allotments and 10-year permit system.
* Multiple Use-Sustained Yield Act of 1960:
  (FS) Mandates multiple use
* Federal Land Policy and Management Act of 1976:
  (BLM) Mandates multiple use
* Public Rangelands Improvement Act of 1978:
  (Both agencies) Maintains records on trends in range condition.
* National Environmental Policy Act of 1969:
  (Both agencies) Requires EISs for activities with impact (BLM and USFS began EISs after suit by NRDC). EISs to be completed in 1988.
* Forest and Rangeland Renewable Resources Planning Act of 1974:
  (USFS) Explicitly related NEPA EISs to USFS plans.

Protection of Riparian Areas on Rangeland

* Public Rangelands Improvement Act of 1987:
  (Both agencies) Reaffirms a national policy to manage, maintain and improve the condition of public rangelands so that they become as productive as possible for all rangeland uses.
* Federal Land Policy Management Act of 1976:
  (BLM) Requires Secretary of Interior to use and observe principles of multiple use and sustained yield.
* Forest and Rangeland Renewable Resources Planning Act of 1974:
  (USFS) Requires Secretary of Agriculture to provide for multiple-use and sustained yield of the forest's products and services.

Fees Charged for Use of Federal Rangeland

* Public Rangelands Improvement Act of 1978:
  (Both agencies) "[To] prevent economic disruption and harm to the western livestock industry, it is in the public interest to charge a fee for livestock grazing . . . which is based on a formula reflecting annual changes in the costs of production [and beef prices]."
* Federal Land Policy Management Act of 1976:
  (Both agencies) It is general policy that ". . . the U.S. receive fair market value of the use of public lands and their resources . . ."

AQUATIC HABITATS

Water flows in California are a highly contested resource. There are ongoing battles over the regulation and control of water supplies, with many environmental concerns at stake. One issue with significant potential impacts on aquatic habitats is whether the state can put environmental conditions on federally permitted water projects. The courts have agreed that the state can decide if adequate water is available in a stream or river on which a federally permitted project is being considered. However, debates continue on whether the state can place any environmental constraints on the operation of federally permitted facilities, and therefore on downstream flows.

The New Melones decision interpreted the "anti-preemption clause" of the Federal Reclamation Act as prohibiting the federal government from preempting state authority over federal dams (California *v.* U.S. 1978). Accordingly, the state has authority to regulate the operation and downstream flows of federal dams. In 1990, the U.S. Supreme Court in the Rock Creek decision (California v. FERC) decided that the SWRCB can only regulate flows to protect consumptive water rights and not to protect the environment below single-purpose FERC-licensed hydroelectric dams. The limits to the authority of SWRCB below multipurpose FERC-licensed dams has not yet been decided.

Control over the operation of dams and other facilities is critically important to protecting instream flows. When the SWRCB has issued water rights, it can reallocate those rights and reconsider minimum flow standards at any time. For example, rights to water in the tributary streams of Mono Lake were recently reallocated to protect the fisheries in these streams. In contrast, FERC licenses are issued for fifty years, and it is very difficult to open them for reconsideration. If FERC controls minimum flow standards, it will be very difficult to respond to new evidence of biological decline.

A state as large and politically complex as California has many separate interests. State policy is not monolithic, nor is the state necessarily a better steward of aquatic resources in California. State interests are taking a stronger environmental position in the preemption fight over state versus federal regulation of water. In contrast, environmental concerns are driving a congressional debate over the management and operation of the Central Valley Project, the federally owned and operated water supply system. Proposed reforms include dedicated water for the environment, allowing water transfers between agricultural areas and urban areas, and reevaluation of federal water subsidies.

Development Versus Conservation: Local Land Use Conflicts

Every county in California is home to several threatened and endangered species; many of these species are threatened by land use changes and habitat loss. Because local governments are the primary decision-making bodies controlling land use, their decisions play a significant role in the conservation or destruction of regional biodiversity. Often development decisions lead to the incremental loss of habitat, without recognition of its significance. When the actions of local governments are added together across the state, the toll on biodiversity is substantial. In many counties, the absence of any biodiversity conservation plan is leading to heated battles that are impeding both conservation and development. Although planning would provide certainty to developers, protection for the resources, and more harmonious community development, there are few examples of regional conservation plans designed by a local government or for a habitat-type.

Many species have very narrow geographic ranges; they may be found only in one county in California. For these species there are few locations where they may be protected, simply because there are few places in the world where they reside. If they also occur in habitat-types that are mainly privately owned, then their fate may be in the hands of the landowner and local government. Protecting these species, particularly before they become endangered, requires a commitment to maintaining viable habitats. In many communities this commitment is not manifest.

THE SANTA ROSA PLAINS: A CASE STUDY

The Santa Rosa Plains of western Sonoma County is an area of ranches and small farms that is rapidly being converted to residential homes due to population pressure and housing costs in the San Francisco Bay area. The region is a patchwork of unincorporated lands and municipalities. The Santa Rosa Plains are also an area of grassland and vernal pools which support migratory waterfowl and five species of rare or endangered plants. Three of these plants, Burke's goldfields, *Lasthenia burkei*, Sonoma sunshine, *Blennosperma bakeri,* and Sebastopol meadowfoam, *Limnanthes vinculans,* are listed as endangered by both the state and federal government.[4]

All of these plant species are restricted to vernal pool habitats, a type of seasonal wetlands that occurs as small pools within grasslands. The pools are filled in the winter by rainwater and dry up during the spring as the water evaporates. Vernal pools throughout California contain many endemic species of plants adapted to the unusual water regime. Historically the five rare plant species were found throughout the Santa Rosa Plains. As urbanization accelerated in the late 1970s and 1980s, vernal pool areas were lost, leading to isolation and endangerment of these species.

Recognizing that all these rare plant species were directly in the path of urban development and that the existing laws would allow incremental loss of habitat until few or no pools remained, in the late 1980s CDFG contracted to have a survey done of Santa Rosa's vernal pools and of the endangered plant populations. In addition, in 1988 CDFG called a meeting of local government officials to discuss a proposal to create a regional vernal pool protection plan and CDFG hired a consultant to write a protection plan proposal (Vilms 1989). The plan determined which sites should be protected as preserves through an Open Space Conservation District and which sites were appropriate for development.

Although the state was trying to encourage a regional approach to protection of vernal pools, no municipality took the lead on protection. Instead, annexation of new areas into cities and permitting of housing developments ranging from several units to several hundred units continued. During the winter of 1988 and the spring of 1989 conflicts arose on several proposals for developments that, if permitted, would eliminate vernal pools and rare and endangered plant species. Vernal pools became a household word in Santa Rosa because of the newspaper and television attention, and two hundred people attended a one-day conference on "Northern California Vernal Pools" that the California Native Plant Society, a nonprofit conservation group, held on a Friday in May 1989 in an attempt to encourage public education and dialogue.

Because vernal pools are wetlands, there are many federal and state regulatory agencies involved in permitting development. The conservation and development conflicts that arose are complex because of the numbers of regulatory actors involved and because of the mitigation for habitat loss proposed by project proponents. All of the projects come under the California Environmental Quality Act. Despite the presence of rare and endangered species, in one case the destruction of vernal pools was permitted by the City of Santa Rosa (with CDFG's tacit approval) using the "mitigated negative declaration" provisions of CEQA. This means that although vernal pool habitat was to be eliminated on the project site, mitigation for this impact had been identified. The mitigation consisted of removing the rare plants from the project site and transplanting them into other pools on another parcel. The "receiver" parcel was to be protected as open space. Transplantation is a new and unproven technique, and many conservation groups objected to this as an unsuitable mitigation for endangered species, particularly since no provision was made to guarantee the success of the mitigation. (For example, it would be possible to establish new populations of the rare plant in a protected locale in advance of eliminating the plants on the project site.) There was no specific mitigation for the loss of the vernal pool *habitat* itself, nor were any provisions made to address the genetic consequences of mixing the plant populations from the two sites (the development site and the "receiver" site).

Due to the controversies, several projects were delayed, numerous plant populations were moved, some before the project had been approved, and at least one homeowners' group brought a CEQA lawsuit against the municipality and a developer. Threats of countersuit and intimidation of landowners brought the Sierra Club Legal Defense Fund into the picture in the spring of 1989.

By the spring of 1992, a Santa Rosa Vernal Pools Task Force had been established, but no effective means of resolving the conflicts in Santa Rosa have been implemented, despite the vernal pool protection plan proposal written by Vilms. Some developers are so concerned that limitations may be placed on proposed projects that they have plowed the vernal pools on their property in an attempt to eliminate the endangered plants, and others have threatened to follow suit. Because agricultural use of land is permissible in these areas, this approach to "solving" the endangered species problem is legal. (However, filling of wetlands without a permit is not legal. Should it be determined that these vernal pools are jurisdictional wetlands, plowing will not change their status as wetlands. Local conservation activists are now considering lawsuits claiming wetlands have been illegally filled.)

The task force includes members from city and county government, the building industry, CDFG, USFWS, and local citizens. A Memorandum of Understanding was drafted in early 1992 agreeing to take a regional planning approach to vernal pool protection. Although the city and county planning staffs are more supportive of a regional planning approach, the building industry is not. There is no agreement over who will bear the costs of the regional planning, and no agreement on how to keep the vernal pools protected while planning continues. Although the debate has now continued for over five years, a resolution has yet to be embraced by local governments. If citizen suits and longer, more drawn-out permitting procedures become commonplace, the time, effort, and expense of a regional conservation plan will look more favorable.

BARRIERS TO LOCAL AND REGIONAL CONSERVATION PLANNING

Although conservation planning to protect biological resources is desirable, there are many barriers to formulating and implementing such a plan. Urban land values in California are very high. As a result, the pressure to convert rural land to suburban uses is substantial. The problem is not unique to biological conservation; the protection of prime agricultural land from conversion is also made exceedingly difficult by the pressure to maximize economic return from land. Once land values in an area increase, either due to speculation that the zoning may soon be changed from agriculture to residential or belief that an area may soon be annexed, the land has essentially already been converted. The land becomes too expensive to buy for less intensive purposes.

Local governments have the power to establish open space districts and to enforce these decisions. Where agricultural uses are compatible with conservation of biodiversity, maintaining land as an agricultural district is an excellent choice. A regional conservation plan need not be elaborate nor oppressive. A great deal of successful conservation can be accomplished by identifying critical habitat areas within a county and establishing a means of maintaining them. Riparian areas can be maintained as natural corridors for wildlife and simultaneously add substantial dollar-value to adjacent real estate. It is difficult, however, to guarantee protection of biodiversity in an area that is urbanizing without acquiring the land as a park. This is because local communities often wish to maximize their revenues and perceive urban growth as more valuable than agriculture or other land uses which have the benefit of also protecting biodiversity. In addition, local government often has a substantial representation of elected officials who favor growth and urbanization because these sectors have the most vocal and often the most wealthy constituencies.

There is considerable resistance to changes in local land use plans that result in a perceived reallocation of development rights. Many land owners have conceptual plans for their property that may or may not be consistent with the County General Plan or the existing zoning. Counties can rewrite General Plans and designate areas as open space and municipalities can down-zone without compensating landowners for the effect these changes have on future development options. Private individuals tend to think it is their "right" to develop their land to the maximum extent possible, despite numerous legal decisions at many levels of the court, restricting or bounding the "bundle" of property rights. Because the values of biodiversity accrue to all and cannot be captured by a single individual, the "right-to-do-whatever-I-please" ethos is often in direct conflict with conservation of biological resources which depends upon action for collective welfare.

Local planning departments rarely have biological experts on their staff. As a result local planners rely heavily on the experts in state and federal regulatory agencies for advice on natural resources issues. Because these agencies often do not take a strict protectionist position, even regarding the most scarce resources, such as wetlands and endangered species, local municipalities can find little reason to refuse to permit development projects.

In summary, although local land use planning could establish preserve zones or open space areas to protect scarce biological resources or more common species and habitats, this rarely occurs (not even when state government provides help). Many of the existing examples of local conservation plans have been completed as Habitat Conservation Plans under the ESA. Although careful mitigation is becoming more common, it is rarely accompanied by any type of regional plan. Rather, each project that results in significant loss of habitat has its individual mitigation action. A patchwork of damaged areas and small fixes are spread across the landscape, and incremental loss of scarce species and habitat continues. State government currently has no means to force regional planning, and resource agencies' staff often do not take a tough stance in conservation and development conflict to encourage regional approaches. Yet the exceedingly high land values for urban land make regional planning as well as biological conservation in urban areas more necessary every day.

Conflicts Between Economic Valuation and Irreplaceable Resources

A variety of economic factors, many of which are influenced by state and federal policies, affect whether the actions of individuals and governments protect or deplete biodiversity. In California, federal subsidies, discount rates, and property values are three of the most important of these. Moreover, pervasive undervaluation of ecological services in California, as elsewhere, tilts the balance of economic decision making away from conservation.

Many economic policies have only unintended consequences for biodiversity. But a few policies lead directly to the rapid depletion of natural resources, chief among these being federal subsidies that are designed to support rural industries and communities through facilitating resource use. These subsidies have been seen as a boon for certain industries, but they have, in fact, contributed to degradation and depletion of the natural resources on which these industries depend.

Subsidies for grazing on federal lands in the western United States cost taxpayers millions of dollars each year, because the fees for grazing privileges are much lower than the costs of the federal rangeland programs. Currently, the government collects $1.54 per animal-unit-month (AUM). In contrast, the marginal costs of operating the BLM and USFS programs were $3.73 per AUM and $3.40 per AUM, respectively, in 1986. Total BLM grazing fee receipts were only 37 percent of program costs, and USFS grazing receipts were barely 30 percent (USGAO 1988a). Fees are also well below fair market value, with leasing rates for comparable private land nearly four times higher, on average (USDA and USDI 1986, CDF 1988). Even public land managed by other federal agencies or the state is leased at rates higher than those charged by BLM or USFS (CDF 1988).

Artificially low fees for use of federal rangelands are related to several environmental problems. Below-market fees encourage overstocking by distorting free-market controls (e.g., by lowering the marginal cost seen by the rancher) on range use. In addition, program deficits severely limit the resources available to the agencies for range management and improvement. For example, the low fee is directly related to the lack of adequate staff or funding for riparian restoration (NRDC 1989). To the extent that these subsidies lower the fees that private landholders can charge for their rangeland and thus reduce the value of private rangeland, federal subsidies also accelerate the rate of conversion of rangeland to urban and agricultural uses. In similar ways, "below-cost" timber sales on USFS lands and subsidies on water from federal water projects provide incentives for unsound environmental and economic practices.

The price of water to farmers and ranchers has also been maintained at an artificially low level (compared to the cost of new deliveries or the estimated market value) and encourages use of water that might not be justified under strictly free-market conditions. For example, farmers currently are typically charged $20–40 per acre-foot for water from the state's massive water storage and conveyance system, whereas domestic consumers typically pay $300–500 per acre-foot. The lower water prices are maintained by huge government subsidies, paid for with tax revenues, that enable consumers to pay less for food grown on irrigated lands. One effective policy for encouraging water conservation may be the adjustment of water prices. Much debate centers around the economic wisdom of subsidized water, but the environmental implications are unambiguous: water is not used in agriculture as frugally as possible, with the result that less water is available for ecologically beneficial uses, and more water is lost to evaporation.

The cost of capital and the opportunity to make high profits in some markets leads to rapid depletion if natural resources are viewed simply as commodity investments to be used today. Unfortunately, industries that extract natural resources often have economic incentive to value only the commodity (extracted resource) itself and not to protect or invest in the ecosystem services that produce commodities. As the case of Maxxam's acquisition and subsequent liquidation of Pacific Lumber's old-growth redwoods demonstrates, resource depletion can be a rational action under the pressure of escalating investment opportunities and high interest rates. In sharp contrast to economic factors or social systems that place emphasis on investing in continuing productivity, the current economic and legal climate encourages us to leave little behind for our children. If some natural resources were considered the property of future generations, rather than available for exploitation by the present generation, market mechanisms would still work to find economically efficient use of resources, but without eliminating all of a resource (Howarth and Norgaard 1990).

Ecological services are undervalued by society in general and by economic analyses in particular, in part because these benefits are poorly understood and taken for granted by the public. The obstacles to fair economic valuation are acknowledged by many economists and attempts are being made to include so-called externalities into formal cost-benefit analyses. In practice, ecosystem services are rarely satisfactorily treated by economics. This is true both for formal cost-benefit analyses of development projects, such as dams and electric power plants, and for less formal economic analyses that local governments perform when they decide whether to approve or disapprove a new housing tract or factory. In general, local governments take little or no account of the consequences of the loss of ecosystem services brought about by loss or degradation of natural habitats. In this way, lasting environmental quality is traded for one-time development opportunities.

With some of the most sought-after real estate in the world, California faces severe economic obstacles to land preservation. The assessed value of all real estate in California in 1987 was $1,243 billion, and it was appreciating at a rate of nearly 10 percent a year or $330 million *per day* (AOR 1990). Thus not only is it difficult to raise adequate funds to acquire parkland, the acreage of parks that can be acquired with appropriated money diminishes with time. The large profit-potential on private land leads to great battles over any attempt to curb the intensity of use of private land. As every developer is aware, the same parcel that is worth millions when slated for high-density development may be worth only a fraction of that amount if its zoning restricts land conversion. In its stewardship of the public welfare, however, government, through zoning, has the power to grant financial windfalls and the authority to restrict the use of privately owned land. The right of government to protect the public welfare is challenged by those who see the concomitant reduction in property values as unfair "taking." Although in the past the Supreme Court has repeatedly ruled on the side of governments, affirming the right to restrict the use of privately owned land for the public good, landowners continue to file "takings" suits against governments attempting to exercise this right. The consequences of this trend are clearly threatening to any habitat protection program; land purchases can be prohibitively expensive whereas restrictive zoning may entail lengthy and expensive lawsuits.

Knowledge Gaps

Often, in both public and private decision making, a tradeoff is confronted between the need to act and the need to know. Consider the case of impending climate warming. To delay preventive or compensatory action until more data and better scientific understanding are available means that, when action is finally taken, it may be too late or far more expensive than if action were taken now. However, to act now, with imperfect information about the problem, risks overreacting or reacting in an ineffective manner. Implicit in many of the recommendations made in the following chapter is the view that knowledge of the threats to biodiversity is now sufficient to permit implementation of wiser and more aggressive biological conservation strategies; we will not conclude that the only need now is for more research. Nevertheless, many important gaps do exist in our knowledge of California's biodiversity and the means by which it is lost. The knowledge gaps that pose serious barriers to effective conservation and the institutional reasons for the persistence of these gaps are reviewed here.

DATA NEEDS

Although numerous surveys and data sets of plant and animal distributions in California exist, the value of these data is limited by the inconsistent methods and definitions used in data collection and compilation. Essentially all of the data are focused on species distributions, with data on the genetic composition of natural populations available for only a fraction of California's species, and with only sporadic coverage of California's habitats. Although there has been a concerted effort to collect data on the locations of the state's rare and endangered species, data on the basic ecology and population biology of these species is usually absent. Almost no data are available to evaluate the status of those species not yet acknowledged to be rare or endangered. The long-term monitoring needed to acquire data on wildlife population trends is also deficient. These gaps make it impossible to evaluate accurately the status of California's biodiversity.

The absence of coordination among the organizations responsible for data gathering and data base management, and their disparate goals, are largely responsible for the problems in quality, consistency, and accessibility of data. For example, there is no consistent classification of habitats or vegetation types among state agencies or between state and federal agencies.[5] Thus we have inadequate knowledge of what vegetation is where in the state and at what rate it is being converted or degraded. The excellent work of the FRRAP program addressed this task at a very large scale of resolution, and broad vegetation types are being mapped at University of California, Santa Barbara as part of the gaps analysis project. Habitat acreage data are not available at a finer scale. Coordinated efforts to know how many acres of different habitats are found within existing protected areas are at their infancy. There appears to be little motivation presently to coordinate the data gathering and management efforts. In addition, because funding for data gathering and management is scarce, there has been a strong push within agencies to centralize data bases.

Long-term monitoring to determine population sizes and natural fluctuations in the populations of selected plants and animals in California is critical if we are to detect trends caused by environmental stresses such as climate change or the chronic effects of pollutants on an ecosystem. Although there are numerous parks and reserves where long-term monitoring could be conducted in different habitats throughout the state, almost no monitoring is being done, primarily because of a lack of funds. The duration of research grants, typically a year or two at the most, is a major barrier to performing such studies because observing such trends often takes a decade. Researchers are unlikely to undertake such studies if they do not have confidence that the funding agencies will continue to support the work through to completion.

The lack of information on genetic diversity at the population level is attributable mainly to priorities within the state agencies that fund biological data base acquisition: knowledge of genetic diversity has not been perceived as a high priority to date. Surveys of genetic diversity are primarily accomplished by academic researchers to test specific hypotheses rather than to understand the distribution of genetic diversity statewide. Carrying out such surveys is more difficult than censusing species distributions and only populations of highest priority could possibly be surveyed. Adequate attention has not been given to identifying these high-priority populations.

SCIENTIFIC RESEARCH NEEDS

Major gaps exist in our ability to foresee the ecological consequences to California of global change, in particular of climate warming and stratospheric ozone depletion. Recent conferences and workshops have made loud and clear the message that more research is needed in these areas, and at least at the federal level, funding is already beginning to close some of these gaps.

Getting less attention is a problem area that has been with us for far longer than global change, yet is no less important—the biological consequences of the incremental loss of habitats (see also *Cumulative Effects*). One excellent study has been carried out that examined the consequences of degradation and fragmentation of habitat accompanying suburbanization on biodiversity (Soulé et al. 1988). But the biological consequences of incremental loss in other habitats such as destruction of riparian forest remain unstudied. Like long-term monitoring, looking at the consequences of incremental loss is difficult under the typical funding cycle. The important consequences may occur on a longer time scale.

The multiplicity of threats facing individual ecosystems poses further scientific challenges to our understanding of threats to biodiversity. In some cases, state agencies are supporting such research, with one example being the California Air Resources Board's program on multiple air pollutant stresses on vegetation. But some multiple threats involve the jurisdiction of several agencies. In such cases, lack of coordination among agency research programs is often a barrier to the funding and execution of effective scientific research.

Three areas are especially worthy of more research: restoration, preserve design, and sustainable timber and range management. We lack understanding of the potential for restoration of already damaged ecosystems. Many locations of the most endangered habitats are badly degraded. To prevent the downward slide of species dependent upon these habitats we need both to protect existing sites and restore habitat. Moreover, under the present policy of using restoration or ecosystem creation as mitigation for habitat loss, there is an urgent need for careful restoration work. In many of these mitigation decisions, the pressure to act now has completely overwhelmed the need to have a greater understanding. It may be years before we recognize the ecological consequences of many of today's mitigation actions.

More research is also needed on the design of preserves, to insure that the money spent to set aside lands is used most wisely. To safeguard critical habitats, more information is needed about the effects of water diversions and of pesticide pollution on our aquatic ecosystems so that sensible standards can be set. In order to be able to use wisely

California's wealth of natural resources we also need a better understanding of techniques for managing forest and rangelands for both commodity production and biodiversity. The Integrated Hardwood Range Management Program has initiated some research on how to successfully produce marketable commodities such as cattle without contributing to loss of wildland habitats such as oak woodlands. More such research is needed. These are critical research areas for California's future.

We have highlighted here what we consider to be the major gaps in our scientific understanding of threats to biodiversity, but it should not be assumed that problems left unmentioned are unimportant. Mysteries abound in all aspects of ecosystem structure and stability and, more specifically, in our knowledge of both the importance of, and threats to, biodiversity. The establishment of conservation biology as a scientific subdiscipline of ecology is one of the most promising academic developments in recent years, for it heralds a more vigorous research effort to probe these mysteries.

Gaps in Education

Although a plethora of educational programs in biology, wilderness living, conservation, natural history, and the like are available in California for nearly all ages, there are many symptoms of failure in science education, generally, and in education about the biosphere, in particular. This book's purpose is not to review these symptoms of failure, for they have been widely studied and discussed.[6] All evidence points to the fact that most high school students have little understanding of natural science and do not perceive how dependent the quality of their lives is on the preservation of biodiversity. The problem is not limited to today's students, of course, for yesterday's poorly educated children have become today's ignorant adults.

As part of a broad attempt to improve science education in the United States, high school biology courses and texts have been revamped in recent years around the "new biology," with molecular biology at the core of the new curricula. Although it is important to convey to students the insights that molecular biology provides about the unity of all life on Earth, these new courses deflect attention from populations and ecosystems. They convey the impression that the most exciting frontiers of biological science lie at the molecular level, whereas, in fact, some of the most exciting developments in biology are at the systems level. More destructively, they fail to teach students the essentials about how our planet works and the linkages between our lives and those of the creatures who share our planet with us.

At the primary school level, ecology and conservation are better established in the classroom. As is appropriate for the lower grades, considerable emphasis in science continues to be placed on helping students gain familiarity with plants and animals. It is also important that engaging exploration of ecology and conservation continue into the middle school/junior high level. This is the stage in which most children lose interest in science. Middle school is also the time that students are increasingly socially aware—a perfect time for socially relevant science courses.

At the college and university level, the last two decades have witnessed the appearance of interdisciplinary environmental programs; some of these emphasize biological conservation and provide students with a state-of-the-art understanding of the major threats to biodiversity. To the best of our knowledge, however, no university has added to their undergraduate curriculum a course requirement in the fundamentals of "How the Biosphere Works," and as a result most students never confront intellectually the ways in which their lives are linked to the fate of their environment. Advanced degrees in economics and in business administration are conferred upon people who have never been taught the basic constraints imposed on both nature and human society by physical laws and the principles of ecology. Yet these same people will, in their professional careers, be making policy decisions that will inevitably undermine the public welfare if those decisions are not based on sound scientific principles.

For professionals, continuing education is needed to assure that the many professional staff people responsible for implementing environmental and natural resource laws receive the benefits of current research. Hundreds of resource professionals are responsible for implementing the policies and managing the lands that are critical to assuring long-term maintenance of healthy ecosystems. New research findings and technical skills need to be made broadly available. Yet, few in-service training programs are available, and when budgets are tight, "optional" training is often foregone. Resource professionals need to be knowledgeable about the most recent research findings and management techniques, just as doctors need to be up-to-date to provide excellent medical services.

CHAPTER SIX

Recommendations: A Strategy for Conservation

Despite the progress made through the acquisition of new parks in California, the passage of the California Environmental Quality Act over twenty years ago, and the creation of several new programs in state government, major threats to biological diversity and numerous barriers to its protection remain. Today, private, nongovernmental organizations are playing leading roles in the conservation of biodiversity, with environmental advocacy groups fighting to improve implementation and enforcement of existing laws and placing bond initiatives on the ballot to buy parks. These actions are each individually effective, but they are also reactions to failures of the existing state governmental structures—legislative and executive—to protect and plan for a workable future. There is a growing recognition that many of the problems in the state (particularly growth management, air pollution, and transportation) cannot be readily solved by a government that is solely reactive, nor one that pits local interests against each other. Loss of biodiversity is yet another problem that requires both a regional and an anticipatory approach. No single municipality acting alone can address these regional problems, in which the actions of individuals add up to a diminished quality of life for many. Leadership at federal, state, and regional levels is needed.

In this chapter we propose a state-level strategy for overcoming the interconnected barriers to biological conservation described in chapter 5. We describe the key components for bringing about a significant, long-term shift in the way California's governing bodies and, more generally, the people of the state manage their ecological heritage. The complexity of the problems demand solutions that are also multifaceted. Some problems can be corrected now by taking *immediate actions* to limit the damages occurring today. Enforcing existing laws and balancing the composition of policy-making bodies will have swift, positive consequences. These are the gains we can and should realize now while we begin the process of making the *long-term institutional changes* needed to improve the management of the state's resources. These long-term institutional changes entail a planning approach using proactive programs to design land use patterns and resource management systems that are sustainable. Finally, *anticipatory action* is recommended to diminish the threats posed by global environment changes: climate change and stratospheric ozone depletion. These problems become harder to reverse with each day no action is taken, and the risks they pose are large.

Our recommendations are not intended as tactical ways to immediately reduce specific threats. Many tactical needs, such as water conservation programs, or stopping a particular development project that threatens a rare plant, or immediately acquiring a critical habitat area, are not dealt with in this report. This is not because tactical solutions are unnecessary—far from it—but rather because the need for them is being addressed by many public interest groups, whereas the design of a conservation strategy for the whole state has been relatively neglected.

1. Mandate that the Protection of Biodiversity Is State Policy

Problem to be solved. Many agencies in California facilitate or regulate the use of biological resources for commodity production, recreational purposes, or development. These activities may be in conflict with protection and maintenance of biodiversity. When these conflicts between immediate human demands and resource protection occur, few agencies perceive the maintenance of biodiversity as their primary responsibility. As a result, conflicts are too often resolved in favor of the consumptive use of resources, and California's biodiversity declines. Perhaps more significant, development of programs that do not include conservation goals and objectives can create institutional obstacles to conservation.

The lack of a clear mandate to protect biodiversity undercuts protection efforts by weakening enforcement of existing laws and regulations, as well as by encouraging tradeoffs that favor commodities and short-term benefits over sustainable practices.

Some agencies and legislators assume the protection of biodiversity is the responsibility of the Department of Fish and Game. However, this agency has neither the authority, financial resources, nor ability to protect biodiversity against the many diverse threats now common in California. Furthermore, nearly every state entity is in some way involved in actions that affect biodiversity. Given the number and magnitude of projects that government agencies are involved with, it is impractical for any one department to screen all state actions that affect biodiversity. However, many agencies do not perceive such review as their own responsibility and hence do not have the necessary programs or expertise for such evaluation.

Goal. Make the conservation and maintenance of biodiversity the responsibility of all the levels and agencies of government in California. Encourage actions that aid protection of biodiversity and discourage actions causing its loss.

Recommendation. Make the conservation of biodiversity a state policy that all agencies are responsible for accomplishing. This can be achieved through legislation.[1] Establish an in-house program in each major agency to help ensure that conservation is achieved. Possible language for such a mandate:

"The economic, aesthetic, ecological, and recreational well-being of California depends upon the conservation of biodiversity. Biodiversity is the basis of the state's life-support system, is irreplaceable, and is of inestimable value to all Californians. It therefore is the policy of the state that all governmental agencies, boards, and commissions will act to conserve, restore, and enhance biodiversity for present and future generations."

2. Establish the California Habitat Protection Act

Problem to be solved. California has no laws specifically protecting its natural habitats. The result has been significant degradation, fragmentation, and loss of certain, critical habitat-types, including streams, riparian forests, wetlands, vernal pools, coastal dunes, and old-growth forests. Many other habitats, including those as common as the valley oak woodland or coastal sage scrub are being degraded and lost at an alarming rate. In addition, since each natural community is crucial to the life cycle of certain species, these losses have an unavoidable impact on species diversity as well.

Existing laws protect endangered species but do little to protect habitats. The federal and California Endangered Species Acts can, in theory, be used to protect the necessary habitat of a listed animal species. Even when a protected species is dependent on a specific habitat, however, the connection between damage to habitat and loss of populations or species may not be sufficiently well understood to permit action under the Endangered Species Acts, or other species protection laws. Moreover, not every rare or threatened habitat is tightly coupled with the survival of a listed rare or endangered species. Even when plant or animal populations are not at risk, protection against degradation is needed because habitats provide a host of goods and services for humanity, and these are diminished as habitat degradation progresses. Furthermore, our knowledge is inadequate to judge how much of any one habitat can be lost before new crises will arise.

The prevailing system of land use controls encourages the incremental loss of terrestrial habitat. Land use is planned and permitted at the local level, where the benefits gained by converting habitat are easily captured in the short term. However, the costs accrue to the general public over a longer period. In general, people know how to value short-term impacts better than they do long-term consequences. Thus, careful planning can play a crucial role by allowing people to see the accumulated impacts of their decisions. The current planning and permitting process is incremental: each county or municipality plans and permits development based on information only for that locale, and most permits or zoning variances are evaluated in isolation from other land use or habitat impacts. Unless permits are granted only in adherence with specific conservation goals, the result is cumulative loss of habitat. Furthermore, unless these conservation goals are based on knowledge of regional or statewide trends in habitat loss from development, logging, grazing, and other factors, they will likely be neither effective nor efficient in protecting California's biodiversity. A regional or state-level perspective is needed to balance the skewed distributions of costs and benefits and to provide the necessary information about trends over the entire range of each habitat.

The dismal status of aquatic habitats in California gives testimony to the failure of present-day approaches to aquatic habitat conservation. Protecting aquatic habitats is hampered by many factors, both physical and political. For instance, protecting any stream or lake requires protecting its watershed and upstream reaches, which may be in a neighboring county, state, or country, yet regulation of these areas may be in different hands. Current laws and institutions are unable to follow a stream's meanders across existing jurisdictional boundaries, leaving many watersheds and rivers at risk.

Habitat degradation and loss is a statewide phenomenon that currently cannot be tracked by any single authoritative body because: (1) land use planning and permitting is a local process with no statewide coordination; and (2) state agencies tend to focus on single causes of decline, such as water use, air pollution, or transportation, whereas a single habitat type is likely to be threatened by multiple threats over its range.

Goal. Protect California's native habitats for their own intrinsic value, for the maintenance of natural goods and services for humanity, and for the preservation of native species. This can be accomplished by identifying threatened and rare habitats, and by providing a means of protecting these habitats. The means to protect habitats must encompass the multitude of factors leading to habitat loss and degradation. Protection from incremental loss requires effective regional and local planning for biodiversity through habitat conservation elements in General Plans throughout California. Emphasis on planning will reduce the uncertainty developers face in the permitting process and lessen the adversarial tone that characterizes conservation/development conflicts.

Recommendation. We propose that the state enact a *Habitat Protection Act* (HPA). The purpose of this act is to ensure that state and local governing bodies shall take no action that further endangers a habitat identified as endangered and to facilitate regional or county planning for habitat conservation. The act should operate at three levels—land-use planning at the county level or regional level, terrestrial and aquatic habitat protection by existing state agencies, and habitat assessment and policy coordination by the proposed California Biodiversity Conservation Board (see Recommendation 3) or some other body capable of the implementation. The HPA should include the following three programmatic tasks:

A. *Identification of threatened and endangered habitats.* The California Biodiversity Conservation Board (CBCB; or implementing board) would define criteria for assessing the degree of endangerment of habitat, and on that basis, create three categories of endangerment. For habitats in the "most-endangered" category, no losses would be permitted. Habitats in the second category, denoted "threatened" habitats, would be protected by a no-net-loss policy, in which development in that habitat would be permitted provided that restoration and protection of some other example of that same habitat-type compensates for the loss, through programs such as mitigation banks. The status of nonthreatened habitats would be periodically assessed but their use would be unrestricted by the HPA. These assessments would be available to state agencies, local planners, and federal land managers. The notion of "loss" would be broadly construed to include degradation and fragmentation as well as outright loss. It is important to incorporate particular species assemblages and ecosystem processes in the definition of a habitat, so that degradation and loss can be assessed and prevented. In contrast, proposals that define habitat solely by dominant vegetation may allow degradation that results in the loss of species and ecosystem goods and services. The HPA should contain provisions promoting effective restoration of degraded habitats, through economic, institutional, and technical means.

We recommend that the CBCB assume the responsibility for this phase of implementation of the act, drawing heavily on the expertise in the Biodiversity Research Institute (Recommendation 4) and existing state agencies and boards charged with environmental protection of California's natural resources. Both the criteria for listing habitats and the specific assignments of habitat types would be reviewed and updated periodically as new scientific information on causes and consequences of habitat degradation and loss becomes available.

B. *Habitat conservation planning.* Individual county planning agencies would be required to formulate land use plans that insure that the no-loss and no-net-loss goals are met for critical habitats within their jurisdiction. The county planning bodies would receive assistance from the CBCB in identifying critical habitats within each county. In instances where a county was prepared to permit development on threatened habitat in return for restoration and protection of equivalent habitat elsewhere, a mitigation banking plan or similar program would be necessary. If a county were willing to plan for the conservation of unlisted habitats in their jurisdiction, staff assistance and funding would be available from the CBCB. Counties would be encouraged to collaborate with regional governing units (such as the Association of Bay Area Governments and the Southern California Association of Governments) to develop regional plans that incorporate a coordinated approach to habitat protection (for example, permitting transfer of development options across county boundaries or preventing the side effects of development in one county from damaging habitat in another). The CBCB would also be responsible for periodic evaluation of the implementation of the Habitat Protection Act and would conduct the monitoring of restoration efforts and mitigation banks.

Habitat conservation planning would also apply to state agencies, departments, and boards whose jurisdiction includes activities that affect California's habitats. Agencies would be required to include in environmental impact reports explicit discussion of how their plans insure that they will take no action that further endangers a listed habitat.

County or regional authority is often inadequate to protect *aquatic* habitats, because the actions threatening many aquatic habitats are regulated by state or federal agencies. For this reason, the State Water Resources Control Board would be required to set minimum flow standards for endangered aquatic habitats and regulate other activities that further endanger listed aquatic habitats.

C. Research on trends in habitat loss and protection. The final programmatic area mandated by the HPA should be research to enable the state to avoid the reactive approach that has plagued species protection and many other conservation efforts. In conjunction with the Biodiversity Research Institute (Recommendation 4), the CBCB would seek to identify trends in threats and habitat loss and to prioritize actions that the state must take to prevent loss and endangerment of new habitats.

Substantial funding will be required for program implementation, including pass-through monies to cover counties' costs and funds to compensate landowners for lands found to have been "taken" by noloss policies for critically endangered habitats. Several funding sources need to be explored but the funding source should probably be tied to activities involving real estate development, hydroelectric generation, and water consumption, or other actions contributing to habitat loss.

3. Establish the California Biodiversity Conservation Board

Problem to be solved. Threats to biodiversity in California do not fall neatly within the jurisdiction of any one or even a few of the state's existing agencies. Departments within the Resources Agency have responsibility for management of land, water, and biological resources, whereas the California Environmental Protection Agency oversees many of the state's pollution problems plus water rights. However, many other departments such as the Department of Food and Agriculture, the State Lands Commission, and the Department of Transportation play important roles in biological resource management or are responsible for programs that threaten biodiversity. Many of these threats could be prevented or solved more effectively and more rapidly if agencies could coordinate their efforts or work cooperatively, but the state does not provide systematically for interagency coordination and cooperation in the protection of biodiversity. Nor does the state have an office with a primary mission of protection of biodiversity.

Given the cast of federal, state, and local government entities that affect biodiversity in California, it is no wonder that there are institutional failures due to both overlapping jurisdictions and problems receiving no attention from any entity. Lack of communication and coordination as well as institutional apathy and lack of knowledge have led to agencies pursuing their goals without regard for biodiversity. CEQA has not proven adequate to ensure consideration of biodiversity. Finally, no existing agency has the mandate or the expertise to conserve biodiversity at the habitat level, nor to assist with regional biodiversity planning.[2]

Goals.

1. Establish an organization with the mandate and expertise to maintain statewide knowledge of the threats to, and protection of, biodiversity.
2. Foster communication, coordination, and cooperation among the local, state, and federal offices affecting biodiversity. In particular, be capable of assisting with regional planning.
3. Provide the oversight and coordination needed to ensure that the

state's agencies and boards properly consider existing and impending threats to biodiversity.

4. Administer and enforce the proposed Habitat Protection Act.

5. Serve as an advocate for biodiversity protection on federal land.

Recommendation. To achieve these five goals, we propose that the California Biodiversity Conservation Board (CBCB) be created within state government. Many possible approaches to solving the institutional problem of a diverse collection of state agencies unable to oversee and protect the state's biodiversity exist, including: creating a new agency with broad responsibilities; restructuring or consolidating existing agencies; or empowering a small office with the institutional vantage point and necessary authority to work with all the state's agencies. We recommend the last of these, formation of a new board under the governor's direction, with the following responsibilities:

A. Oversight of actions and coordination of responsibilities of existing state agencies for protection of biodiversity.

To promote more effective solutions to the many problems that cross agency boundaries, the CBCB would provide institutional auspices for interagency communication and for education of agency staff on significant environmental issues. The CBCB would also convene interagency workshops to coordinate policies and responsibilities among agencies. The CBCB would periodically assess the threats to biodiversity in California and the effectiveness of existing policies and actions taken by existing governing bodies.

Where the CBCB determines that biodiversity is being adversely affected by either an agency's actions or its failure to act, or by the absence of a coordinated approach to specific problems among state government entities, the CBCB would recommend to the governor appropriate actions that should be taken by agencies with responsibility for executing or enforcing existing laws.

B. Administration and enforcement of the Habitat Protection Act. With advice from the proposed Biodiversity Research Institute (Recommendation 4) and the existing state agencies, departments, boards, and commissions concerned with natural resources and environment, the CBCB must develop and apply criteria for classifying the native habitats of the state with respect to their degree of endangerment. This process would be analogous to listing endangered species. The CBCB would also develop planning criteria and priorities for the counties so that they can fulfill their planning responsibilities under the Act. The CBCB would review habitat conservation elements of county or city General Plans and approve those that comply with the Act.

The CBCB would assist counties and municipalities in completing habitat conservation elements for General Plans. The CBCB would be responsible for the design and implementation of a compensation program for lands with habitat subject to the no-loss requirement to the extent necessary to address constitutional "takings" issues, as well as designing mitigation banking programs and other means of achieving no-net loss goals. The CBCB should also investigate and recommend means of establishing incentive programs to encourage private landowners to protect unlisted habitats. Finally, through coordination with the proposed Biodiversity Research Institute, the CBCB would evaluate the regional status of habitats in the state.

C. Ensure consistency of state and federal policies. The CBCB should serve as an advocate for the state's interest in protecting biodiversity in situations where the federal government (e.g., U.S. Forest Service, Bureau of Land Management, Bureau of Reclamation, and Army Corps of Engineers) are taking actions that contradict or undermine state laws and policies regarding the conservation of biodiversity. The CBCB would work with the federal agencies to resolve those problems and ensure that the state policy to protect biodiversity is respected.[3]

4. Establish the California Biodiversity Research Institute

Problem to be solved. Despite the competence of the universities of California and other private and public research programs, there are vast gaps in our knowledge of the status of biodiversity in California and the causes and consequences of its decline (see chapter 5, *Knowledge Gaps*). Particularly lacking is an understanding of the fundamental role of habitats, specifically the roles of habitat quality and the patterns of habitats on the landscape, in maintaining species and genetic biodiversity. These gaps exist, in part, because the questions are tough ones, but also because limited effort is being focused on their solution. One explanation for this is that these kinds of research are not encouraged at the existing research institutions in California. Much of this needed research is applied, in contrast to the fundamental research that is heavily emphasized in universities. Although existing state and federal agencies do support some in-house and extramural research on natural resources, only limited funds go to research on managing and maintaining biodiversity.

Policies must be based on information that is not only timely but also credible. Scientific advice on policy-relevant issues can become sharply polarized when it emanates from groups with a political agenda, whether that agenda is environmental protection or development. To avoid this problem, any proposed new research entity should have the same degree of financial and political independence from vested interests as that enjoyed by the California Academy of Sciences and universities. Nevertheless, such an entity must be able to work closely with industry, environmental groups, and the state and federal agencies concerned with resources and environment so that the important problems are addressed in a coordinated fashion.

Goal. Provide a coordinated and more substantial body of knowledge on biodiversity in California, particularly in the areas of the causes and consequences of its decline and positive measures such as sustainable management and restoration. Ensure that credible, policy-relevant data and research on the status of biodiversity in California and the causes and consequences of its decline are available to decision makers. Conduct research of the highest caliber on these issues.

More specifically, the goals are to:

1. Support research on:
   the nature of existing and emerging threats to biodiversity;
   responses of habitats and species to these threats;
   consequences to society of loss of biodiversity;
   restoration techniques;
   mitigation techniques;
   incentives and policy alternatives that encourage conservation;
   landscape level processes critical to maintaining biodiversity;
   management strategies for sustainable uses of wildlands;
   population genetics relevant to gene pool management;
   techniques for in-situ and ex-situ gene conservation.
2. In collaboration with existing state programs, maintain and disseminate information on:
   species distribution and status;

habitat distribution and status;

conservation techniques such as maintaining genetic stocks or managing viable populations;

threats to habitat and species, including:

air and water pollution;

land development and conversion;

water diversion;

suburbanization;

global threats.

3. Assist in the implementation of the Habitat Protection Act by providing to county planners and the California Biodiversity Conservation Board the data and scientific expertise needed to carry out the provisions of the Act.

Recommendation. The State of California should create a research institute, hereafter called the Biodiversity Research Institute (BRI), that would provide the State of California with the best possible scientific information and advice on the status of biodiversity in California and the causes and consequences of its decline. Applied research should be emphasized at the BRI, thereby complementing and rendering practical the more basic research conducted in universities. Several recent studies have identified critical research areas in conservation biology (for example Soulé and Kohn 1989). In addition to its primary research function, the BRI would also be a coordinating body and clearinghouse for the various data bases on natural resources assembled or used by existing state agencies and the proposed California Biodiversity Conservation Board.

The important link between preservation of species and preservation of habitats suggests that the BRI be organized into approximately ten distinct departments organized by biomes, or general habitat-types, to encourage statewide studies on the status and trends of biodiversity. To achieve a proper balance between independent research and policy relevance, the governing board should include representation from existing governmental agencies, academia, and private-sector professionals. The BRI should receive sufficient line-item support from the state to maintain a significant ongoing level of effort. Additional support from state or federal agencies or from nongovernmental organizations would be available. The BRI should make grants available to researchers at the University of California, the State Universities, or within state agencies in all situations where such extramural activity would take best advantage of existing facilities and talents.

To ensure that the research is policy-relevant and that duplication of effort with existing research programs conducted by state agencies is avoided, the BRI must maintain close ties with the proposed California Biodiversity Conservation Board and the existing agencies charged with responsibilities for resources and environmental protection as well as with natural reserve professionals in the University of California's Natural Reserve System, the Nature Conservancy, and industries such as forestry and agriculture. Simultaneously, institutional independence is important to assure that no single entity exerts undue influence. Appropriate representation on the governing board of the BRI will help achieve this. Sabbatical appointments to BRI for faculty from universities and for scientists from such industries as forestry and agriculture should be encouraged.

5. Ensure Implementation and Enforcement of Existing Laws

Problem to be solved. California already has in place a multifaceted array of laws, regulations, and programs that could potentially help to protect the state's biodiversity. Unfortunately, the effectiveness of many of these is diminished by inadequate funding and staffing or poorly written statutes. The legislature has passed many laws designed to protect resources without also allocating the funds or staff necessary for implementation, rendering these laws ineffectual. Entire agencies such as the Coastal Commission, as well as much smaller programs have been weakened by reductions in funding. Some laws and regulations contain minimal or no penalties for noncompliance, encouraging lack of compliance particularly when the stakes are high and the likelihood of enforcement action is low. Additionally, in the case of certain pollutant impacts and with mitigation of habitat destruction by habitat restoration, the information necessary to prove a violation of the law is prohibitively expensive to develop. Thus, many regulations are unenforceable with current technology and staff resources.

Goal. Successfully use existing laws to decrease loss of biodiversity.

Recommendation. Successful enforcement requires both adequate staffing to check for violations and penalties to encourage compliance. Existing agencies should identify staffing needs in programs responsible for implementing laws in key areas such as water quality, water quantity, mitigation monitoring, pesticide use, endangered species, review of environmental documents, and timber harvest. The legislature should review these needs and then adequately fund these programs to ensure consistent and effective application of California's existing laws.

The legislature should add or increase penalties in existing laws to provide an incentive to comply with the law, easing the enforcement burden. For example, establish substantial financial penalties for persons who willfully damage or harm endangered species. Funds collected could either go to increase the budget of the agency enforcing the law or to support habitat conservation and restoration in the local community.

6. Acquire and Protect Significant Natural Areas

Problem to be solved. Despite the recognition that parks are a critical component of any strategy to protect biodiversity, some habitat-types are dramatically under-represented in the state's parks and preserves. Overcoming this weakness in our collection of protected areas will require coordinated acquisition and coordinated management, as well as action by many levels of government.

Many parks and protected areas require active monitoring and management to ensure they are capable of sustaining the species and ecosystems for which they were acquired. Yet funds for maintaining and operating these parks are often absent.

Creation of a system of preserves that could protect the state's biodiversity is not a feasible task for any single agency. Nor can it be accomplished by state government alone. Many county and regional parks contain significant examples of the state's biodiversity, and 46 percent of California is federally managed. All our parks, but particularly urban parks and open spaces, would benefit from more thoughtful preserve designs—using corridors between habitat patches, encompassing watersheds, and other techniques—to guarantee each park's conservation potential is maximized. Acquiring new parks to ensure more complete representation of biodiversity in our system of protected areas will require funds to purchase and manage land, but some of the need for new acquisition could be diminished by land use planning that incorporates biodiversity conservation (see chapter 5).

Goal. Maximize the conservation benefit that is achieved from California's parks and preserves and guarantee that representative examples of California's ecosystems are included within preserves and protected areas. Design and build a protected area's network in the state capable of being the core of a sustainable conservation program. The goal should be to complete this network within the next twenty-five years, when California's population is projected to reach 45 million.

Recommendation. An effective coordinated approach to park protection is needed. The Interagency Natural Areas Coordinating Committee (INACC) and its regional committees are beginning to facilitate coordination of both park acquisition and management. A successful program would include several features:

A. Establish an inventory of protected areas that includes a frank evaluation of each area's current conservation value. The habitats included within these protected areas and their acreage and condition is essential to this inventory. The groundwork for such an inventory has been laid by the Significant Natural Areas Program in the Department of Fish and Game, but this program has had limited success due to its small staff.

B. Identify and fill gaps in the existing park system through coordination among and between agencies. The identification and acquisition of critical wildlife corridors will both maximize the benefits provided by existing parks and help combat the problems caused by habitat fragmentation.

C. Create stable funding sources for acquisition of new parklands. When annual funding levels fluctuate wildly, no state agency can marshal a staff that is appropriate for both the high and low funding years. Some funds should be spent by state agencies, and some should be allocated to local governments or local interest groups. Local citizen groups have often proved both the most dedicated and most effective organizations at raising both awareness and dollars to add land to existing parks.[4]

Although acquisition dollars are often scarce, the public strongly supports parks and wildlife projects. Recent evidence comes from the successful passage in 1988 of Proposition 70, the California Parks and

Wildlife Bond Act, which established a $770 million bond act for parks, open space, urban greenbelts, and endangered species habitat.

D. *Include funds for operating and managing parks and reserves when allocating monies for acquiring parkland.* As with acquisition, consistent funding for operations and management of parks is needed for parks to achieve their conservation potential.

E. *Improve management of parks for conservation.* Evaluate the management practices in each park, and the suitability of these practices for protecting biodiversity. Encourage coordinated management of parks among government agencies and nonprofit organizations. With assistance from the Biodiversity Research Institute, park and resource professionals should evaluate existing management practices and develop new techniques for ecological management. In some parks, where sensitive ecosystems, such as dune ecosystems, are suffering from recreational use, the park designation should be changed from multiple use to natural reserve to specify a management priority on conservation.

F. *Establish several habitat-oriented "Conservancies"* with goals and objectives similar to those of the existing Coastal Conservancy, Santa Monica Mountains Conservancy, and Tahoe Conservancy. Rather than a geographic focus, such entities should have a habitat-specific mission. Possibilities include a wetlands conservancy and a riparian forest conservancy.

7. Reduce Environmental Illiteracy

Problem to be solved. Most students are inadequately educated in the principles of ecology and environmental science, leaving them ill-prepared to be responsible citizens. Professionals in environmental and natural resource fields have few means of continuing their education to give them the skills they need to understand and address the rapidly growing and changing threats to biodiversity.

The fields of environmental science and natural resource management are also rapidly changing. Our understanding of the causes and consequences of environmental pollutants and benefits of different types of resource management practices is growing daily. Too often, new insights from the research community do not get transferred rapidly to the managers—those responsible for the stewardship of our natural resources.

Two young volunteers in the Habitat Restoration Team of the Golden Gate National Park Associaton pull out French broom. A special tool had to be developed in California to remove these invasive introduced species. (Photo by Charles Kennard)

Goal. All high school and college students should achieve familiarity with the basic scientific principles governing the behavior of the biosphere. Professional training in environmental science, resource management, and conservation biology should be available for natural resources and environmental professionals and for county and municipal planners.

Recommendation. Colleges and universities should require *all* undergraduates to take a course (from a list prepared by each school) that focuses on the biosphere, emphasizing both the laws that govern its behavior and the dependence of humanity upon it. Knowledge of this subject is as vital today to our survival and welfare as are the contents of the current requirements of many colleges and universities (such as composition, basic mathematics, foreign language, or cultural studies).

The high school biology curriculum should provide a balance of emphasis among three domains of biology: the biology of whole systems (population biology, ecology, evolution, and the biological aspects of environmental science), biology at the organismic level, and biology at the cellular and molecular level. Although early exposure to plants and animals in the primary grades is important, it is no substitute for a sound high school level exposure to the concepts and insights about the living world provided by the ecological sciences.

Classroom discussions of environmental issues should not be restricted to biology classes, for all academic disciplines, from history to physics, are pertinent. To promote such discussions, we recommend that all secondary school teachers receive some training in environmental science and ecology, with emphasis placed on the relevance of the teacher's discipline to environmental problems.

In most universities, sabbaticals provide professors an essential means of keeping up in rapidly changing fields of academia. Paid sabbaticals for high school teachers would provide an ideal way for them, too, to learn of new developments in those subjects that are also rapidly evolving. Some public school teachers involved in ecology and environmental science education would find it particularly valuable to spend sabbatical time in a government or nongovernmental agency or a university program. To reach a larger number of teachers and at less cost, opportunities should be provided so that teachers can take short (perhaps one to four weeks) courses in ecology, environmental science, or conservation biology in nearby colleges or universities.

To help resource management and environmental professionals keep up on changes in their fields, a collection of two-day to five-day courses on current issues in environmental science and natural resource management should be developed and made available. It is particularly important that cross-training occur. If only the staff responsible for protection of endangered species take conservation biology courses, the staff of other agencies responsible for programs and activities that harm species will not understand the consequences of their actions. A separate series on current issues in conservation biology, environmental science, or resource management designed for planners could also be developed.

8. Broaden Representation on State Policy-Making Bodies

California's policies on the management of natural resources and the control of pollutants and other threats to biodiversity must balance both the demand for benefits today from our natural resources and the necessity of assuring the long-term health and condition of the state's ecosystems and species so that future generations may also share these benefits. The composition of many of the state's boards, commissions, and advisory groups is skewed toward representation of the interests of industries and organizations that extract goods and value from our natural resources with a short-term perspective. There is an urgent need for wider representation on these policy-making bodies to guarantee that the long-term protection and management of biodiversity receives fair representation.

This problem has been recognized by others. In 1990, the Little Hoover Commission study made a similar finding regarding the California Fish and Game Commission, recommending that the membership of the Fish and Game Commission include representation by "biologists, environmentalists, developers, ranchers and sportspersons." We concur with this recommendation, and further believe that the Fish and Game Commission is only one of the policy-making bodies in state government that needs substantial broadening of the composition of membership.

9. Close the Loopholes in the California Endangered Species Act

Although the California Endangered Species Act (CESA) is perceived by the public to be a legal safety net that guards against the extinction of species, there are several holes in the legislation which allow the legal elimination of endangered species. Endangered plants do not receive protection from destruction (discussed in *Land Use Conflicts,* chapter 5). Nor are the habitats of endangered species adequately protected; without essential habitat a species will certainly not survive. The authority of the Fish and Game Commission to list endangered insects is ambiguous, although the federal government has listed several butterflies as endangered. California's listing process is slow and more cumbersome than need be. These problems must be overcome to secure protection of the species already pushed to the edge of extinction. In addition, some provisions of the Native Plant Protection Act overlap with the CESA creating confusion over the protection of rare plants. This could be solved by repealing the Native Plant Protection Act.

There are no provisions of the Endangered Species Act that work to prevent habitat endangerment. To address this, we have recommended a Habitat Protection Act and the statewide mandate for the protection of biological diversity.

10. Protect Biodiversity in the Face of Global Atmospheric Change

Problem to be solved. Global atmospheric changes threaten the environment of every species and habitat, not only in California but throughout the world. One likely consequence of global change is that ecosystems in the future will be less resilient and less productive than they are today. Although the California Energy Commission has taken the lead on most state policies regarding the prevention of climate change, California has no agency able to take the lead in protecting biodiversity from climate change or stratospheric ozone depletion. In addition, current frameworks for comprehensive regulation or planning, such as CEQA, do not in practice incorporate the threat of global atmospheric change.

Goal. Protect the habitats and species of California from global atmospheric changes by taking steps both to prevent further ozone depletion and climate warming and to minimize the overall ecological impact of the environmental changes that do occur.

Recommendation. California must take a two-pronged approach to addressing global atmospheric change: prevention of further atmospheric pollution and management of the impacts. Many of the individual recommendations made below can be executed by an existing agency.

A. Provide leadership in slowing the rate of atmospheric change. Because the greenhouse effect and ozone depletion are the product of actions occurring all around the world, California cannot stop the warming or depletion by itself. Nevertheless, California can and should lead the way in slowing down and eventually stopping emissions of greenhouse gases and ozone depletors. California is a major source of these gases. The state is responsible for one-sixth of U.S. emissions of ozone-destroying chemicals and 5 percent of total global emissions each year. California is the source of nearly 10 percent of the country's emissions of greenhouse gases. Furthermore, California has the technical ability, the economic flexibility, and the worldwide status to take a leadership role in protection of the atmosphere.

We recommend that the state government:

1. Promote energy conservation to reduce CO_2 emissions from fossil fuel combustion, through mass transit and energy-efficiency standards for buildings, industrial processes, appliances, and other technologies.

2. Increase the use of alternative energy technologies such as cogeneration, wind, and solar to reduce CO_2 emissions.

3. Implement strict emissions controls on non-CO_2 greenhouse gases such as CFCs and methane. For example, require collection and combustion of methane from sewage treatment plants and require leak checks on all natural gas distribution lines.

4. Support research and development of chemical substitutes for ozone depletors and of technologies that have the potential to reduce emissions of greenhouse gases (such as hydrogen- or electric-powered vehicles).

5. The California Air Resources Board and the Regional Air Quality Control Boards should develop a comprehensive and coordinated approach to controlling air emissions to ensure that attempts to solve one air pollution problem do not exacerbate another. Such conflicts have already arisen and are likely to continue, since some substitutes for smog-forming chemicals are ozone depletors or greenhouse gases, and some substitutes for ozone-depleting chemicals are greenhouse gases or cause local smog problems.

6. Regulate industrial use of CFCs through requirements for recycling of ozone-depleting chemicals, greater efficiency in processes employing these chemicals, and the use of substitutes.

B. Mitigate the impacts:

1. Increase the number and diversify the location of parks in the state and maintain habitat corridors between protected areas wherever possible. Guidelines for coastal wetlands protection should take into account the likely rise in sea level.
2. Support research to identify the likely impacts of ozone depletion and climate warming on California's ecosystems and to identify those species and habitats that appear most vulnerable to these impacts.
3. Where clear information exists, include the impacts of ultraviolet radiation and climate warming in the cumulative impact analysis of projects with significant environmental impacts.
4. Support research to identify viable policy options for conservation and mitigation in the face of rapid global change.

Concluding Remarks

Drafting a strategy for conservation of biodiversity is only a first step in a successful plan of action. Sustaining California's natural riches and their many benefits will require the participation and commitment of many people. The government and the private sector must work together to design, implement, and carry out a wise plan for our future and for the future of California.

Our descriptions of these recommendations are incomplete in that we have not specified the best sequence of steps to implement them. We hope these recommendations serve as a catalyst and resource for the many organizations in California interested and able to plan and implement the steps needed to translate these recommendations into specific legislative proposals. For the most innovative recommendations that promote institutional change and a long-term planning approach, particularly the California Biodiversity Conservation Board and the Habitat Protection Act, some combination of workshops and forums for discussion might be a useful early step. The Biodiversity Research Institute and the education recommendations require the attention of experts in environmental and natural resource sciences and science education respectively. Other recommendations are sufficiently straightforward in their attention to immediate problems that they could be taken up in legislative hearings. The recommendations about global environmental problems draw attention to the need to improve our ability to anticipate future environmental problems and design solutions before irreversible consequences occur.

Recent years have seen a change both in the public's awareness of the importance of the natural environment and in resource specialists' knowledge about the fragility of ecosystems and methods of sustainably managing them. Together these have led to a call for a new focus on biodiversity. The proposed ten-part strategy for state action provides a framework for a future California where growth and development can occur in concert with the conservation and enhancement of the biological resources. Biodiversity conservation and protection must be an ongoing process for the state and as such will require an ongoing commitment of time, energy, funding, and wisdom. The state is at a critical juncture—the decisions made in the next ten years will decide the fate of many of the species and ecosystems in California. In doing so, we decide our own fate, and the fate of Californians forever. The choice is in our hands.

CHAPTER SEVEN

Epilogue: Policy Trends

Awareness among state, national, and international policy makers and the public about loss of biodiversity has skyrocketed since this work was first published as a report to the state government in April 1990. Policy discussions in California about biodiversity have changed from "What is biodiversity and why should we care about it?" to the more challenging question "How can we protect biodiversity?" This significant change in focus from "what and why" to "how" has occurred rapidly—due, in part, to the heightened awareness of environmental problems since Earth Day 1990. Media attention to a few very contentious fights over endangered species protection, particularly the spotted owl, has also contributed to bringing conservation issues to the nation's attention.

International debates over how to conserve biodiversity have also captured public attention. Biodiversity conservation was a central concern at the U.N. Earth Summit held in Rio de Janeiro in June of 1992. Leaders of nations from all over the world met to confer on environmental issues of international importance including global climate change, tropical forests, and biodiversity. The United States' stance opposing the biodiversity conservation treaty focused a media spotlight on biodiversity. President Bush was called a "villian" by the press (Kay 1992) for refusing to sign the international treaty on biodiversity despite the agreement of many nations, including Japan and Britain, to sign the treaty. Although the administration agreed with the central provisions of the treaty, they disagreed with many of the proposed mechanisms for conservation (Stevens 1992).

As in the international arena, in California there is now agreement that biodiversity conservation is a problem that must be addressed, but there is no consensus on California's biodiversity policy goals. This final chapter describes some of the major themes that cut across current policy debates about biodiversity and outlines fundamental disagreements over the nature of the problem of loss of biodiversity. We expect that, in the next decade, these issues will be central to many debates over how to conserve biological resources. Many changes have occurred because Governor Pete Wilson's administration is actively engaged in confronting environmental problems and environmental organizations are now recognized as political players that cannot be overlooked. However, the problems identified in chapter 5 still persist, and only parts of the recommendations in chapter 6 are being implemented, while others have been ignored.

The contemporary themes of the debate—the government's mandate to conserve biodiversity, the need for habitat conservation, the challenge of sustainable management, the debate over who should decide how resources are used, and efforts to seek negotiated solutions—show that current policy proposals are addressing only a portion of the problem and are still not guided by a strategic vision. The biodiversity conservation policy arena is increasingly complex and activities that engender both resolution and divisiveness are evident. A successful biodiversity strategy must incorporate the many levels of biodiversity and include actions designed to effect a long-term shift in our management of natural resources, as well as short-term corrective measures. Institutional change, public commitment, and increased understanding will be essential.

Biodiversity Mandate

Growing awareness and citizen concern are prompting changes in the role of government in the protection of biodiversity. Although the California legislature has not yet passed a bill that focuses on biodiversity as a significant policy issue, in 1991 the state and federal resource agencies agreed to work together to conserve biological diver-

Table 7.1. *California's Coordinated Regional Strategy to Conserve Biological Diversity*

Original signatories to the MOU include:
    U.S. Bureau of Land Management
    U.S. Forest Service
    U.S. Fish and Wildlife Service
    U.S. National Park Service
    University of California
    California Resources Agency
    California Department of Fish and Game
    California Department of Forestry and Fire Protection
    California Department of Parks and Recreation
    California State Lands Commission

---

sity in California. To overcome the artificial boundaries between agency jurisdictions that are too often barriers to sound management actions and policies, a few leaders in government agencies wrote a Memorandum of Understanding (MOU) called "The Agreement on Biological Diversity." Ten state and federal agencies signed the MOU. The stated purpose of the memorandum is to "develop guiding principles and policies, design a statewide strategy to conserve biological diversity, and coordinate implementation of this strategy through regional and local institutions" (California Resources Agency 1991). By participating in this effort for a coordinated strategy, state and federal agencies have acknowledged that their mandate explicitly includes conservation of biodiversity.

Several components of the Biodiversity MOU, as it is called, are noteworthy. First, it affirms that maintenance of biological diversity is as much a part of the mandate of our resource management agencies as is the production of various commodities. The signatory parties (table 7.1) agreed to "make the maintenance and enhancement of biological diversity a preeminent goal in their protection and management policies." Second, there is an acknowledgment that state and federal interests do not always concur (as discussed in chapter 5) and that successful conservation depends on coordination of many agencies and organizations. Finally, the MOU recognizes that conservation decisions should be made on biogeographically defined boundaries, rather than on units defined solely by political or historical conventions.

To accomplish these tasks, the MOU establishes an Executive Council chaired by the Secretary of the Resources Agency and composed of

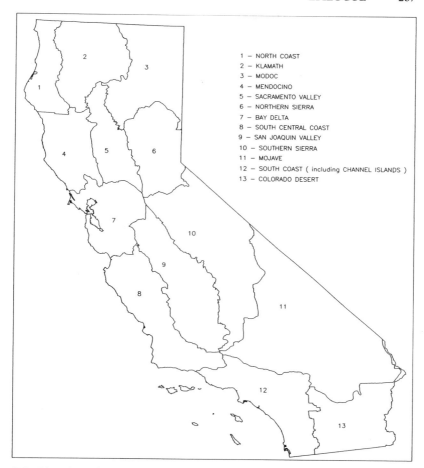

1 – NORTH COAST
2 – KLAMATH
3 – MODOC
4 – MENDOCINO
5 – SACRAMENTO VALLEY
6 – NORTHERN SIERRA
7 – BAY DELTA
8 – SOUTH CENTRAL COAST
9 – SAN JOAQUIN VALLEY
10 – SOUTHERN SIERRA
11 – MOJAVE
12 – SOUTH COAST (including CHANNEL ISLANDS)
13 – COLORADO DESERT

7.1. Bioregions of California.

the top official in each of the signatory agencies in California. Much of the substantive work, however, is expected to occur at the county or regional level through the establishment of Bioregional Councils and Landscape or Watershed Associations[1] (figure 7.1). The bioregional and watershed groups are expected to include representatives from local governments, industry, conservation groups, and concerned citizens. There is an expectation that local and regional conservation strategies and solutions will be developed and implemented.

The Biodiversity MOU simultaneously contains innovations and acknowledges existing activities occurring around the state. State and federal agencies previously initiated several programs to coordinate agencies' activities. For example, the Coordinated Resource Management Program[2] establishes means of local problem solving by including staff from several agencies, local government, and private land owners. The Interagency Natural Areas Coordinating Committee[3] encourages collaboration among agencies to facilitate the establishment and management of protected areas. The Timberlands Task Force[4] helps coordinate timber harvest policies across the many different jurisdictions in the state. None of these programs has as broad a scope or as integrated a vision as the MOU.

In some sense the Biodiversity MOU simply validates some of the activities that are already occurring rather than creating any new activity. In many parts of California, groups of concerned citizens are talking together about the future of their region, recognizing that haphazard growth has led to incremental and irrevocable loss of their quality of life. Some are creating planning documents for the future, like LA 2000 and Bay Vision 2020.[5] Other local groups are working to resolve conflicts between development and endangered species. Others are taking a more comprehensive approach. For example, the San Diego Board of Supervisors has initiated a land use planning process to facilitate wildlife conservation throughout the county.[6] Although the MOU did not initiate any of these projects, it does encourage other people to attempt similar efforts and creates a forum for sharing ideas across regional or landscape councils.

Within several of the eleven Bioregions identified by the MOU, "discussions" among land owners, industry, agency staff, and citizens are addressing resource management concerns and how to balance conservation and development. Five areas have ongoing activities that address concerns over a broad geographic area—the Klamath province, the Sierra Nevada, the San Joaquin Valley, the South Coast, and the Santa Cruz Mountains. Dialogues began in each region as a result of specific region-wide concerns—timber harvest in the Klamath, multiple threats to forests in the Sierra, resource use conflicts in the Santa Cruz Mountains, and endangered species in both the San Joaquin Valley and the South Coast. The controversy and policy debates in the South Coast and the San Joaquin areas have focused on endangered species and have not yet addressed broader biodiversity issues. None of these regional discussions began solely because of the MOU. Nevertheless, Bioregional Councils or Landscape Councils may develop out of these existing forums, and the state government is supporting the effort to form a Klamath Bioregional Council. The MOU may help accelerate the process of finding solutions by encouraging these efforts to ensure biodiversity conservation in the face of increasing threats from land use development, pollution, and resource extraction.

Because each region has distinct resources, land uses, and community values, lasting solutions will differ from place to place, and much of the work to find solutions must be accomplished at the local or regional level. The MOU and the state and federal agencies involved recognize this and anticipate that a bottom-up approach, with most suggestions being identified locally, will be more successful. By recognizing that a top-down approach won't always succeed and that local entities must be involved from the start, the MOU encourages diverse groups to become involved.

Ironically, the MOU has wakened the wrath of many local government officials who are very concerned that the state and federal agencies working together will "gang up" on local government. There were hot words at the second meeting of the Executive Council in early 1992, challenging the authority of the group to convene and to make any decisions. Efforts to "develop principles and policies, and to design a statewide strategy" could lead to additional environmental regulation, which many people oppose. Particularly with the current tight budgets, no local government wants additional requirements from Sacramento. Some officials believe the MOU is an effort to wrest land use authority from local government, concentrating authority in the state capitol. Despite the stated goal of a bottom-up approach, the only organizational level formally developed is the Executive Council—fueling concern that the MOU means increased control by state and federal agencies.[7]

Despite the fears of some local government officials and some landowners, the MOU does not make any demands or require any particular conservation action. Instead, it provides a forum for discussion, and relies entirely on existing legislation and authorities. Perhaps the real complaint of local government is that the MOU encourages establishing policy dialogues outside the existing institutions and structures, suggesting that local government is not adequately addressing these problems. By saying something new is needed, the MOU indirectly critiques local government. If arguments over power and control and suspicions about the motivation for the MOU do not damage the efforts for coordinated management, the MOU and the types of processes it encourages may contribute substantially to conservation success.

Agency coordination and local government action are both critical steps in a long-term conservation strategy. The MOU encourages both of these steps. However, the agencies currently involved include only those that already work regularly on biodiversity concerns. Neither the California Department of Food and Agriculture, nor the newly created California Environmental Protection Agency are included. Because of this, the effects of pollutants and agricultural impacts may be overlooked. Moreover, the current emphasis is on terrestrial biodiversity—wildlife, forests, and rangelands—ignoring aquatic biodiversity. Thus resources and threats are both viewed fairly traditionally, instead of a more comprehensive and integrated vision.

The goals and efforts of the MOU should be encouraged and enhanced to adequately address biodiversity conservation. Where a forum for discussion is enough we can anticipate success. In the long run, talking and sharing knowledge could contribute to changing the way we think about managing California's natural resources. Establishing Landscape and Watershed Councils to plan for conservation and development should also have long-term benefits. However, where stronger measures than dialogue or planning are needed, or where a crisis is now occurring, the MOU will make little difference. For many species and conservation issues, the time available for finding solutions is very short. Rather than an end in itself, the MOU is only a beginning. For all its potential strengths, it cannot resolve all of California's conservation problems. Forums for identifying and solving problems and responsible contributions to biodiversity conservation are necessary but not sufficient components of a conservation strategy.

Habitat Conservation

Habitats, ecosystems, and landscapes are rapidly gaining favor as appropriate scales for conservation actions. Attention to habitat conservation is simultaneously an outgrowth of species protection efforts, a recognition of the need to conserve biodiversity on the ecosystem scale, and a response to changing perceptions of acceptable losses. The question of the correct scale for conservation action is presently under discussion, with proposals to work only at the level of habitat conservation sometimes in conflict with efforts to work on both habitat and species scales.

Recent research in conservation biology suggests incorporating larger scales into our conservation actions, both to ensure the protection of individual species from habitat fragmentation and to ensure the perpetuation of ecosystem processes. Piecemeal development leads to incremental loss of habitat, which can only be avoided by planning over larger geographic areas and incorporating biodiversity considerations into land use planning. Conflicts are growing between conservation and land development as development spreads through the state and increasing numbers of species are endangered and then listed under the state or federal ESA. For these reasons, we included in our recommendations a Habitat Protection Act to encourage county land use planning that incorporates ecosystem conservation.

In 1991, attempting to resolve conflicts between conservation and development while preventing further species endangerment, the California legislature established a new program for Natural Community Conservation Planning (NCCP) administered by the California Department of Fish and Game. The goal of a Natural Community Conservation Plan "is to conserve long-term viable populations of the State's native animal and plant species, and their habitats, in landscape units large enough to ensure their continued existence" (CDFG 1991*e*). To achieve this goal the CDFG will enter into agreements with other public agencies and private interests to develop and implement a plan to protect certain biological communities adversely impacted by growth and development. A pilot project has been started for the coastal sage scrub community in southern California.

Some perceive this new approach as the best possible means of resolving conflicts between conservation and development, whereas others insist the NCCP process is simply a means of getting around the Endangered Species Act. These viewpoints are both accurate assessments of the potential directions the NCCP process may take. The consequences for California's biodiversity are quite different if state policy encourages choosing between species and habitats rather than choosing to protect both species and habitats.

In San Diego, Orange, Los Angeles, and Riverside counties (all areas undergoing rapid urban development) numerous species are threatened by habitat loss and fragmentation. Several of these species, in particular two birds, the California gnatcatcher and the coastal cactus wren, depend on coastal sage scrub habitats. Proposals to list these species under the federal and state ESAs have created controversy—if the birds were listed, the pace and pattern of development in these counties would be greatly restricted. The development community does not want the birds listed, fearing that listing will result in slowing down every project to allow review of the potential impacts of the project on the gnatcatcher or cactus wren.

The NCCP process establishes a Scientific Review Panel to identify the data collection needs and the guidelines for conserving the target natural community. Land owners and local governments voluntarily enter into agreements to be part of the planning area and to cooperate in surveys of their lands to determine the habitats and species present. Enrolled properties are included in an eighteen-month planning process to assess impacts and design NCCP conservation plans to assure the long-term protection of the habitat-type and the species that depend on it. Landowners agree not to change the land use of their property during the enrollment period. By participating in the NCCP process landowners expect to enjoy a streamlined environmental review process because concerns about endangered species and habitat loss will be addressed in the conservation plan. The NCCP is anticipated to be considered equivalent to completing appropriate sections of the environmental review requirements of CEQA and will provide state and federal permits for impacts to listed species.

Although modeled after habitat conservation efforts under the federal ESA, the NCCP process is quite different from what would occur if the gnatcatcher or cactus wren were federally listed. Once an animal has been listed the strong protective requirements of the ESA greatly limit the permissible activities on property containing the listed animal or its critical habitat. Actions that eliminate either the habitat of the listed species or an individual animal are usually prohibited. To obtain permits for development, landowners, in conjunction with government agencies, are required to complete a Habitat Conservation Plan (HCP). Typically, HCPs allow a portion of the listed species' habitat to be lost, in exchange for insuring long-term protection of the remainder of the habitat through acquisition and dedication of the area as a park or reserve.[8] The process of designing and implementing an HCP is time consuming because many individuals and organizations must work together to collect the necessary biological data, identify reserve areas and agree on their boundaries, and create a funding mechanism to acquire and maintain the reserved areas. Once a listed species is involved, HCPs are considered preferable to the uncertainty and confusion that would result from each individual landowner potentially violating the ESA and trying to resolve the problem alone.

NCCPs are intended to be an improvement on the HCP process. The time and expense in designing HCPs[9] has led some analysts to recommend that HCPs include all the listed or candidate species in the area (Bean et al. 1991). In addition, as argued in our recommendation for a Habitat Protection Act, the development community wants to have increased certainty in the development permitting process. HCPs are usually long and complex negotiations between several parties—conducting more than one in the same geographic area is time consuming and wasteful of resources. In comparison, NCCPs will also require significant data collection efforts, but will accommodate several species simultaneously, are expected to be limited to an eighteen-month planning period, and are voluntary.

IS THE NCCP APPROACH AN IMPROVEMENT IN PRACTICE OR ONLY IN THEORY?

The NCCP process is still so new that it is not now possible to evaluate its ultimate success or failure. NCCPs differ from HCPs by focusing on many species and on a larger scale, namely "natural communities" (which are, for practical purposes, synonymous with habitat-types). One motivation for moving toward habitat or natural community conservation in coastal southern California is that numerous species are at risk within the coastal sage scrub habitat. Not only are two birds proposed for listing but several other species found in the coastal sage, the San Diego horned lizard and the orange-throated whiptail lizard, are also species of concern. In addition, over forty other rare plants and animals live in the region. To prevent further endangerment of these species land use planning must insure no further habitat fragmentation. NCCPs are expected to plan for many species at once, eliminating the need for numerous separate HCPs.

Habitat Conservation Plans and NCCPs sound like ideal solutions: a negotiated balance between conservation and development. But they are limited by our scientific knowledge and by the process of negotiating which lands are ultimately protected. Therefore, the scientific difficulties of a habitat/multispecies approach will first be discussed here, followed by an exploration of some of the compromises in the proposed process.

Just designing a Habitat Conservation Plan that can guarantee the long-term preservation of a single species is a difficult task. Rarely are enough data available to make confident predictions about the total area of habitat required or its spatial distribution. The scientific complexity of designing a plan for many species in a geographic area, even if the species are dependent on the same habitat-type, and are all subjected to the same threats, is much greater. A multispecies conservation plan entails identifying the biological requirements of each one of the group of species and delineating the actual geographic boundaries necessary for the conservation of the group. Because each species has different requirements for survival, a multispecies reserve will have boundaries that differ from a single species reserve. Even so, a conservation plan designed for several species may not meet all the needs of the ecosystem or habitat-type. Defining requirements for a habitat-type necessitates looking at the ecological processes that affect the success of all the resident species, plants, and animals, not just the threatened species.

To develop a multispecies conservation plan, parcels are identified that contribute to the conservation of one or more species, with each parcel chosen reducing the risk of loss of one or more species. As the numbers of species at risk increases so does the complexity of alternatives. There is no purely technical way to choose between a parcel important for the gnatcatcher and a parcel important for the cactus wren or for a plant species. Explictly or implicitly, priorities are made to protect one parcel over another, thereby favoring one species or conservation goal over the others. The preserve design decisions then become negotiated in a complex array of risk assessment decisions which include biology, land uses, economics, and politics. Ultimately, the process of drawing preserve boundaries results in an agreement to sacrifice additional habitat for species already known to be endangered. The area outside the preserve boundary is eventually fully developed. Using the best information possible, the U.S. Fish and Wildlife Service endorses the final HCP plan when federally listed species are involved.

Unfortunately, as we move from single species conservation planning to multispecies planning and then to habitat-type or natural communities conservation planning, our knowledge of what components are necessary for success declines dramatically. Scientists often know a great deal about individual species, but their knowledge of ecosystem conservation is much more limited. Because of limited knowledge of appropriate preserve designs at the habitat-type or ecosystem level, it is much more difficult to predict the likelihood of success and thereby to assess the risk of choosing between different, alternative conservation plans.

The NCCP process is an evolving experiment. Some components of the NCCP process may hinder its ability to achieve its objectives in the pilot project in southern California—protecting coastal sage scrub and the sage scrub species. First, the planning process does not necessarily include all undeveloped coastal sage scrub in the region. Only those lands voluntarily enrolled by land owners and local government are included. Enrollment by owners of large acreages of coastal sage scrub may minimize the importance of this problem, but if small owners do not enroll in the program the habitat loss and fragmentation that endangers coastal scrub species will continue. Second, in the desire to provide a more predictable process for landowners, the time line is very short—eighteen months. Decisions will then be made based on the data at hand. The technical complexity combined with the short time line insures that many unknowns will persist. Yet the wildlife agencies are being asked to agree that NCCPs will meet the conservation requirements of the state and federal ESAs.

NCCPs will be designed by local governments with input by wildlife agencies and scientists. The agreements for each NCCP are still being worked out. Local governments are being given a large amount of discretion to implement the NCCP law. Will a regional overview of habitat linkages be incorporated into the final design? Will wildlife agencies have substantial oversight authority or will the final say reside with local government? The NCCP program is promoted as a proactive approach to avoiding further threats to species. In the coastal sage scrub communities many species are already endangered; the time is late for a truly anticipatory approach. Because the process allows continued loss of habitat, many conservationists are not sanguine that NCCPs can achieve their goal of conserving coastal sage scrub and its species. The specific details of each NCCP will affect how successful the program is at conservation.

As the exact terms and the exact boundaries of the NCCP are negotiated, tradeoffs are made—portions of the species' habitat or natural community are determined to be expendable. In doing so, the policy goal subtly shifts from prohibiting extinction (the goal of the ESA) to defining acceptable loss. NCCPs will allow loss of part of a greatly diminished habitat-type without knowing the consequences for the full suite of species that dwell there. In this way, NCCPs are part of a trend toward ecological triage. Arguments for triage are becoming more common. Those promoting the triage argument suggest that since we cannot protect everything, we should focus on habitats, protect those species that easily are accommodated within a habitat protection approach, and admit that some species will fall through the cracks.

Many conservation advocates argue that the NCCP is being used to avoid listing species that merit listing, rather than being a mechanism to plan ahead to diminish the threats (Silver 1992). For example, the Resources Agency spoke against listing the gnatcatcher under the California ESA in August of 1991. They argued in favor of allowing a new conservation process (the NCCP process) to be attempted, while allowing development to continue.[10] At the same hearing, academic researchers and CDFG biologists testified that the bird merits listing on scientific grounds. The Fish and Game Commission chose not to list the bird at that time. Although technically there was no reason that state or federal listing should jeopardize the NCCP process, politically there was. The development community did not want to face the constraints the ESA imposes and was willing to enroll land to avoid the listing.

California conservationists are being encouraged to choose between the Endangered Species Act, an admittedly reactive approach, and a new, unproven process. Most are wisely refusing to consider these as mutually exclusive alternatives, preferring to work for the success of both approaches. Conceptually the NCCP is an outstanding approach—it designs a scientifically supported plan to protect habitat to avoid the endangerment of plants and animals. The hope is that the animals will be protected, federal listing will not occur, and conservation and development will both occur. Unfortunately, sufficient motivation to undertake the massive effort of an NCCP may only occur when such a large extent of a habitat-type has been lost that one or more species are already endangered, because only the threat of federal listing motivates people to cooperate to find a resolution. By this stage, it may be too late for a truly proactive approach. There is no assurance, however, that the NCCP process will succeed. As one CDFG staff person says, "We'll just have to take a crap shot. This process has got to be one or two steps better than the postage stamp pieces of sage scrub being left [undeveloped] now. We just don't know if one or two steps better is enough." Sadly, the coastal sage is another example of incremental loss of habitat leading to habitat fragmentation and species endangerment. The choice of a truly anticipatory approach is no longer available for coastal sage.

The coastal sage scrub NCCP experiment is quite remarkable. The NCCP process is trying to invent a new conservation approach in the toughest of circumstances, the rapidly disappearing coastal sage scrub habitat, rather than attempting an easier pilot project. NCCPs may prove to be marvelous conservation approaches only if they do not become a hidden argument for protecting the habitat-type in such a way that many of the resident species are left unprotected. One measure of successful habitat protection must be the presence of its component species. If the habitat-type cannot support the species that depend upon it, then the habitat-type itself must not be healthy. To succeed, conservation efforts must be directed at both species *and* habitat-type conservation, not at species *or* habitat-types.

If the public policy goal is to protect biological diversity, then the only alternative is to work both on protecting endangered species (those organisms already on the edge) *and* on habitat conservation to avoid the endangerment of even more species in the future. Habitat protection is touted as a proactive approach, yet most of the recent attention has been over habitat-types so altered that many of their inhabitants are rare or endangered species. The California gnatcatcher is but one example. Others include the Delta smelt, the winter-run Chinook salmon, and the northern spotted owl. What about the more common species and habitats? We cannot really "get ahead of the curve" and insure their conservation before they are endangered without working on conserving many types of habitats, not simply the most endangered habitats.

Is Sustainable Management an Option?

Sustainable management of California's biological resources is a challenge of increasing urgency. The debate over the appropriate use and stewardship of public and private wildlands (80 percent of the state) reflects a dialogue that is also occurring internationally. In the past, short-term benefits have been garnered at the expense of longer-term gains. The goal is now shifting from primary attention to securing commodities and livelihoods from the land to a broader goal of assuring the long-term health of ecosystems.

To understand both the nature of sustainable management controversy and the possible solutions, the dimensions of the problem must be sorted out. What are the arguments for a new approach to wildland management? Is it technically feasible to produce commodities while maintaining the long-term health of ecosystems? Are any institutions trying new approaches, or is it all talk? What are the barriers to success? Finally, there is the head-on collision between two sets of values regarding the proper uses of public and private lands. Answering the question

"Who decides the appropriate management and use of private and public wildlands?" will be part of the policy dialogue well into the next century. We discuss the management issues in this section; the conflict over who decides will be discussed in the next section.

CHANGING MANAGEMENT GOALS FOR WILDLANDS AND OPEN SPACE

Sustainable management is now at the core of many conservation controversies. Conservation attention has switched from identifying and protecting small set aside areas to focusing on the management of the vast acreages that are used for resource production. Some argue that public and private forest and rangelands of California and the rest of the western states are being mined rather than managed as renewable resources. One arena for this debate is the old-growth forests in the Pacific Northwest. The media has focused on the northern spotted owl, listed as threatened in 1990, but the crux of the dispute is over management goals for the forests. Should the forests be managed to maximize short-term gain, sustainable yield, or ecosystem health? The argument for sustainable management reflects a desire to insure the continued productive capacity of the landscape in perpetuity rather than undue attention to the annual production of commodities. In the re-evaluation of management goals for forest lands, many activities are being questioned. Timber harvest practices such as the acceptable sizes of clear cuts and the consequences of timber harvest in riparian zones are all being scrutinized, as is the amount and distribution of the remaining old-growth forests.

Concern over timber production targets mandated for national forest lands by administration officials in Washington received public scrutiny when the USFS's Regional Forester from the Northern Rocky Mountains claimed he was fired for refusing to meet timber production targets that would have caused extensive environmental damage and violated federal laws (Egan 1991). The series of news stories brought to the public's attention a debate that had been brewing in the agency. Should production targets be set by the ecological capacity of the land or by political agreement in Washington? If administration officials require production targets that the forests cannot meet without damaging consequences for forest ecosystems, sustainable management and the achievement of diverse environmental goals cannot be met.

In rural landscapes, the choices are rarely as simple as conservation versus development. In many areas timber harvest, agriculture, and grazing are compatible with conservation goals. A continuum exists in the sensitivity of species and habitat-types to the disturbances caused by various land uses. Some species can tolerate the intensity and frequency of disturbance caused by clear cutting. Others can only tolerate timber harvests done by selective logging rather than clear-cutting. We have also learned that not only harvest practices but also the scale of harvest across the landscape affects the ability of species and habitat-types to persist. Similarly, aquatic species are differentially sensitive to projects that alter rivers. Many fish can tolerate water diversions if the quantity isn't too large and the time of year is carefully chosen. The challenge is to determine how much timber harvest and grazing can proceed without irreversible loss of biodiversity, a necessarily site-specific determination because some areas need more protection than other areas.

Certain areas should be managed exclusively for natural values because they contain habitat-types or resident species that are so fragile that any other use of the land cannot co-occur without causing irreparable damage. Most lands are not extremely sensitive, yet unrestrained resource use can cause damage to the most robust of ecosystems. Unsustainable harvest has been the norm in too many areas and within these regions, sensitive species have not been protected. Some areas have been abused—restoration is needed before they once against support productive resource industries. In wildlands where commodity production has been the major use of the land, the best formula is a combination of zoning conservation areas to protect sensitive areas like streamside zones or critical wildlife habitat, and managing harvest levels on other areas to assure both economic return from the land and long-term conservation of biodiversity.

Innovative techniques for managing landscapes for productivity and ecosystem health are being tested in many regions of California and elsewhere. In the forestry industry some scientists (particularly a group from the Pacific Northwest) are promoting "New Forestry," timber practices that acknowledge and try to ameliorate management or harvesting effects on ecosystem processes and species diversity. Like any novel approach, New Forestry is often criticized, but the growing collection of books and research reports on such practices indicate that many ecologically sound timber harvest techniques are feasible.

URBAN LANDSCAPES

The intensity of land use in urban and suburban developments has resulted in the loss of many species and habitat-types. The means of preventing further loss of biodiversity in these areas has been to design parks or open space areas—to "zone" dedicated-use areas. As a result, in urban communities the controversies over conservation appear relatively straightforward because both conservation and development cannot co-occur on the same piece of land. The solution has been to decide where development can occur and where conservation must occur. In fact, in urban areas similar sustainable management issues are debated in the context of appropriate uses of open spaces and parks. Recreational uses such as hiking, mountain biking, or horseback riding must be accommodated with watershed protection, fire management, and ecosystem management. Managing urban parks and open spaces for ecosystem conservation is still a new, untested idea in many communities.

AQUATIC ECOSYSTEMS

In terrestrial ecosystems we have the option of zoning some areas as exclusive conservation areas while allowing multiple uses in other areas. Such zoning is not so easy for aquatic resources. Environmental controversies over water resources in California are mainly battles over how much of the natural streamflow should remain in the rivers and how much can be withdrawn for urban, industrial, and agricultural uses. Some threats to rivers and wetlands can be minimized by excluding activities in streamside zones that cause significant erosion, or by regulating the filling of wetlands. However, restricting the withdrawal of water from one area of a river and simultaneously permitting withdrawals upstream is ineffective protection for riverine systems. Clearly, it is not possible to set aside one side of the Sacramento River to receive natural streamflows and withdraw water only from the other side. Typically, all uses of the rivers of the state must coexist. Some accommodations may be made with respect to *timing* of flows, but spatial, zoning-type arrangements are not possible. The requirement that multiple uses co-occur within the same river makes the most common solution to conservation and development conflicts on land unobtainable for most of California's aquatic resources.

NEW FEDERAL POLICY FOR ECOSYSTEM MANAGEMENT

The major federal land management agencies are also considering new approaches. Starting in 1989–1990 the U.S. Forest Service encouraged a new paradigm in land management through its "New Perspectives" program. This program encouraged national forests and USFS staff to explore land management projects that are not focused primarily on commodity production, but have "a new perspective" focused on assuring the long-term health of the ecosystem. The goals of the program are to work for ecosystem management, biological diversity, long-term productivity, sustainable yields and uses, and landscape aesthetics (Salwasser 1990, Kessler 1992).

The New Perspectives pilot program has led to a change in USFS policy, indicating a movement away from the commodity production orientation which has dominated over the past several decades to an ecosystem management orientation. In 1992, the Chief of the USFS announced that an ecological approach will be used to achieve the multiple-use management of national forests and grasslands. This new policy directive acknowledges the public's concern for the environment by encouraging higher sensitivity to environmental values in land management. For example, clear-cutting has been eliminated as a standard way of harvesting timber of national forests. Each region of the USFS will develop its own strategy for implementing this new policy directive.

The ecological consequences of this new policy directive will not be immediately manifest—forest ecosystems grow and change slowly. An ecosystem management philosophy cannot change the status or condition of national forests overnight. In addition, the USFS continues to have a mandate to produce many commodities and achieve many objectives simultaneously. Conflicts over the management of particular parcels of land will continue to occur. Finally, the USFS is a large, complex institution—rapid change is difficult in big bureaucracies. Nevertheless, the shift to ecosystem management is quite significant politically. Sustainable, ecologically oriented management is the goal today and for the future.

Questions about how to implement sustainable ecosystem management practices are being raised both nationally and internationally. For example, a national policy dialogue examining the conservation of biodiversity on federal lands agreed both that biodiversity was important and that present efforts were not adequate to ensure conservation.

However, no agreement could be reached on how to ensure biodiversity conservation on federal lands (Keystone 1991). In the international effort to conserve biodiversity the Global Biodiversity Strategy has an objective of "incorporating biodiversity conservation into the management of biological resources" (WRI 1992). Sustainable development and biodiversity conservation were also central issues at the United Nations Conference on Environment and Development (Earth Summit) held in Brazil in 1992. There are still many technical difficulties to be overcome in learning how to maintain healthy ecosystems while simultaneously providing resource commodities and economically viable communities. Agreeing to do so is the first step.

Private and Public Resources Use—Who Decides?

As it becomes increasingly obvious that conservation solutions must encompass a more comprehensive scope both through ecosystem protection and inclusion of biodiversity considerations in land management and land use planning, it must be acknowledged that people's current means of livelihoods may be affected in order to achieve conservation goals. This is not a popular conclusion. Even while citizens, conservation groups, and federal, state, and local government organizations begin to discuss means of protecting natural resources while assuring growth, other organizations are forming and meeting to fight what they perceive to be an assault on private property rights.

A national coalition of groups referred to as the Wise Use Movement (WUM) is resisting constraints on the use of private property and working to continue private access to resources on public lands (Satchell 1991). Its goals are to weaken environmental regulations, assure continued resource extraction on public lands, reduce the role of government in decision making about natural resources and private business, and assure that private landowners can use their property as they wish. Although not a monolithic movement, there are efforts to coordinate the activities of the many diverse groups. Many small, independent grassroots organizations concerned with local issues are now being initiated and nationally coordinated by people such as Charles Cushman of the National Inholder's Association and Ron Arnold, Center for Defense of Free Enterprise. Nationally, the movement has worked

*Grazing cattle and rancher on Mount Diablo, where controversy continues over allow-
ing grazing in the State Park. (Photo by Charles Kennard)*

to kill legislation that would increase grazing fees on public land and
would prevent reform of the 1872 Mining Law.

In California, small and large organizations with values similar to
the Wise Use Movement are beginning to fight against the environmental policies that protect natural resources—whether or not these
laws or conservation actions directly affect the organization or its constituents. For example, the California Farm Bureau's 1992 political
platform recommends requiring an Environmental Impact Report before listing species under the state ESA, opposes any increase in wilderness acreage in California, recommends exemption of commercial timber harvest from CEQA, and opposes expansion of the federal or state
Wild and Scenic River systems.

At the same time, public support for environmental protection has
been growing in California and nationally—demonstrating that the public
wants sound conservation policies implemented. The WUM has responded by fighting conservation policies and actions on both public
and private lands. The northern spotted owl case is a prime example.
The listing of the northern spotted owl focused tremendous attention
by both the environmental community and the WUM on management
goals for the forests of the Pacific Northwest. Each side argues for dif-

ferent goals for management of the forest lands and for a different role for government in resource management.

To protect the northern spotted owl from the threat of extinction, owl Habitat Conservation Areas have been proposed. These would require setting aside federal land from timber harvest. No private land is included in these Habitat Conservation Area proposals. Deciding to protect the northern spotted owl is a small part of a larger group of decisions to manage the federal forests for long-term benefits.

Opponents to listing the owl are concerned about values other than long-term sustainable management of the forests. They blame the listing of the owl for the loss of jobs, even though massive cutting on private lands and automation have already cost thousands of jobs. They argue against "locking up" more federal land. Although forestry practices have not been sustainable, resulting in damage to ecosystems and lost jobs, the WUM argues that the federal Endangered Species Act is the problem.[11] This is consistent with their goal to fight federal policies that protect ecosystem values rather than commodity values.

The debate regarding the appropriate use of the California desert is also a debate over the appropriate use of public lands. Much of the California desert is a patchwork of lands owned by the Bureau of Land Management and lands in private ownership. Recreational use of the deserts is increasing, and grazing and mining continue as significant industries in this region. Despite the design and implementation of a California Desert Conservation Plan in the early 1980s by the BLM, many fragile desert ecosystems are being damaged, and the desert tortoise has been listed as a threatened species under the federal ESA. Frustrated by continued problems in the desert, conservationists have proposed turning large areas of California's deserts into national parks rather than allow any continued commodity use.

Although the commodities on these forest and rangelands provide economic livelihood to many people in California, directly and indirectly, they are public resources managed by the federal government for the benefit of all the citizens of the United States. Nationwide, citizen concern for environmental protection is demanding a shift in management of all federal lands from a focus on commodity production to assuring long-term sustainable management.

Proponents of the Wise Use Movement disagree with the goal of management for biodiversity conservation and often use flamboyant rhetorical statements about conserving endangered people or lifestyles.

But the Wise Use Movement is not alone in taking outlandish positions. Some environmentalists have taken extreme positions, such as declaring that no timber harvest and no grazing should be allowed on public lands. For example, "Cattle-free in '93" is a slogan that refers to an effort to eliminate grazing from public lands by 1993. Such positions may be based on skepticism that sustainable resource use can be achieved and are certainly a response to years of inadequate management for ecological values. Federal land management goals are being reevaluated and are shifting toward ecosystem management and protection. Both sides are hoping to sway decisions in their favor and are trying to gain popular support.

Actions that affect private lands are also coming under increasing anti-environmental backlash. Since the late 1960s, government has regulated private actions that cause air or water pollution or that generate hazardous materials. The authority for many environmental laws comes from the power of government to protect human health and welfare. Government regulation and zoning of land uses has a much longer history than environmental regulation. Because it is now widely evident that the actions of individuals are resulting in damage that affect many people and places, solutions to environmental problems will affect individual economic practices to assure public benefits. Like most government regulation there is a tension between private rights and the well-being of the community. But attempts at coordinated protection/conservation are decried as unreasonable government intrusion into the affairs of private landowners.

Efforts to achieve regional conservation strategies as proposed in the Biodiversity MOU are being attacked by groups who are concerned that their way of life and livelihoods are threatened. Rather than seeing a benefit from having state and federal agencies work in a more coordinated fashion, they are concerned about creating another level of government, more regulation, and loss of control over private property. Opponents to the MOU simply have different values and priorities.

The appropriate role of government in the conservation and use of public and private natural resources is under debate. As the evidence grows that current practices in land development, water use, and resource use are causing environmental damage, individual actions are increasingly implicated. Heated debate about the effect of the Endangered Species Act on private property owners will not diminish the numbers of species at risk. Only sound management and planning can achieve this. Nevertheless, there is not yet consensus on either the most important values or uses of wildlands, nor on who decides, nor on how to achieve these goals.

Negotiated Solutions Achieving New Favor

As environmental values become more widely held, the organizations promoting these concerns have begun to move from a reactive position by using lawsuits or other means, to an anticipatory approach by constructing new policies, laws, and solutions. Many examples, in California and elsewhere, show that the tactic of fighting every small battle has not resulted in lasting solutions. Negotiations and consensus-building are currently perceived by many as the most appropriate means of breaking the stalemate over environmental problems both in California and nationally.

In the fall of 1990, after numerous unsuccessful attempts at passing innovative environmental statutes in the California legislature, frustrated environmental advocates went to the public. Numerous initiatives were placed on the ballot that would have significantly and in some cases radically changed the natural resource and environmental laws in California. Groups opposed to the environmental initiatives wrote separate initiatives, so that the ballot included numerous competing measures. The media campaigns were expensive and dramatic. In the end, all the initiatives, both from industry and the environmentalists, failed.

Although the environmentalists' forestry initiative, Forests Forever, lost, it received 48 percent of the vote despite a blistering media campaign against it. When the environmental community threatened another initiative, a small group agreed to try an alternative approach: a negotiated agreement among the various interests. Representatives from the environmental community and the timber industry met, talked, negotiated, and finally agreed on a package of forest practice reforms that were written into four bills in the California legislature. The bills were amended, changed, and passed in the Assembly and Senate as the "Sierra Accord." Governor Wilson, however, vetoed the package. After another round of negotiations, a new package of bills was produced, "The Grand Accord."

No consensus exists on the merits of the proposals that emerged from these negotiations on forest practices. Many industry representatives and environmental organizations found the negotiated outcome completely unacceptable and walked away from the negotiations before they were completed. Some environmentalists saw the Grand Accord as an improvement over current timber harvest practices, whereas others felt the package was entirely too weak. Similarly, some industry representatives found the compromises acceptable whereas others felt they were intolerable. The fact that these negotiations are occurring at all represents a marked change in the process of formulating forestry policy. Environmentalists are now widely recognized as significant players in the policy-making process.

Another negotiation process is working to find agreement on water supply issues. Referred to as the three-way process, agricultural, urban, and environmental water interests have been meeting since 1990 in an effort to resolve the stalemate over water supply and instream flows in California. Environmental improvements, new environmental standards, new water facilities, water transfers, water conservation, and water pricing are among the long list of issues being discussed by this group.[12] A small number of individuals are striving to draft an agreement that would help break the stalemate over water issues in California. Even if the three-way process does lead to some agreements, it is not certain the current administration will support their results. Governor Wilson has established his own water policy separate from the three-way process. In addition, only a few groups are represented in this negotiation. Whether or not the small group of negotiators can reach an agreement, and whether or not this agreement will be acceptable to the larger community are both unresolved questions.[13]

The timber negotiations and the water negotiations were started in large part by private interest groups. Now the state and federal government, through signing the Biodiversity MOU, are validating and encouraging consensus-building forums at both watershed and regional levels. In addition to the regional councils fostered by the MOU, several areas of the state have home-grown watershed or landscape scale efforts. Groups are meeting in diverse areas from the Mattole River Watershed Alliance in Humboldt County to the Sierra Nevada, to the Santa Cruz Mountains. People from government, industry, development, and environmental groups are discussing their differences and looking for common ground, in an attempt to find solutions rather than simply find new fights. A common refrain is "We got tired of fighting, and wondered if we couldn't resolve some of these problems by sitting down and putting our heads together." To date the successes have been modest, but the conversations are becoming more numerous.

The spirit of trying new approaches is generating new ideas and broadening the understanding of those interested in finding sound management policies for our natural resources. Dialogue will continue to be part of any problem-solving package. But dialogue cannot resolve all the problems. Many of these discussion processes are occurring only because the different interest groups were unable to accomplish their individual goals alone. Strong laws, strong advocates, and increasing public pressure for resolution has brought the diverse parties to the bargaining table. To the extent that this continues to happen and that participants have honest intentions of finding solutions that allow both conservation and development, we may be able to create innovative answers. Right now, trust is in short supply. Many species and habitats are already pushed to their ecological limits and need immediate attention. If discussions are used as an excuse not to implement environmental laws, or if they encourage the perpetuation of damaging practices, or if they are designed to slow down economic enterprises, they will fail. Dialogue and consensus building cannot be our only tool, but they can help.

Cautious Optimism for the Future

Conservation policy in California is changing quickly, a consequence of the state's search for a more sensible future for its human and wild inhabitants. Some current trends in conservation policy in California are promising, whereas others threaten to hinder progress toward a long-term biodiversity conservation strategy for the state. New endeavors such as the Biodiversity MOU and Natural Community Conservation Plans contain visions of long-term institutional changes that can improve the management of California's biodiversity. They show a willingness to anticipate conservation crises and to begin to establish proactive rather than reactive responses. Many people and projects are recognizing the need to work at several scales for successful conservation—both species and habitats must be included, and both local and bioregional approaches must be taken. In addition, disparate groups are trying to overcome their polarities and discuss means of reaching solutions acceptable to many parties.

Despite this evidence of progress and increased commitment to conservation, many other activities are antagonistic to new conservation efforts. On many fronts no tangible progress has been made. Dialogue and negotiation may lead only to the illusion of solutions. Many are talking at cross-purposes; some propound the merits of biodiversity conservation, whereas others organize to defeat the Endangered Species Act or to assure no change in the status quo management of public and private wildlands. A biodiversity conservation strategy is still needed that will take immediate action to limit actions currently causing damage, that will assure a long-term shift in how California manages its ecological heritage, and that looks ahead to take anticipatory actions to diminish and avoid future threats.

One reason for the slow progress toward a conservation strategy is that the options to stem species' losses are politically much more difficult than in the past. For example, the plight of the Delta smelt, a declining species that dwells in the Sacramento-San Joaquin river delta, has been inaccurately compared to the snail darter (Gross 1991). Although both are small endangered fish, the political circumstances and the policy choices in these two cases are very different. The snail darter case was a decision about whether to take a future action (building the Tellico dam) which would likely have an adverse effect on a species. The Delta smelt case, like many issues debated now, questions whether to stop present actions that are already having a known detrimental effect on a species. These are much harder decisions to make. There are many established interests at stake, including those whose current livelihoods are at risk. To protect the Delta smelt may require diverting less of the natural stream flows of the Sacramento and San Joaquin rivers for human use. Furthermore, the Delta smelt is only one of a suite of species adversely affected by the altered streamflows in the Bay-Delta. Nevertheless, it is much easier to decide not to start a new project than to decide to make a change, maybe even a fundamental change, in our practices when current practices cause environmental damage. The stakes are very high on both sides—no wonder the debate is loud.

These are fundamental questions: can we decide as a society to make changes in practices that we know cause environmental harm? how are we going to make these decisions? where on the conservation-development continuum will that decision fall? and who will decide? Our choices appear to be either reducing the damage per unit benefit, be that benefit water, timber, or agriculture, or reducing the benefit we receive now, or else accepting the loss of genes, species, and ecosystems, as well as reduced benefits for future generations. Different parties are calling for each of these as the best answer. Some say reduce the damage, some say reduce the benefits, and some say accept the losses.

Many current ways of doing business are demonstrably destructive—be that business agriculture, industry, housing, manufacturing, or forestry. We have already caused sufficient environmental harm to necessitate restoration for some ecosystems. To avoid more damage will require changes in our practices. Changes will affect private property owners and will require planning and tough decisions. Most people are willing to support conservation if it affects land uses far from their daily lives. Saving endangered species is also easily supported unless it requires changing our plans for urban growth or changing the operation of our water delivery systems. We have already used up many of our easy choices. Now we are being tested by the difficult decisions.

Accomplishing our conservation goals and accommodating both human and ecosystem needs in California will take time, ideas, and information. Solutions will not be arrived at overnight, but must instead be achieved by a long-term commitment to California's future. The challenges California faces are large, yet many steps have been taken toward creating a strategy that will truly protect the biological heritage of California. Success will not be measured by rhetoric from the governor's office, the legislature, industry, or environmentalists nor by the number of signatories on the MOU. The true test will be the census figures for the northern spotted owl, the winter-run chinook salmon, the California gnatcatcher, and other endangered species twenty years from now. We will know if we have moved forward on a course for conserving biodiversity by the acres of healthy forests, wetlands, and deserts left to our grandchildren.

Notes

Chapter 3

1. Because patterns of genetic variation often follow environmental gradients or geographic patterns, activities that eliminate a geographically distinct portion of the species range are likely to eliminate localized genetic patterns. For example, actions that eliminated all the southern populations of a species might eliminate genes that helped the species cope with hot temperatures.

2. Scientists use many different indices to quantify species diversity. Most combine both the number of different species in an area and the relative abundance of each. For simplicity, throughout the report, "species diversity" will refer to a simple count of the number of different species present in an area. This count of species present is called "species richness" by some authors.

3. Vascular plants include all plants that have specialized tissue for transporting water and nutrients. Ferns, cycads, conifers, and flowering plants are the major groups of vascular plants. Algae, mosses, and liverworts are nonvascular plants.

4. Throughout the text, "species" will refer to both species and subspecies unless specifically noted as either full species or subspecies. Subspecies are identifiable variants within a species. Because many of the characteristics that distinguish one subspecies from another are genetically based, subspecies are considered by scientists as distinct biological entities. We have counted them as separate entities to fully incorporate the range of biological variation in our numbers.

5. The Jepson Herbarium at the University of California, Berkeley is currently editing a new manual of the plants of California. This massive effort is expected to be completed in 1993.

6. This total includes full species of vertebrates and includes those birds that regularly occur in California, rather than all the species that have been sighted. Many species, such as migratory waterfowl, occur in California each year and depend upon California's ecosystems, but breed elsewhere.

7. The California Native Plant Society considers a plant extinct if it has not been sighted for over thirty years despite repeated searches.

8. One hundred and forty-four plants were listed as threatened or endangered by the State of California in the fall of 1991. In addition, the federal government listed thirty-four plants, six of which were not also listed by the state. Thirty-six vertebrates were listed by both the state and the federal government. An additional twenty-one vertebrates were only on the federal list and an additional thirty-four were included only on the state list. The total also includes fifteen invertebrates listed by either the state or federal government.

9. For example, the Yosemite onion, *Allium yosemitense,* is known from only a few populations, but these are in inaccessible areas in Yosemite National Park and not vulnerable to human threats (Howard 1980).

10. Because both species and subspecies can be listed under the ESA, the comparison of numbers species of concern to the total number of species in California has to be done carefully. Fifty-five species have more than one subspecies listed or on a species of concern list. Both species and subspecies are counted to give the total of 306 vertebrates at risk, as different subspecies include distinct genetic traits. However, to attain a percentage of the total fauna at risk, we compared only the numbers of full species. No invertebrates are included in either of these counts.

11. Many salmon species have distinct "runs" or geographically distinct populations that are also genetically differentiated. Because of its distinct characteristics, the winter-run Chinook is considered to be racially distinct from all other runs of Chinook salmon.

12. Throughout the text ESA will be used to refer to the Federal Endangered Species Act and CESA to refer to the California Endangered Species Act.

13. Millions of acres of California are rural and have low levels of development (fewer than six structures per ten acres). Rural areas are included in the wildland acreages, not in the urban or agricultural acreages. Agriculture is here defined as cultivated lands or irrigated pasture land.

14. In addition to the fifteen million acres of urban land or irrigated agriculture, the American Farmland Trust (1986) reports an additional two million acres are dryland farmed.

15. See Mount Diablo General Plan 1989 and Angel Island Focused Environmental Plan 1988, California Department of Parks and Recreation, Sacramento.

16. The water quality agreement known as D1485 was a four-agency agreement that determined target water flows in the Suisun marsh. It was designed to provide adequate water to protect *waterfowl* areas in the marsh. Unfortunately, the water quantity and water quality needs of other species that reside in the tidally influenced marsh, including several species of endangered plants and animals, were overlooked.

17. The USFS is finishing this round of its land management planning pro-

cess. Although National Forest managers are charged with maintaining the diversity of plant and animal communities, it is too early to tell if the Forest Service will achieve this goal. Many organizations and scientists are critical of the Forest Service's progress to date (Wilcove 1988). Nearly every Forest Plan in California has been contested, many on issues related to biodiversity.

18. Ellison's biotically oriented classification system provides more insight into the biodiversity of California's aquatic types than does the USFWS classification, which is based on physical parameters (Cowardin et al. 1979).

19. An acre-foot is the volume of water that will cover an acre of land to a depth of one foot. It is equal to 325,851 gallons.

20. This figure includes open water, mud flats, and marshes.

21. A major reservoir has a dam height of at least 190 feet or a storage capacity over 100,000 acre-feet.

Chapter 4

1. Because of higher harvest efficiency and water conservation measures, average carrying capacity (value as feeding ground for waterfowl) of flooded cropland is much lower than it was in the 1960s (Dennis and Marcus 1983).

2. Rural land has fewer than six structures per ten acres.

3. Nonfarm rural settlement is associated with more wildfire starts and more difficult fire management (Conservation Foundation 1987). The number of fires on nonfederal land has doubled since 1970 as a result of increased population and recreation (CDF 1988).

4. Sources for population projections in California include the Department of Finance, U.S. Commerce Department, U.S. Census Bureau, and Center for Continuing Study of California Economy. No state or private organization monitors or forecasts land use and habitat conversion statewide. Although urbanization is highly correlated with population a more accurate assessment is warranted given the impacts of development and the necessity of planning for the future.

5. In the early 1980s, an average of 1.7 acres were urbanized in California for every seven people added to the state's population (AFT 1986). The American Farmland Trust estimates that an additional 1.7 million acres will be developed by the year 2000 as the state grows by seven million people. Because population density tends to increase with urbanization, FRRAP estimates that an average of 1 acre will be urbanized for every seven people added, or about 1 million acres total, will be converted to rural or urban use by the year 2000. However, another reason for the higher AFT estimate is that AFT anticipates more rural conversion than does the FRRAP analysis.

6. California's total net offstream water use was 23 percent of water consumed by the entire United States in 1985, according to the U.S. Geologic Survey (Solley et al. 1988). California's consumption is the highest in the na-

tion, with the second-most thirsty state using less than half as much water as California.

7. California has 102 dams 190 feet high or with a capacity over 100,000 acre-feet (Fay et al. 1987) and more than 1,200 dams that are either over 25 feet high with a capacity over 15 acre-feet or with a dam height over 6 feet and capacity over 50 acre-feet (CDF 1988).

8. The Mono Lake Committee, with the help of the National Audubon Society, Sierra Club, and others, is fighting to save Mono Lake by limiting water diversions from its tributary streams. In 1983, the California Supreme Court ruled that the public trust values of Mono Lake must be considered before Los Angeles' water demands are met. Preliminary injunctions issued by Judge Finney, in 1989 and 1991, bar Los Angeles from diverting water from any of the four streams flowing into Mono Lake until the lake rises 3 feet (to elevation 6377 feet) or until the SWRCB issues a decision, expected in summer of 1993. In a related decision, Judge Finney ordered Los Angeles DWP to restore the complex of stream and riparian habitats that had supported the stream fisheries before the diversions. To this end, DWP, the Mono Lake Committee, and other parties are currently embarked on a major restoration project.

9. Since initiating hearings in 1987, the State Water Resources Control Board has been struggling with its court-ordered mandate to set water quality standards for the San Francisco Bay-Delta. To a large extent, the *quantity* of freshwater flows through the Bay-Delta determines the estuary's water *quality* (e.g., appropriate salinity gradients). The standards are expected to require increased flows through the estuary and therefore to affect many existing water use permits. On the basis of testimony by hundreds of technical experts, the state board issued a Draft Water Quality Control Plan in 1988, recommending significant increases in springtime flows for fishery protection. This plan was withdrawn, however, under political pressure. As of spring 1992, the Board had not promulgated new flow requirements.

10. Overdraft refers to the quantity of groundwater pumped which is greater than the annual replenishment.

11. Water statistics by DWR are often presented for "net water use" instead of for total withdrawals or delivered supply (also termed total consumption, total water use, or total applied water use). Compared to total withdrawals, net water use is a much smaller number that subtracts sewage effluent, agricultural runoff, and other waste water from withdrawals (DWR 1987).

12. The potential impact of global warming on rain and snowfall has introduced new uncertainty in assessing future water supplies. This uncertainty is being used as a rationale for building more and larger dams as measures against possible flooding or water shortages. Yet careful analysis shows that only under a few, highly prescribed climate change scenarios would dams yield these benefits. Due to the serious consequences of building more dams on the state's remaining riverine habitats, and due to the scientific uncertainty in predictions of rain and snowfall, much more study is needed before climate change can be considered a legitimate rationale for building or enlarging dams.

13. California's forests supply 10 percent of the U.S. timber harvest from

only 3–4 percent of the nation's commercial timberland. Most of the lumber is used in California, with 28 percent shipped to other states and only 1 percent exported out of the country (CDF 1988).

14. The beef produced on California rangeland forage was worth $318 million in 1985 (ranking thirteenth among the state's agricultural products). Counting both range and feedlots production, beef had a commodity value of $1.09 billion in 1985 (ranking second behind dairy products). California's sheep industry is the nation's second largest, with a commodity value of $52 million (CDF 1988). In 1982, the range industry was one of the top three grossing industries in fifteen counties.

15. Results of a CDF timber harvest model, CALPLAN, show harvestable timber resources stable from 1990 to 2000, followed by a statewide decline through 2030. They project that tree biomass on industry lands will decline (because cutting exceeds growth by 22 percent annually) while biomass on nonindustrial land is projected to increase because harvesting on nonindustrial private land is only 29 percent of annual tree growth, whereas harvesting is 69 percent of growth on public lands and averages 79 percent of growth statewide (CDF 1988).

The factors controlling future stand inventory and forest biomass, in addition to harvest rate, include state and federal policies, private investment in forest management, and conversion of forests to housing. Trends in these factors suggest continued overharvesting and reductions in forest stands. Current demographic, social, and economic trends are creating an unfavorable climate for investment in forest management (CDF 1988). Although the shift in private forest ownership, from industrial to nonindustrial holdings, tends to preserve stands because cutting is less intense, these nonindustrial lands are also more likely to be converted to urban or rural use.

16. Many human activities result in nutrient loading and accelerated eutrophication, including agricultural runoff and soil disturbance from logging, grazing, and urban development.

17. Lake Tahoe and Eagle Lake attempt to meet the CWA "no discharge" rule by using tertiary sewage treatment and improved septic tank systems, respectively. The "no new discharge" policy for the San Francisco Bay has inspired creative solutions such as the creation of the Martinez Wetlands, which act as evaporation ponds that allow no discharge to reach the Bay. Wetlands are also used to achieve tertiary treatment in Humboldt County. The use of natural or created wetlands to filter out pollutants—and achieve tertiary treatment of sewage—demonstrates the importance of ecosystem functions for human welfare.

18. The Clean Water Act identifies 135 "priority" toxic pollutants common in discharge; these include PCB, dioxin, pesticides, solvents, and poisonous metals such as lead and cadmium. Nutrients in wastewater and other nontoxic pollutants are also recognized by CWA.

19. We discuss here only those pollutants for which the ecological damage done in California results mainly from California emissions. Mountain ranges and prevailing wind patterns limit the input of air pollution from other states.

The threat to California from global atmospheric change, in particular from climate warming and stratospheric ozone depletion, is discussed under *Global Atmospheric Change*.

20. In addition to acute toxicity and bioaccumulation, pesticides also affect biota indirectly. For example, marsh crabs exposed to the insecticide Temofos experience increased bird predation due to insecticide-inhibited escape responses.

21. For example, the goal of the Pesticide Contamination and Prevention Act of 1986 (PCPA) is to prevent further pesticide contamination of groundwater and drinking water by requiring CDFA to collect data on transport of pesticides, monitor soil and water for chemicals, and suspend use of any pesticides found in groundwater or deep soil that are not specifically exempted. Through selective interpretation and implementation, CDFA has stalled PCPA.

22. Most plant species tested so far show a decrease in photosynthetic rate, water-use efficiency, plant yield, and/or leaf area. The net effect on plant growth can be dramatic; soybean yields were reduced up to 25 percent by a UV increase corresponding to a 25 percent decrease in the ozone layer (an unrealistically high level of ozone depletion). Most experiments have used high doses of UV, but two factors suggest their results indicate sensitivity to lower doses. First, experiments have found that plant growth is inhibited by even very small increases in UV radiation. Second, in laboratory tests, photo-inhibition is a cumulative and nearly linear response to UV exposure (Caldwell 1981).

23. Until recently, a single portion of the UV spectrum, UV-B, was thought to be responsible for UV damage to plants. Accordingly, many experiments exposed organisms to only UV-B light and not the whole UV spectrum. New evidence suggests that UV-C may also be biologically active; thus experiments using only UV-B may have underestimated total biological response to increases in solar ultraviolet radiation striking the earth's surface.

24. Deforestation leads to a net increase in atmospheric CO_2 in two ways. First, the vegetation, usually grasses and shrubs, which replaces the mature forest typically stores much less carbon in its biomass; the difference in storage is released into the atmosphere. Second, deforestation usually results in the loss of soil organic matter, in part due to erosion but also due to decomposition releasing CO_2 into the atmosphere.

Chapter 5

1. The CEQA guidelines (section 15355, subd. (b)) define "cumulative impacts [as] the change in the environment which results from the incremental impact of the project when added to other closely related past, present and reasonably foreseeable probable future projects. Cumulative impacts can result from individually minor but collectively significant projects taking place over a period of time."

2. Reasons cited for lack of grazing reductions on allotments identified as overstocked were, in descending order, insufficient data, permittee resistance, outside political climate, agency political climate, pending range improvement, and permittee nonuse.

3. Both the Forest Service and the Bureau of Land Management have regulations pertaining to their land use plans and resource management that require consistency with state and local agencies and set general guidelines for the communication and coordination of germane plans and policies. A small excerpt of these regulations is given for each agency.

U.S. Forest Service, under the Secretary of Agriculture
Subchapter II—land use planning and land acquisition and disposition. U.S. Code 43 1712(c). In the development and revision of land use plans, the Secretary shall . . . (8) provide for compliance with applicable pollution control laws, including State and Federal air, water, noise, or other pollution standards or implementation plans; and (9) coordinate the land use inventory, planning, and management activities of or for such lands with the land use planning and management programs of other Federal departments and agencies and of the State and local governments . . . the Secretary shall . . . assure that consideration is given to those State, local and tribal plans . . . and shall provide for meaningful public involvement of State and local government officials, both elected and appointed, in the development of land use programs, land use regulations, and land use decisions for public lands . . . Land use plans of the Secretary under this section shall be consistent with State and local plans to the maximum extent he finds consistent with Federal law and the purposes of this Act.

Bureau of Land Management, under the Secretary of the Interior
43 CFR Ch II Subchapter A—General Management subpart 1610.3–1. Coordination of planning efforts. (a) The objectives of coordination are to . . . provide for meaningful public involvement of other Federal agencies, State and local government officials . . . in the development of resource management plans.

1610.3–2 consistency requirements. (a) Guidance and resource management plans and amendments to management framework plans shall be consistent with officially approved or adopted resource related plans and the policies and programs contained therein, of other Federal agencies, State and local governments . . . including Federal and State pollution control laws as implemented by applicable Federal and State air, water, noise and other pollution standards or implementation plans.

4. These three plants were federally listed in 1991.

5. The California Native Plant Society, a nonprofit private organization, has a two-year project to design a vegetation classification system for California. The group undertaking this task includes representatives from academia, state and federal agencies, industry, and knowledgeable citizens. They hope to complete their work by the end of 1992.

6. See, for example, LaPointe, A. E., Mead, N. A., and Phillips, G. W., "A World of Differences: An International Assessment of Mathematics and Science" (Princeton: Educational Testing Service, 1989); or Carnegie Council on Adolescent Development, *Turning Points: Preparing American Youth for the 21ˢᵗ Century,* The Report of the Task Force on Education of Young Adolescents (Washington, D.C.: Carnegie Corporation of New York, 1989).

Chapter 6

1. In 1991, ten state and federal agencies signed a Memorandum of Understanding (MOU), agreeing to make maintenance of biological diversity a management goal and to work together to coordinate their policies and actions.

2. Although the 1991 Biodiversity MOU, mentioned in note 1 and described in the Epilogue, is a valuable step in this process, only a fraction of the agencies whose actions affect biological diversity are involved. For example, agencies with authority over water rights (SWRCB), pollution control (Calif. EPA), and agricultural practices (CDFA) were notably absent from the initial signatories. By mid-1992 additional agencies were invited to sign the MOU.

3. In the Wilson administration, the Resources Agency is taking a leadership role in coordinating state and federal agencies' activities on biodiversity. The Resources Agency and the Department of Fish and Game are also working to assist local governments in a regional, habitat-conservation planning effort. These efforts do not encompass many of the different agencies in state government. Nor are they integrated with the Governor's Growth Management Task Force, which is being directed by the Office of Planning and Research.

4. Two examples of the role of private citizens groups that have contributed significantly to the protection of individual parks: in the Santa Monica Mountains National Recreation Area citizen activists have flown to Washington to lobby for dollars to expand this park; Save Mount Diablo is a twenty-year-old group that has successfully spearheaded the expansion and protection of Mount Diablo State Park.

Chapter 7

1. Eleven bioregions have been identified in the state. Landscape Associations are smaller units within these regions, and Watershed Associations are units within landscapes.

2. CRMP includes fourteen state and federal agencies.

3. INACC includes ten state, federal, and private member organizations.

4. TLTF includes ten state, federal, and private member organizations.

5. Neither of these planning documents address biodiversity conservation.

6. In February of 1991, the San Diego Board of Supervisors adopted the findings and recommendations of our original report and directed staff to develop a program to deal with wildlife habitat preservation and regional open space strategies. The County Open Space and Multiple Species Wildlife Habitat Conservation Plan will identify sensitive species and habitat and establish means of protecting these areas. The primary focus is the unincorporated area that comprises 85 percent of the county.

7. The Executive Council on Biodiversity agreed at their August 1992 meeting to invite other agencies and organizations to participate in the Biodiversity MOU. In addition to the ten original signatories, the following organizations were invited to participate: six Regional Associations of the California State Association of Counties, the South Central Coast Regional Association of Counties, the Regional Council of Rural Counties, the California Department of Water Resources, the California Department of Conservation, the California Association of Resource Conservation Districts, the U.S. Soil Conservation Service, the U.S. Bureau of Reclamation, and the U.S. Agricultural Stabilization and Conservation Service.

The organizations invited to join are either already members of one of the other multiagency cooperative agreements or representatives of local government. Although there was some discussion of including both the State Water Resources Control Board, because of its responsibility for water quality and water rights, and the USEPA, neither were included. The Executive Council acknowledged that some new members would want the MOU modified. No modifications had yet been made when this book went to press.

8. Once an HCP has been designed and a funding mechanism for the acquisition of protected lands established the U.S. Fish and Wildlife Service grants permits for "taking" of listed species and habitat in the areas that are outside the designated conservation area.

9. The Coachella Valley HCP (for the Coachella Valley fringe-toed lizard) took over three years to complete, and the land acquisition alone cost $22 million. Additional costs include the dollars spent on staff time and research (Beatley 1992).

10. The NCCP process does not require interim controls on development, so development and habitat loss continues during the planning period.

11. Many organizations in the WUM have targeted the reauthorization of the federal Endangered Species Act. They hope to stop the ESA or greatly amend it.

12. In 1991 a separate coalition of urban water agencies and environmental organizations crafted an agreement to use "best management practices" to help conserve water. The alliance between northern and southern urban water agencies was much heralded (for example, see Mayer 1991). Although an agreement was reached on water conservation, no agreement was reached on how to allocate or use the water conserved. The environmental negotiators wanted a commitment to restore aquatic fish and wildlife habitats with the saved water. The urban water officials wanted some of the saved water to go to municipal growth. No conclusion was reached.

13. See, for example, Redmond and Gottlieb (1992). They argue that the members of the three-way negotiation represent limited concerns and constituencies and are therefore unlikely to find meaningful solutions.

Acronyms

The following acronyms are those used for citing references in the text.

AFT	American Farmland Trust
AOR	Assembly Office of Research
BCDC	Bay Conservation and Development Commission
CARB	California Air Resources Board
CDF	California Department of Forestry and Fire Protection
CDFA	California Department of Food and Agriculture
CDFG	California Department of Fish and Game
CNPS	California Native Plant Society
DPR	California Department of Parks and Recreation
DWR	California Department of Water Resources
FERC	Federal Energy Regulatory Commission
FRRAP	Forest and Range Resources Assessment Program (in CDF)
IHRMP	Integrated Hardwood Range Management Program (in CDF)
NDDB	Natural Diversity Data Base (in CDFG)
RWQCB	Regional Water Quality Control Board
SWRCB	State Water Resources Control Board
USBLM	U.S. Bureau of Land Management

USDA   U.S. Department of Agriculture
USEPA   U.S. Environmental Protection Agency
USFWS   U.S. Fish and Wildlife Service
USGS   U.S. Geologic Survey
USNPS   U.S. National Park Service
USSCS   U.S. Soil Conservation Service
WRI   World Resources Institute

References

Airola, D.
    1989   Testimony to California Senate Committee on Natural Resources and Wildlife, Natural Diversity Forum. 29 August 1989.

American Farmland Trust
    1986   *Eroding Choices, Emerging Issues: The Condition of California's Agricultural Land Resources* (San Francisco: American Farmland Trust).

Anderson, D. W., J. R. Jehl, Jr., R. W. Risebrough, L. A. Woods, Jr., W. R. Deweese, and W. G. Edgecomb
    1975   "Brown Pelicans: Improved Reproduction Off the Southern California Coast," *Science* 190:806–808.

Arnold, R. A.
    1986   "Decline of the Endangered Palos Verdes Blue Butterfly in California," *Biological Conservation* 40:203–217.

Assembly Office of Research
    1985   *The Leaching Fields* (Sacramento: Assembly Office of Research).
    1990   Letter of March 9, 1990 to Assemblyman Lloyd Connelly, signed by Steven Thompson, director, responding to request for information on establishing a real estate transfer tax for funding parks and open space.

Axelrod, D. I.
    1977   "Outline History of California Vegetation," in *Terrestrial Vegetation of California,* ed. M. G. Barbour and J. Major (New York: John Wiley and Sons), 139–193.

Bailey, Steven.
    1992   Personal communication. Curator of Birds and Mammals, California Academy of Science, San Francisco.

Bakker, E.
    1984   *An Island Called California: An Ecological Introduction to its Natural*

Communities. 2d ed. rev. and expanded (Berkeley, Los Angeles, London: University of California Press).

Barbour, M., B. Pavlik, F. Drysdale, and S. Lindstrom
1991   "California Vegetation: Diversity and Change," *Fremontia* 19(1):3–12.

Barnes, P. W., S. D. Flint, and M. M. Caldwell
1987   "Photosynthesis Damage and Protective Pigments in Plants from a Latitudinal Arctic/Alpine Gradient Exposed to Supplemental UV Radiation in the Field," *Arctic and Alpine Research* 19(1):21–27.

Bean, M. J., S. G. Fitzgerald, and M. A. O'Connell
1991   *Reconciling Conflicts Under the Endangered Species Act. The Habitat Conservation Planning Experience* (Washington, D.C.: World Wildlife Fund).

Beatley, T.
1992   "Balancing Urban Development and Endangered Species: The Coachella Valley Habitat Conservation Plan," *Environmental Management* 16(1):7–19.

Belliveau, M., and J. May
1989   *A Fragile Shield Above the Golden State: California's Contribution to the Chemical Destruction of Earth's Protective Ozone Layer* (San Francisco: Citizen's for a Better Environment).

Bittman, R.
1989   Personal communication. Botanist, California Department of Fish and Game.
1992   Personal communication. Botanist, California Department of Fish and Game.

Bolsinger, C.
1988   The Hardwoods of California's Timberlands, Woodlands, and Savannas. USDA Forest Service. Research Bulletin PNW-RB-148.

Bowman, K. P.
1988   "Global Trends in Total Ozone," *Science* 239:48–50.

Botkin, D., W. S. Broecker, L. G. Everett, J. Shapiro, and J. A. Wiens
1988   *The Future of Mono Lake* (Santa Barbara: University of California Community and Organization Research Institute).

Branson, F. A.
1985   *Vegetation Changes on Western Rangelands.* Range monograph no. 2. Society for Range Management, Denver.

Brown, C.
1989   Personal communication. Environmental specialist. California Department of Transportation, Marysville.

Brown, R.
1987   "Toxics and Young Striped Bass." Working Paper for the Interagency Ecological Studies Program's Striped Bass Report. California Department of Fish and Game. August 1987.

Caldwell, M. M.
1981   "Plant Response to Solar Ultraviolet Radiation," in *Encyclopedia of Plant Physiology 12A, Physiological Plant Ecology I,* ed. O. L. Lange,

P. S. Nobel, C. B. Osmond, and H. Ziegler (Berlin, Heidelberg, New York: Springer-Verlag), 170–194.

Caldwell, M. M., R. Robberecht, and S. D. Flint
1983   "Internal Filters: Prospects for UV-acclimation in Higher Plants," *Physiol. Plant.* 58:445–450.

California Air Resources Board
1988   *The Health and Welfare Effects of Acid Deposition in California: An Assessment.* California Air Resources Board.

California Department of Finance
1988   *California Statistical Abstract* (Sacramento: California Department of Finance).

1989a   *State and County Population Estimates to July 1, 1988 (provisional).* Department of Finance, Demographic Research Unit. Report 88 E-2, March 1989.

1989b   *Population Estimates vs. Population Projections: 1988.* Department of Finance, Demographic Research Unit, March 1989.

1991   *California Statistical Abstract* (Sacramento: California Department of Finance).

California Department of Fish and Game
1987   *Final EIR.* White Bass Management Program. July 1987.

1988a   *Wildlife Habitats Relations Data Base.* California Department of Fish and Game.

1988b   Memo to Secretary for Resources: Draft Planning Criteria and Pre-planning Analysis for Bishop Resource Management Plan, U.S. Bureau Land Management sch 88110304. 5 December 1988.

1989a   1988 Annual Report on the Status of California's State Listed Threatened and Endangered Plants and Animals. March 1989.

1989b   Wildlife Habitat Relationship System. Species Comparison Report. Database version. 10 September 1989.

1991a   State and Federal Endangered and Threatened Animals of California. Revised October 1991.

1991b   *Designated Endangered, Threatened, or Rare Plants.* Endangered Plant Project, Nongame-Heritage Program. April 1991.

1991c   *Special Animals List.* Natural Diversity Data Base, Natural Heritage Division. August 1991.

1991d   *1990 Annual Report on the Status of California's State Listed Threatened and Endangered Plants and Animals.* March 1991.

1991e   *Natural Community Conservation Planning: A Partnership to Conserve California Ecosystems.* Concept Paper, Natural Heritage Division. 6 October 1991.

California Department of Food and Agriculture
1971   *Pesticide Use Report by Commodity, 1970.* Pesticide Registration and Agricultural Productivity Program, California Department of Food and Agriculture.

1987   *Pesticide Use Report by Commodity, 1986.* Pesticide Registration and Agricultural Productivity Program, California Department of Food and Agriculture.

California Department of Forestry and Fire Protection
    1986   *1985 Wildfire Activity Statistics*. California Department of Forestry and Fire Protection.
    1988   *California's Forest and Rangelands: Growing Conflict over Changing Uses*. Forest and Rangelands Resource Assessment Program (Sacramento: California Department of Forestry and Fire Protection).

California Department of Parks and Recreation
    1988   *California Wetlands: An Element of the California Outdoor Recreation Planning Program*. September.

California Department of Water Resources
    1983   *The California Water Plan: Projected Use and Available Water Supplies to 2020*. Bulletin 160–83. December.
    1987   *California Water: Looking to the Future*. Bulletin 160–87. (Sacramento: California Department of Water Resources).
    1988   *Statistical Appendix to California Water: Looking to the Future*. Bulletin 160–87.
    1992   Memorandum on Winter Run Salmon. From Sheila Greene to Randy Brown, California Department of Water Resources. 19 August 1992.

California Gene Resources Program
    1982   *Anadromous Salmonid Genetic Resources: An Assessment and Plan for California*. Prepared for the State Department of Food and Agriculture (Contract No. 9146) by The National Council on Gene Resources, Berkeley, Calif.

California Native Plant Society
    1988   Information retrieved from computer data base on rare and endangered plants. Sacramento.

California Resources Agency
    1991   Memorandum of Understanding. California's Coordinated Regional Strategy to Conserve Biological Diversity: "The Agreement on Biological Diversity." 19 September 1991.

California State Lands Commission
    1989   Press release. 18 April 1989.

Campbell, F. T., and J. H. Wald
    1989   *Areas of Critical Environmental Concern: Promise vs. Reality* (San Francisco: Natural Resources Defenses Council).

Cappaert v. United States
    1976   426 U.S. 128, 48 L. Ed. 2d 523.

Cervantes, R., J. Ferguson, A. Rivasplata, and G. Stober
    1989   "Tracking CEQA Mitigation Measures under AB3180." California Office of Planning and Research. April 1989.

Cochrane, S. A.
    1986   *Programs for the Preservation of Natural Diversity in California*. Department of Fish and Game, Nongame Heritage Program, Administrative Report No. 84-2. Revised March 1986.

Cohen, A. N.
    1989a   "New Types of Justifications for Traditional Types of Water Proj-

ects." Master's thesis, University of California, Berkeley, Energy and Resources Group.

1989*b*   "Threatened in the Nest," *Pacific Discovery* Fall 1989:6–13.

1992   Personal communication. Board of Directors, East Bay Municipal Utility District.

Conservation Foundation

1987   *State of the Environment: A View Towards the Nineties* (Washington, D.C.: The Conservation Foundation).

Cowardin, L. M., V. Carter, F. C. Golet, and E. T. LaRoe

1979   *Classification of Wetlands and Deepwater Habitats of the United States.* U.S. Fish and Wildlife Service. FWS/OBS-79/31.

Dasmann, R. F.

1966   *The Destruction of California* (New York: Collier Books).

1981   *California's Changing Environment.* Golden State Series (San Francisco: Boyd and Fraser Pub. Co.).

D'Avanzo, C.

1990   "Long-term Evaluation of Wetland Creation Projects," in *Wetland Creation and Restoration: The Status of the Science,* ed. J. A. Kusler and M. E. Kutula (Washington, D.C.: Island Press), 487–496.

Davis, F. W., J. E. Estes, B. C. Csuti, and J. M. Scott

1991   *Geographic Information Systems Analysis of Biodiversity in California. Final Report—Year 1.* Submitted to National Fisheries Foundation and Southern California Edison. Department of Geography, University of California, Santa Barbara.

Davis, L.

1989   "Legal Update: Lake Granted Reprieve—But Not Out of Danger Yet," *The Mono Lake Newsletter* 12(2):4–5.

Day, A. M.

1949   *North American Waterfowl* (Harrisburg, Pa.: The Stackpole Co.).

de Becker, S., and A. Sweet

1988   "Classification Crosswalk," in *A Guide to Wildlife Habitats of California,* ed. K. E. Mayer and W. F. Laudenslayer, Jr. (Sacramento: California Department of Forestry and Fire Protection).

Dennis, N. B., and M. L. Marcus

1983   *Status and Trends of California Wetlands* (Novato, Calif.: ESA/ Madrone, Environmental Science Associates, Inc.).

DeSante, D. F., and P. Pyle

1986   *Distributional Checklist of North American Birds* (Lee Vining, Calif.: Artemisia Press).

Diringer, E.

1992   "U.S. Agencies Square Off Over Water for Salmon," *San Francisco Chronicle,* 11 February 1992, p. A1.

Dreistadt, S. H., and D. L. Dahlsten

1986   "Medfly Eradication in California: Lessons from the Field," *Environment* 24(6):18–44.

Duggan, S., J. G. Moose, and T. Thomas

1988   *Guide to the California Environmental Quality Act,* 2d ed. (Berkeley: Solano Press).

Duggins, D. O., C. A. Simenstad, and J. A. Estes
    1989   "Magnification of Secondary Production by Kelp Detritus in Coastal
            Marine Ecosystems," *Science* 245:170–173.
Egan, T.
    1991   "Forest Supervisors Say Politicians Are Asking Them to Cut Too
            Much," *New York Times,* 16 September 1991, p. A1.
Eliot, W.
    1985   *Implementing Mitigation Policies in San Francisco Bay: A Critique.* A
            report of the California Coastal Conservancy. Oakland, Calif.
Ellison, J. P.
    1984   *A Revised Classification of Native Aquatic Communities in California.*
            Department of Fish and Game, Planning Branch. Administrative
            Report No. 84-1.
El-Sayed, S.
    1988   "Life Under the Ozone Hole," *Natural History,* October, 72–
            80.
Faber, P. M., E. Keller, A. Sands, and B. M. Massey
    1989   *The Ecology of Riparian Habitats of the Southern California Coastal
            Region: A Community Profile.* U.S. Fish and Wildlife Service Bio-
            logical Report 85(7.27).
Fay, J. S., S. W. Fay, and R. J. Boehm
    1987   *California Almanac,* 3d ed. (Santa Barbara: Pacific Data Re-
            sources).
Fried, J., and M. Torn
    1990   "Analyzing Localized Climate Impacts with the Changed Cli-
            mate Fire Modeling System," *Natural Resource Modeling* 4:229–
            253.
Gilmer, D. S., M. R. Miller, R. D. Bauer, and J. R. LeDonne
    1982   *California's Central Valley Wintering Waterfowl: Concerns and
            Challenges.* Transactions of the 47th North American Wildlife and
            Natural Resources Conference, Wildlife Management Institute,
            Washington, D.C.
Gleick, P.
    1988   "Regional Hydrologic Consequences of Increases in Atmospheric
            CO_2 and Other Trace Gases," *Climatic Change* 10:137–161.
Goddard, F.
    1988   Personal communication. CDF [California Department of For-
            estry and Fire Protection] Unit Forester, Region 4, Lassen and
            Modoc Counties.
Goldman, C. R., and E. R. Byron
    1986   *Changing Water Quality at Lake Tahoe: The First Five Years of the
            Lake Tahoe Interagency Monitoring Program.* Tahoe Research Group,
            Institute of Ecology, University of California, Davis.
Goldman, C. R., and A. J. Horne
    1983   *Limnology* (New York: McGraw-Hill).
Granholm, S., et al.
    1989.   *Endangered Habitat: A Report on the Status of Seasonal Wetlands in*

San Francisco Bay and a Recommended Plan for Their Protection. Prepared for the National Audubon Society.

Gray, Brian E.
1989   "A Reconsideration of Instream Appropriative Water Rights in California," *Ecology Law Quarterly* 16:667–717.

Greenbelt Alliance
1989   *The Bay Area's Greenbelt: At Risk*. First findings of the Greenbelt Mapping and Assessment Program. San Francisco.

Gross, J.
1991   "Dying Fish May Force California to Sacrifice Its Thirst for Water," *New York Times,* 27 October 1991, p. A1.

Gunther A. J., J. A. Davis, and D. J. Phillips
1987   *An Assessment of the Loading of Toxic Contaminants to the San Francisco Bay-Delta* (Richmond, Calif.: San Francisco Bay-Delta Aquatic Habitat Institute).

Harris, L. D.
1984   *The Fragmented Forest* (Chicago: University of Chicago Press).

Harte, J., and E. Hoffman
1989   "Possible Effects of Acid Deposition on a Rocky Mountain Population of the Salamander *Ambystoma tigrinum,*" *Conservation Biology* 3:149–158.

Harte, J., M. Torn, and D. B. Jensen
1992   "The Nature and Consequences of Indirect Linkages Between Climate Change and Biological Diversity," in *Global Warming and Biological Diversity,* ed. R. L. Peters and T. E. Lovejoy (New Haven: Yale University Press), 325–343.

Hayes, M. P., and M. R. Jennings
1986   "Decline of Ranid Frog Species in Western North America: Are Bullfrogs *(Rana catesbiana)* Responsible?," *Journal of Herpetology* 20(4):490–509.

Heady, H. F.
1975   *Rangeland Management* (New York McGraw-Hill).
1977   "Valley Grassland," in *Terrestrial Vegetation of California,* ed. M. G. Barbour and J. Major (New York: John-Wiley and Sons), 491–514.

Hickman, J.
1989   Personal communication. Editor of the Jepson Manual, University of California, Berkeley.

Hinrichsen, D.
1988   "Parks in Peril," *The Amicus Journal* 10:3–5.

Holland, R. F.
1986   "Preliminary Descriptions of the Terrestrial Natural Communities of California," Department of Fish and Game. Nongame Heritage Program. October 1986.

Hornbeck, D. L.
1983   *California Patterns: A Geographical and Historical Atlas* (Mountainview, Calif.: Mayfield Publishing Company).

Horner, G. L., C. V. Moore, and R. E. Howitt
    1984   "Increasing Farm Water Supply by Conservation," in *Western Water: Can Farm Water Conservation Save Californians from Building More Water Projects?* Western Water Education Foundation, Sacramento. November/December.
Howard, A.
    1980   "In Search of the Yosemite Onion," *Fremontia* 8(1):15–18.
Howarth, R. B., and R. B. Norgaard
    1990   "Intergenerational Resources Rights, Efficiency and Social Optimality," *Land Economics* 66(1):1–11.
Howell, J. T.
    1972   "A Statistical Estimate of Munz' Supplement to a California Flora," *The Wasmann Journal of Biology* 30(1–2):93–96.
Huntsinger, L., W. Tietje, and R. Schmidt
    1988   *Integrated Hardwood Range Management Program: Research Update.* California Department of Forestry and Fire Protection.
Hurst, E., M. Hehnke, and C. C. Goude
    1980   "The Destruction of Riparian Vegetation and Its Impact on the Avian Wildlife in the Sacramento River Valley, California," *American Birds* 34:8–12.
Jennings, M. R.
    1987   *Annotated Checklist of the Amphibians and Reptiles of California.* Southwestern Herpetologists Society. Sp. Publ. No. 3.
Jensen, D. B.
    1983   *The Status of California's Natural Communities.* (Sacramento: California Department of Fish and Game).
    1987a   "Concepts of Preserve Design: What Have We Learned?" in *Conservation and Management of Rare and Endangered Plants,* ed. T. S. Elias (Sacramento: California Native Plant Society), 595–604.
    1987b   "Mitigation Banking: Protecting Resources or Minimizing Enforcement Costs?" Master's thesis, University of California, Berkeley, Energy and Resources Group.
    1988   "Induced Rarity and Threats to California's Biota." Paper presented at 1988 annual meeting of Society for Conservation Biology, Davis, Calif.
Johnson, K. N., J. F. Franklin, J. W. Thomas, and J. Gordon
    1991   *Alternatives for Management of Late-successional Forests of the Pacific Northwest.* A Report to the Agriculture Committee and the Merchant Marine and Fisheries Committee of the U.S. House of Representatives. Scientific Panel on Late-successional Forest Ecosystems. 8 October.
Jones and Stokes Associates
    1987   Sliding Toward Extinction: The State of California's Natural Heritage. Sacramento. A report commissioned by The California Nature Conservancy.

Katibah, E. F.
   1984   "A Brief History of Riparian Forests in the Central Valley of Cal-
            ifornia," in *California Riparian Systems,* ed. R. E. Warner and
            K. M. Hendrix (Berkeley, Los Angeles, London: University of
            California Press), 23–29.
Kay, J.
   1989   "State Delays Decision on Redwood Cuts," *San Francisco Exam-*
            iner, 19 December 1989.
   1992   "Bush the Villian at Rio Talks." *San Francisco Examiner,* 7 June
            1992, p. A1.
Kessler, W.
   1992   "A Parable of Paradigms," *Journal of Forestry* 90(4):18–20.
Keystone Center
   1991   *Biological Diversity on Federal Lands.* Report of a Keystone Policy
            Dialogue.
Kuchler, A. W.
   1977   "Appendix: The Map of the Natural Vegetation of California," in
            Terrestrial Vegetation of California, ed. M. G. Barbour and J. Major
            (New York: John Wiley and Sons), 909–938.
Laudenslayer, W. F., Jr., W. E. Grenfell, and D. C. Zeiner
   1991   "A Check-list of the Amphibians, Reptiles, Birds, and Mammals
            of California," *California Fish and Game* 77(3):109–141.
Ledig, F. T.
   1988   "The Conservation of Diversity in Forest Trees," *Biosci-*
            *ence:*38(7):471–479.
MacArthur, R. H., and E. O. Wilson
   1967   *The Theory of Island Biogeography* (Princeton: Princeton University
            Press).
McClaran, M. P.
   1990   "Livestock in Wilderness: A Review and Forecast," *Environmental*
            Law 20:857–889.
McGriff, D.
   1992   Personal communication. Wildlife biologist, California Depart-
            ment of Fish and Game, Sacramento.
McGuire, P. E., and C. O. Qualset, eds.
   1986   *Genetic Resources Conservation Program Annual Report 1985–1986.*
            Report No. 1. University of California Genetic Resources Conser-
            vation Program.
McNeely, J. A., and K. R. Miller, eds.
   1984   *National Parks: Conservation and Development* (Washington, D.C.:
            Smithsonian Institution Press).
Maser, C., R. F. Tarrant, J. M. Trappe, and J. F. Franklin, tech. eds.
   1988   *From the Forest to the Sea: A Story of Fallen Trees.* USDA Forest
            Service General Technical Report PNW-GTR-229.
Mayer, J.
   1991   "Interests Sign Major Water Pact." *Sacramento Bee,* 12 December
            1991, p. B1.

Mayer, K. E., and W. F. Laudenslayer, Jr., eds.
    1988   *A Guide to Wildlife Habitats of California* (Sacramento: California Department of Forestry and Fire Protection).

Melack, J. M., S. D. Cooper, T. M. Jenkins, L. Barmuta, S. Hamilton, K. Kratz, J. Sickman, and C. Soiseth
    1989   *Chemical and Biological Characteristics of Emerald Lake and the Streams in Its Watershed and the Responses of the Lakes and Streams to Acidic Deposition.* Final Report, Contract AG-184-32, California Air Resources Board.

Millar, C. I., and W. J. Libby
    1989   "Restoration: Disneyland or Native Ecosystem?," *Fremontia* 17(2):3–10.

Miller, A. H.
    1951   "An Analysis of the Distribution of the Birds of California," *University of California Publications in Zoology* 50(6):531–644.

Moffatt and Nichol, Engineers, Wetlands Research Associates, Inc., and San Francisco Bay Conservation and Development Commission Staff
    1987   *Future Sea Level Rise: Predictions and Implications for San Francisco Bay.* Prepared for San Francisco Bay Conservation and Development Commission.

Mooney, H. A., S. P. Hamburg, and J. A. Drake
    1986   "The Invasions of Plants and Animals into California," in *The Biology of Ecological Invasions of North America and Hawaii,* ed. H. A. Mooney and J. A. Drake (New York: Springer-Verlag), 250–272.

Moore, S. B.
    1989a   "Selenium in Agricultural Drainage: Essential Nutrient or Toxic Threat?," *J. of Irrigation and Drainage Engineering* 115(1):21–28.
    1989b   Telephone interview. Drainwater Studies Coordinator, San Joaquin Valley Drainage Program, U.S. Fish and Wildlife Service, Sacramento, 6 February 1989.

Moyle, P. B.
    1976   *Inland Fishes of California* (Berkeley, Los Angeles, London: University of California Press), 405 pp.
    1986   "Fish Introductions into North America: Patterns and Ecological Impact," in *The Biology of Ecological Invasions of North America and Hawaii,* ed. H. A. Mooney and J. A. Drake (New York: Springer-Verlag), 27–44.
    1992   Personal communication. Professor, Department of Wildlife and Fisheries Biology, University of California, Davis.

Moyle, P. B., and J. E. Williams
    1990   "Biodiversity Loss in the Temperate Zone: Decline of the Native Fish Fauna of California," *Conservation Biology* 4(3):275–284.

Moyle, P. B., J. E. Williams, and E. D. Wikramanayake
    1989   *Fish Species of Special Concern of California.* Final report submitted to the California Department of Fish and Game, Inland Fisheries Division, Rancho Cordova, Calif. October 1989.

Munz, P. A., and D. D. Keck
    1968   *A California Flora and Supplement* (Berkeley and Los Angeles: University of California Press).

Murphy, D. D.
    1988   Petition for listing *Euphydryas editha* "quino" as endangered species. Sent to G. Edwards, Acting Regional Director, U.S. Fish and Wildlife Service. 26 September 1988.
    1989   Personal communication. Director, Center for Conservation Biology, Stanford, Calif.

National Oceanic and Atmospheric Administration
    1987   *National Status and Trends Program for Marine Quality—Progress Report.* U.S. Department of Commerce. January.

Natural Resources Defense Council
    1989   Testimony by Johanna H. Wald regarding reauthorization of the BLM to the Subcommittee on National Parks and Public Lands of the U.S. House of Representative's Committee on Interior and Insular Affairs. 11 April 1989.

The Nature Conservancy
    1989   Data from National Heritage Computer Inventory, Boston.

Newman, A.
    1990   *Tropical Rainforest* (New York: Facts on File).

Nichols, F. H., J. E. Cloern, S. N. Luoma, and D. H. Peterson
    1986   "The Modification of an Estuary," *Science* 231:136–144.

Nichols, F. H., and M. Pamatmat
    1988   *The Ecology of the Soft-bottom Benthos of San Francisco Bay: A Community Profile.* Prepared for U.S. Fish and Wildlife Service, National Wetlands Research Center, Washington, D.C.

Nickelson, T. E., M. F. Solazzi, and S. J. Johnson
    1986   "Use of Hatchery Coho Salmon *(Oncorhynchus kisutch)* Presmolts to Build Wild Populations in Oregon Coastal Streams," *Canadian Journal of Fisheries and Aquatic Sciences* 43:2443–2449.

Paine, R. T.
    1966   "Food Web Complexity and Species Diversity," *American Naturalist* 100: 65–75.

Palmer, T.
    1986   *Endangered Rivers and the Conservation Movement* (Berkeley, Los Angeles, London: University of California Press).

Parker, I., and W. J. Matyas
    1981   *CALVEG: A Classification of Californian Vegetation.* USDA Forest Service Regional Ecology Group, San Francisco.

Parsons, G. L., G. Cassis, A. R. Moldenke, J. D. Lattin, N. H. Anderson, J. C. Miller, P. Hammond, and T. D. Schwalter
    1991   *Invertebrates of the H. J. Andrews Experimental Forest, Western Cascade Range, Oregon. V: An Annotated List of Insects and Other Arthropods.* USDA PNWRS General Technical Report. PNW-GTR-290.

Peakall, D. B., and L. F. Kiff
  1988   "DDE Contamination in Peregrines and American Kestrels and Its Effect on Reproduction," in *Peregrine Falcon Populations,* ed. T. J. Cade, J. H. Enderson, C. G. Thelander, and C. M. White (The Peregrine Fund, Inc.), 337–350.

Pease, W., and K. Taylor
  1992   *Derivation of Site-specific Water Quality Criteria for Selenium in San Francisco Bay.* Technical Report for the San Francisco Regional Water Quality Control Board.

Perkins, G.
  1989   Personal communication. Association for Bay Area Governments. San Francisco.

Peters, R. L.
  1988   *Effects of Global Warming on Species and Habitats: An Overview.* Endangered Species Update, vol. 4, no. 7.

Peters, R. L., and J. D. Darling
  1985   "The Greenhouse Effect and Nature Reserves," *Bioscience* 35:707–717.

Peters, R. L. and T. E. Lovejoy, eds.
  1992   *The Consequences of the Greenhouse Effect for Biological Diversity* (New Haven: Yale University Press).

Planning and Conservation League
  1990   Draft: The 21st Century Report. Sacramento.

Powell, J., and C. Hogue
  1979   *California Insects* (Berkeley, Los Angeles, London: University of California Press).

Raven, P. H., and D. I. Axelrod
  1978   "Origin and Relationship of the California Flora," *University of California Publications in Botany* 72:1–134.

Redmond, J., and R. Gottlieb
  1992   "The Select Few Who Still Control State's Water Policy Discussions." *Sacramento Bee,* 1 July 1992.

Remsen, J. V.
  1978   *Bird Species of Special Concern in California.* An Annotated List of Declining and Vulnerable Bird Species Compiled for the California Department of Fish and Game.

Riggs, L. A.
  1986   *Genetic Considerations in Salmon and Steelhead Planning.* Final report. Northwest Power Planning Council.
  1990a   *Principles for Genetic Conservation and Production Quality.* Northwest Power Planning Council (contract no. C90-005) by GEN-REC.
  1990b   "Conserving Genetic Resources On-site in Forest-ecosystems," *Forest Ecology and Management* 35(1–2):45–68.

Ringold, P. L., and J. Clark
  1980   *The Coastal Almanac for 1980—The Year of the Coast* (Washington,

D.C.: The Conservation Foundation, and San Francisco: W. H. Freeman & Co.).

Risebrough, R. W.
1969 "Chlorinated Hydrocarbons in Marine Ecosystems," in *Chemical Fallout,* ed. M. W. Miller and G. G. Berg (Springfield: Charles C. Thomas Publisher), 5–23.

Rosener, J. B., and H. B. Gregersen
1987 "Non-legislative Deregulation: A Study of the California Coastal Act and the Forest Practices Act." Unpublished, Graduate School of Management, University of California at Irvine.

Roy, B.
1989 Personal communication. Botany Department, Pomona College, Claremont, Calif.

Roye, C.
1989 Personal communication. Associate resource ecologist, Department of Parks and Recreation, Sacramento.

Sacramento Valley Waterfowl Habitat Management Committee
1983 *Pacific Flyway Waterfowl in California's Sacramento Valley Wetlands.* California Wetland Association, Redwood City.

Sailer, R. I.
1978 "Our Immigrant Insect Fauna," *Bulletin of the Entomological Society of America* 24:3–11.

Salwasser, H.
1990 "Gaining Perspective—Forestry for the Future," *Journal of Forestry* 88(11):32–38.

San Joaquin Valley Drainage Program
1987 *Developing Options: An Overview of Efforts to Solve Agricultural Drainage and Drainage-Related Problems in the San Joaquin Valley.* San Joaquin Valley Drainage Program, December.

Satchell, M.
1991 "Any Color But Green," *U.S. News and World Report,* 21 October 1991, 74–76.

Save-the-Redwoods League
1979 *Save-the-Redwoods League: Guardians of Nature's Elders.* Fund Raising Management. January/February.

Schaffer, W. M., D. B. Jensen, D. E. Hobbs, J. Gurevitch, J. R. Todd, and M. V. Schaffer
1979 "Competition, Foraging Energetics and the Cost of Sociality in 3 Species of Bees," *Ecology* 60(5):976–987.

Schneider, K.
1989 "Science Academy Says Chemicals Do Not Necessarily Increase Crops; Policy Shift on Aide Urged to Discourage Pesticides," *New York Times,* 8 September 1989, p. 1.

Schonewald-Cox, C. M.
1988 "Boundaries in the Protection of Nature Reserves," *Bioscience* 38(7):480–486.

Schroeder, R. A., D. U. Palwski, and J. P. Skorupa
    1988   *Reconnaissance Investigation of Water Quality, Bottom Sediment, and Biota Associated with Irrigation Drainage in the Tulare Lake Bed Area, Southern San Joaquin Valley, California, 1986–1987.* U.S. Geological Survey, Water Resources Investigation Report 88-4001, U.S. Geological Survey, Sacramento.

Schultz, A. M.
    1985   "Background and Recent History," in *Selenium and Agricultural Drainage: Implications for San Francisco Bay and The California Environment,* ed. W. Davoren, Proceedings of the 2nd Selenium Symposium, 23 March 1985, Berkeley. The Bay Institute, San Francisco.

Senate Concurrent Resolution 28
    1979   *Wetlands Resolution.* Resolutions, Chap 92 1979.

Shabecoff, P.
    1987   "Pesticide plight," *New York Times,* 27 May 1987, p. A9.
    1988   "Survey finds hundreds of native plants in imminent danger," *New York Times,* 6 December 1988, p. B7.

Shapovalov, L., A. J. Cordone, and W. A. Dill
    1981   "A List of the Freshwater and Anadromous Fishes of California," *California Fish and Game* 671:4–38.

Shea, C. P.
    1988   *Protecting Life on Earth: Steps to Save the Ozone Layer.* Worldwatch paper 87, Worldwatch Institute, Washington, D.C.

Shevock, J., and D. W. Taylor
    1987   "Plant Exploration in California: The Frontier Is Still Here," in *Conservation and Management of Rare and Endangered Plants,* ed. T. S. Elias (Sacramento: California Native Plant Society), 91–98.

Silver, D.
    1992   "A Special Report. Natural Community Conservation Planning as of March 1992," *Endangered Habitats League Newsletter* 2(2):3–4.

Skinner, J. E.
    1962   *An Historical Review of the Fish and Wildlife Resources of the San Francisco Bay Area.* California Department of Fish and Game, Water Projects Branch, Report No. 1. June.

Skinner, M.
    1992   Personal communication. Botanist. California Native Plant Society, Sacramento.

Skorupa, J. P.
    1989   Personal communication. Wildlife Research Biologist, Department of Wildlife and Fisheries Biology, University of California, Davis.

Skorupa, J. P., and J. M. Ohlendorf
    1988   *Deformed Waterbirds Embryos Found Near Agricultural Drainage Ponds in the Tulare Basin.* Research Information Bulletin, U.S. Fish and Wildlife Service, no. 88–49. July.

Smith, J. P., Jr.
1987   "California's Endangered Plants and the CNPS Rare Plant Program," in *Conservation and Management of Rare and Endangered Plants,* ed. T. S. Elias (Sacramento: California Native Plant Society), 1–6.

Smith, J. P., Jr., and K. Berg, eds.
1988   *Inventory of Rare and Endangered Vascular Plants of California.* Spec. Publication No. 1. 4th ed. (Sacramento: California Native Plant Society).

Smith, J. R.
1979   "Toxic Substances: EPA and OSHA Are Reluctant Regulators," *Science* 203:28–32.

Smith, K.
1989   Testimony to the California Senate Committee on Natural Resources and Wildlife Natural Diversity Forum. 29 August 1989.

Solley, W. B., C. F. Merk, and R. R. Pierce
1988   "Estimated Use of Water in the United States in 1985." United States Geologic Survey, Circular 10004.

Soulé, M. E., T. B. Bolger, A. C. Alberts, J. Wright, M. Sorice, and S. Hill
1988   "Reconstructed Dynamics of Rapid Extinctions of Chaparral-requiring Birds in Urban Habitat Islands," *Conservation Biology* 2(1):75–92.

Soulé, M. E., and K. A. Kohn, eds.
1989   *Research Priorities for Conservation Biology* (Washington, D.C.: Island Press).

Speth, J. G.
1988   "Environmental Pollution—A Long-term Perspective." Proceedings of the Centennial Symposium Earth '88: Changing Geographic Perspectives. National Geographic Society, Washington D.C.

State Water Resources Control Board
1988   *Draft Water Quality Control Plan for Salinity in San Francisco Bay/Sacramento-San Joaquin Delta-Estuary,* October 1988. Sacramento.
1990   *1990 Water Quality Assessment* (Sacramento: Division of Water Quality, State Water Resources Central Board).

Stebbins, G. L.
1978   "Why Are There So Many Rare Plants in California?," *Fremontia* 5(4):6–10.

Stebbins, R. C.
1990   "A Desert at the Crossroads," *Pacific Discovery*, Winter.

Steinhart, P.
1990   *California's Wild Heritage: Threatened and Endangered Species of the Golden State.* California Department of Fish and Game, California Academy of Sciences, and Sierra Club Books.

Stevens, W. K.
1992   "To U.S., Treaty's Flaws Outweigh Benefits," *New York Times,* 6 June 1992, p. 5.

Stork, R.
    1989   Personal communication. Director of Conservation. Friends of the River. Sacramento.
    1992   Personal communication. Director of Conservation. Friends of the River. Sacramento.
Strauss, E., and L. Davis
    1989   "A Reasonable Compromise: Lake Elevation 6388'," *Mono Lake Newsletter* 12:9–15.
Taylor, K.
    1992   Personal communication. San Francisco Bay Regional Water Quality Control Board. Oakland.
Terborgh, J., and B. Winter
    1980   "Some Causes of Extinction," in *Conservation Biology,* ed. M. E. Soulé and B. A. Wilcox (Sunderland, Mass.: Sinauer Assoc.), 119–133.
Thompsen, C. D.
    1985   "An Assessment of Noxious Range Weeds in California." Master's thesis, Department of Range Management, University of California, Davis).
Thompson, K.
    1961   "The Riparian Forests of the Upper Sacramento Valley," *Annals of the Association of American Geographers* 51(3):294–315.
Torn, M. S., and J. S. Fried
    1992   "Predicting the Impacts of Global Warming on Wildland Fire," *Climatic Change* 21:257–274.
Toxic Substance Monitoring Program
    1984   *Water Quality Monitoring Report.* No. 86-4-WQ. State Water Resources Control Board.
U.S. Department of Agriculture, Forest Service and U.S. Deprtment of Interior Bureau of Land Management
    1986   *Grazing Fee Review and Evaluation: Final Report 1979–1985.* A report from the Secretary of Agriculture and the Secretary of the Interior, Washington D.C.
U.S. Department of Agriculture, Soil Conservation Service
    1984   *California's County Resources Inventory.* Summary tabulations. USDA, Davis, Calif.
U.S. Environmental Protection Agency
    1984   *Report to Congress: Nonpoint Pollution in the U.S.* Office of Water Program Operations.
    1988   *Endangered Species Protection Program,* Federal Register 53(46):7716–7721.
U.S. Fish and Wildlife Service
    1978   *Concept Plan for Waterfowl Wintering Habitat Preservation, Central Valley, California.* U.S. Fish and Wildlife Service, Portland.
U.S. General Accounting Office
    1988a   *Rangeland Management: More Emphasis Needed on Declining and Overstocked Grazing Allotments.* GAO/RCED-88-80. June.

1988*b*   *Rangeland Management: Some Riparian Areas Restored But Wide-spread Improvement Will Be Slow.* GAO/RCED-88-105. June.

Vilms, J.
1989   *Mechanisms of Vernal Pool Protection.* Report for the California Department of Fish and Game, Natural Heritage Division.

Vogel, N.
1991   "Aquatic Life in S.F. Bay Reels from Drought." *Sacramento Bee,* 11 February 1992.

Wake, D. B.
1980   Letter to Mr. Guy Martin, commenting on the BLMs Final Environmental Impact Statement and Proposed Plan for the California Desert Conservation Area. 17 November 1980, from University of California, Berkeley.

Wald, J. H., and A. Notthoff
1989   "Offshore Oil Drilling on the Central California Coast: Response to the Central Coast OCS Regional Studies Program to the Call for Information and Nominations for the Pacific OCS Lease Sale 119." Central Coast OCS Regional Studies Program, San Francisco.

Webb, R. H., and H. G. Wilshire
1983   *Environmental Effects of Off-road Vehicles: Impacts and Management in Arid Regions* (New York: Springer-Verlag).

Western, D., and M. C. Pearl
1989   *Conservation for the Twenty-first Century* (New York: Oxford University Press).

Westman, W. E.
1977   "How Much are Nature's Services Worth?," *Science* 197:960–964.
1979   "Oxidant Effects on California Coastal Sage Scrub," *Science* 205:1001–1003.
1987   "Implications of Ecological Theory for Rare Plant Conservation in Coastal Sage Scrub," in *Conservation and Management of Rare and Endangered Plants,* ed. T. S. Elias (Sacramento: California Native Plant Society), 133–140.

Whitcomb, R. F., C. S. Robbins, J. F. Lynch, B. L. Whitcomb, M. K. Klimkiewicz, and D. Bystrak
1981   "Effects of Forest Fragmentation on Avifauna of the Eastern Deciduous Forest," in *Forest Island Dynamics in Man-Dominated Landscapes,* ed. R. L. Burgess and D. M. Sharpe (New York: Springer-Verlag), 125–206.

White, J. R., P. S. Hoffman, D. Hammond, and S. Baumgarten
1987   *Selenium Verification Study/1986.* California Department of Fish and Game.

Wilcove, D.
1988   *Protecting Biological Diversity.* Vol 2. of *National Forests: Policies for the Future* (Washington, D.C.: The Wilderness Society),

Williams, P. B.
1985   *An Overview of the Impact of Accelerated Sea Level Rise on San*

Francisco Bay. Report by Philip Williams and Associates, San Francisco.

Wilson, B. C.
    1990   "Gene-pool Reserves of Douglas Fir," *Forest Ecology and Management* 35(1–2):121–130.

Woodman, J. N., and E. B. Cowling
    1987   "Airborne Chemicals and Forest Health," *Environmental Science and Technology* 21:120–126.

World Resources Institute, World Conservation Union (IUCN), and United Nations Environment Programme
    1992   *Global Biodiversity Strategy* (Baltimore: World Resources Institute Publications).

Zedler, J.
    1989   Presentation given at the Society of Ecological Restoration and Management Conference. Claremont Hotel, Oakland, Calif., January 1989.

Index

Photographs are indicated by italic type.

Designer:	U.C. Press Staff
Compositor:	Maple-Vail Book Manufacturing Group
Text:	10/13 Galliard
Display:	Galliard
Printer:	Maple-Vail Book Manufacturing Group
Binder:	Maple-Vail Book Manufacturing Group